Nature, Reality, and the Sacred

TITLES IN THE SERIES

Nature, Reality, and the Sacred

The Nexus of Science and Religion

Langdon Gilkey

FORTRESS PRESS
MINNEAPOLIS

NATURE, REALITY, AND THE SACRED
The Nexus of Science and Religion

Scripture quotations unless otherwise noted are from the New Revised Standard Version Bible, copyright © 1989 by the Division of Christian Education of the National Council of the Churches of Christ in the United States.

Excerpts from *The Anthropic Cosmological Principle* by John D. Barrow and Frank J. Tipler (Oxford: Clarendon Press, 1986) are reprinted by permission of Oxford University Press.

Chapter 4 is based in part on Langdon Gilkey, "Whatever Happened to Immanuel Kant?" in *The Church and Contemporary Cosmology,* James Miller and Ken McCall, eds. (Pittsburgh: Carnegie Mellon) and appears by permission of Carnegie Mellon University Press.

Material in chapters 1-5 is adapted from Langdon Gilkey, "Nature, Reality, and the Sacred," in *ZYGON: Journal of Religion and Science* (Vol. 24, September 1989) and is reprinted by permission of Blackwell Publishers.

Chapters 2, 5, and 11 are based in part on Langdon Gilkey, "What Theology Can Learn from Science," in *Science, Technology, and the Christian Faith,* Brent Waters and Vernon L. Barbour, eds. (United Ministries in Higher Education, 1991).

Cover design: Keith McCormick

Library of Congress Cataloging-in-Publication Data

Gilkey, Langdon Brown, 1919-
    Nature, reality, and the sacred : the nexus of science and
religion / Langdon Gilkey.
       p. cm.—(Theology and the sciences)
    Includes bibliographical references (p. xxx–xxx) and index.
    ISBN 0–8006–2754–7 (alk. paper) :
    1. Nature—Religious aspects—Christianity. 2. Nature.
3. Religion and science. I. Title II. Series.
BT695.5.G55 1993
261.5'5—dc20   93–14308
                                                                      CIP

The paper used in this publication meets the minimum requirements of American National Standard for Information Sciences—Permanence of Paper for Printed Library Materials, ANSI Z329.48–1984. ∞™

Manufactured in the U.S.A.   1–2754

97   96   95   94   93   1   2   3   4   5   6   7   8   9   10

Dedicated, with love and admiration, to
Amos Welcome Gilkey

"It isn't life that matters. . . .
T'is the courage that you bring to it."
Hugh Walpole, *Fortitude*

Contents

Acknowledgments

This book has been in preparation for several years, which is another way of saying that its final unity represents a bringing together—by reworking, rewriting, and eventual expansion—of any number of course lectures; addresses; and papers conceived, written, delivered, and, every once in a while, published over the previous decade. Nothing is unusual about this; books neither appear out of the blue nor have direct descendents so much as direct ancestors, not only in the many other thinkers who have influenced the ideas in a volume (whom I hope are recognized in the endnotes) but also in the experiments, the first efforts, the trial balloons that each teacher and author floats off into academic space before the unified, finished, and inclusive work appears. What is important is citing these early ancestors or genetic forebears, especially where the addresses or lectures given were hosted so thoughtfully and received so graciously by the departments, colleges, seminaries, and conferences that sponsored them—as was the case for each paper listed below.

Before these papers are listed, however, I wish to recognize the far more significant influences in the coming-to-be of a work such as this, namely, the people whose hard work, passionate concern, and astounding patience made possible the events for which all of this was conceived and written. These are the people whose quiet, often unrecognized labor conceives and brings to birth the continuing conversation of science and religion. Without them, no dialogue would occur; nor would clarity or understanding increase. In fact, fewer papers, courses, and books on this important subject would be available.

First among these "heroes and martyrs" is Philip Hefner, director of the Chicago Center for Religion and Science, associated with the Lutheran School of Theology at Chicago. At least half of what I have thought and written on this broad subject has developed under his generous and patient auspices, in seminars, lecture series, conferences, and so forth, organized and led by him in both Chicago and Germany.

Ken McCall of the Presbyterian Church (U.S.A.) and James Miller of the University of Pittsburgh have—both separately and together—organized conferences at which some of the papers in this book were given. These papers, like caterpillars, eventually through rewriting were transformed into what I hope are the more graceful chapters that follow.

Three other impresarios of religion–science events—namely, Robert

Russell and Ted Peters of the Center for Theology and the Natural Sciences, Berkeley, and Holmes Rolston III of Colorado State University—should be mentioned because their example and their organizing talents have encouraged a great deal of my work in this field.

Finally, I recall with affectionate gratitude my longtime colleague at the University of Chicago Divinity School, David Tracy. David was willing to team-teach courses that, as we stipulated, we "knew little enough about"; in successive years in study and lectures, we both dove into virtually unknown waters, first in a course on nature and then in one on archaic religion. Out of that risky, happy, and creative time (inspired, needless to say, by our then colleague Mircea Eliade) came many of the thoughts on the following pages.

Below are the papers that have come together, in rewritten and reassembled form, to constitute elements in the chapters of this book. These are listed in the order of delivery and include any publication prior to this volume that may have resulted.

1. "What Ever Happened to Immanuel Kant?" Paper presented at a meeting of the Taskforce for Theology and Cosmology of the Presbyterian Church (U.S.A.), Berkeley, California, December 9–12, 1987. Published in *The Church and Contemporary Cosmology*, ed. James Miller and Ken McCall, Carnegie Mellon. (Chapter 4.)
2. "The Principle of Order in the West." Paper presented at Confucian–Christian Conference, Hong Kong, June 1988; arranged by Peter Lee, Hong Kong, and John Berthrong, Boston University. (Chapter 8.)
3. "Nature, Reality, and the Sacred." Paper presented at the Lutheran School of Theology at Chicago, March 2, 1989. Later published under same title in *Zygon: Journal of Religion and Science* 24 (September 1989): 283–95. (Chapters 1 and 5.)
4. "What Theology Can Learn from Science." Paper presented at the Commission for Religion and Science, United Ministries in Higher Education, Jacksonville Beach, Florida, May 6–7, 1989. Published in *Science, Technology, and the Christian Faith*, ed. Brent Waters and Vernon L. Barbour, United Ministries in Higher Education, 1991. (Chapters 2, 4, and 11.)
5. "Nature, Religion, and the Sacred." Paper presented at the Midwest American Theological Society, November 3, 1989; arranged by James Nelson, North Park College, Chicago. (Part Two.)
6. "Cosmos, Conscience, and Creation." Paper presented at the National

Association for Science, Technology, and Society, Washington, D.C., February 3, 1990. (Chapters 1 through 5.)

7. "The Human Care of Creation." Paper presented at the Conference on Ecology, sponsored by the Hillel Fellowship of the University of Denver, February 13, 1990. (Chapter 10.)

8. "What Does Science Have to Learn from Religion?" Paper presented at the annual meeting of the American Association for the Advancement of Science, New Orleans, February 15, 1990; arranged by James Miller, University of Pittsburgh. (Chapters 10 and 13.)

9. "Caring for Creation." Paper presented at the North American Conference on Religion and Ecology, Washington, D.C., May 17–19, 1990. (Chapter 10.)

10. "Can We Speak of God in Our Day?" Paper presented at Saint Catherine's School, Richmond, Virginia, December 1990; arranged by Susan Eaves. (Chapters 12 and 13.)

11. "The Human Care of Nature" and "The God of Nature." Papers presented at Hardin-Simmons University, Logsdon School of Theology, Abilene, Texas, October 14–16, 1991; arranged by Professor George Knight of the Logsdon faculty. (Chapters 12 and 13.)

12. "Human Viability in a Nature That Is Mortal." Paper presented at the Templeton Conference, the Lutheran School of Theology at Chicago, November 17–18, 1991; sponsored by the Chicago Center for Religion and Science. (Chapter 11.)

These scattered pieces on various aspects of the interplay between religion and science were brought together into three series of lectures that also preceded the final reworking of this book.

13. The Albert W. Meyer Lectures, Saint Mary of the Lake Seminary, Mundalein, Illinois, April 1989. Four lectures.

14. The Anthony Jordan Lectures, Newman Theological Seminary, Edmonton, Alberta, Canada, March 8–10, 1990. Three lectures.

15. The Richard Lectures, University of Virginia, Charlottesville, November 14–16, 1990. Three lectures. (The Richard Lectures are the official sponsors of this volume.)

I wish to thank three people especially who have helped me in the preparation of a volume that brings together this decade of work. Joseph Pettit of the Divinity School, University of Chicago—and formerly of Georgetown University—has prepared the index and bibliography. Gwendolyn Barnes, a friend who has done a multitude of good things for all of us, has typed, retyped, and retyped again the manuscript at each of its many stages. Timothy Staveteig, academic editor, Fortress Press, has overseen the editorial details on this, our second book together.

None of this could have been done without the interest, patience, and affection—evident in innumerable and hilarious narrations and discussions around the table—of my family: Frouwkje, Amos, and my love, Ram Rattan.

Misapprehensions of Reality

Ever since I participated as a witness in the creationist trial in Little Rock, Arkansas, in 1981, the relations of religion and science to each other, on the one hand, and of both to a beleaguered and endangered nature, on the other, have been my nearly constant focus through speeches, articles, and even a book. But that controversy over "creationist law" was important to me not because it meant the advent of a new lecture circuit but because it made two things evident.

First, a purely "religious" apprehension of nature, void of any influence of the scientific understanding of nature, is indefensible. Such a view is utterly antithetical to almost all that modern inquiry and modern life "know" about the nature around us. And as Western history shows, such a purely "religious" interpretation, at least in the Christian tradition, leaves nature empty of real significance, a mere stage provided for the human drama with God but a realm lacking in reality or value for itself.

Second, a purely "scientific" apprehension of nature, void of any influence of the religious understanding of nature, is equally indefensible. This side, also presented at the creationist trial, is thoroughly dominant in our culture. It won the day in court but may in its own way be helping to lose the struggle to save our natural environment. This "scientistic" or "empiricist" understanding of nature is precisely what the physical sciences, especially physics and chemistry, say about nature, namely, that it is an objective, causally determined realm of external relations, of matter–energy in motion, mindlessly hurrying here and there—a realm as void of meanings as it is of any trace of inwardness. So thoroughly objectified, nature is made ready, as Herbert Marcuse said, to become mere raw material for our use, an object of dubious human purposes.

Oddly, then, the purely scientific understanding is more devastating than the purely religious apprehension of nature, because the scientific apprehension provides the intellectual legitimation for the industrial and commercial exploitation of nature. The fault lies not in what science says of nature; its knowledge is, on its own terms, unquestionably valid in the way that all science is valid. Rather, the fault lies in how this scientific understanding of nature is itself understood, that is, in the assumed philosophy of science that accompanies most scientific and technological practice.

My critique is not of science, its methods, or its results but of this way of knowing as understood in relation to other, complementary ways of knowing. The view of science that I criticize (1) sees science as the only way to know reality and so the only responsible means for defining reality for us and (2) views the results of science as providing an exhaustive account of reality or nature and hence as leaving no room for other modes of knowing, such as aesthetic, intuitive, speculative, or religious modes. As a consequence, the various nonscientific ways through which humans have apprehended the nature around them—and the artistic, literary, philosophical, and theological disciplines, among others, that monitor these ways of understanding—are construed by this scientistic perspective as having merely subjective referents. According to this view, even the subject who might prattle on in such nonscientific ways can be known only by "objective" scientific analysis.

In this scientific view, therefore, no *Lebensraum* is left for the humanities, for reflection on the human condition, for rational consideration of the moral and political context of science or culture, or for discussion of the convictions and presuppositions fundamental to that context and so to any creative civilization. This book devotes its first attention, then, to a critical investigation of the scientistic side of the debate present at Little Rock. Such a critique and reinterpretation of scientific knowing represent the initial step toward developing a fuller, more variegated understanding of nature and the science that knows nature.

Centrally, this book is about nature. Yet, because physical science is, for us moderns, that main avenue into understanding and so into knowing nature, this book is also about science and nature. And because I am a theologian and hence a student of religion, this book finally concerns itself with some (but not all) of the many human "religious" apprehensions of nature. The themes that course through this book, therefore, concern nature; the scientific knowledge of nature; and religious, especially archaic religious, apprehensions or intuitions of nature.

The search here is for some deeper understanding of the reality of nature. This search is motivated by the conviction that though both scientific understanding and religious apprehension tell us much of this reality, neither science nor religious apprehension alone can provide us with a definitive or exhaustive understanding of nature's power, creativity, and mystery. Nevertheless, both science and religion—the cognitive par excellence and the

intuitive—represent authentic expressions of the *human* response to nature. Hence scientific knowing and religious sensibility may, if taken together, usher us into a new "knowing" of natural process and a new sense of nature's reality in itself, valued for itself.

The discussion unfolds on three levels, or stages. First, I broach the subject of the knowledge of nature. This is the fundamental issue, because what we humans think that we know of any object determines for us what we believe its reality to be. A religious knowing of nature that ignores or even counters a scientific understanding (the Creationist view) is briefly discussed and rejected. The burden of Part One is devoted to creationism's opposite, that is, the scientific realism, empiricism, or positivism that claims (1) that science alone knows anything of nature's reality and (2) that nature is precisely and exhaustively as science describes it. Part One, then, is composed of a critical examination of these claims and an attempt to provide a more intelligible, coherent, and inclusive interpretation of scientific knowing, namely, a form of critical realism. Science surely is our most dependable and accurate mode of knowing the natural world around us. But other modes of knowing through which reality—the nature around us and in us—discloses itself to us are possible, indeed, modes on which science itself depends for its possibility. Part One poses the question: How are these modes to be used with science to deepen our knowledge of nature's reality?

Part Two continues these reflections by juxtaposing what modern science says about nature with what primal religion apprehended of nature. In principle and with great profit, other nonscientific apprehensions, or intuitions, of nature could be analyzed and juxtaposed to a scientific understanding: common experience of nature, the visual arts, literature, philosophy—all represent ways through which nature has disclosed itself to humans. Analyses of these modes of apprehension of nature could, like primal religion, serve to enrich our understanding of nature's reality, were they also correlated in some systematic way with modern scientific understanding.

Primordial religion was, however, the earliest and unquestionably the longest lasting of the various forms of human encounter and interpretation of nature. The focus in this part is on what early religion thought of nature, not on what it may or may not have said about God or the gods. This juxtaposition of science and early religion on the single issue of nature is made possible (and coherent) by the interesting fact that for both science and early religion, nature discloses itself in or through the same four categories: (1) nature as power, (2) nature as life, (3) nature as order, and (4) nature as dialectical unity of life and death. As the discussion shows, much remains the same at the most fundamental level in our relation to nature, even though the implications drawn from the archaic view and the modern view are quite different. The hoped-for benefit is that this attempt to explore another human apprehension of nature will enrich and correct our modern, clearly deplorable interpretation of nature. As Chapter 10 argues, the mortal seriousness of the environmental crisis makes such enrichment and correction not only desirable but also mandatory.

Part Three broaches the question of the religious dimension of nature. Is such a dimension possible in our modern encounter with nature? This dimension was available to primal religion and for nearly all the archaic religion that preceded modern life. Is the religious dimension, which might be termed the "sacred" in nature, still present in any way? If so, what are its forms in a scientific age, that is, in a civilization where the scientific understanding of nature (within limits) is also affirmed and the technological manipulation of nature (possibly within stricter limits!) is also accepted?

The conditions for such a sacred disclosure are framed within the correlation of Part Two—that is, particular "limit questions" are not answerable from within the scientific understanding. Power, life, order, and unity—these puzzles are raised by the sciences but are not answerable in the limited terms of those disciplines. These puzzles call for philosophical and possibly theological reflection. Moreover, any such reflection on these questions uncovers in them traces or signs of something more within nature and also perhaps something beyond it. Proof is not readily at hand here; nonetheless these traces imply the need for further articulation of a systematic sort.

Chapter 13 attempts such an articulation, namely, reflection on these questions, on these traces and signs as pointers to the divine itself. These are only the beginning—if they are that, because they are there only "for eyes that see"—of discourse about God. Much more is known of the divine through history's unique events and through communal and personal experience, through what religious traditions have called "revelation." Nonetheless, what is known of the divine in nature, or what is seen by serious attention to be disclosed there, is an integral part, if only a part, of what can be said of God by faith.

Most important for our current dilemmas with regard to nature, however, is the fact, repeated through Parts Two and Three, that an enrichment of our modern view of nature—of its reality, integrity, and value for us—is dependent on the presence of the sacred dimension of nature in our modern consciousness. Through this dimension nature is granted an integrity of its own, a richer, more mysterious being, creativity, and value than an objectifying, scientific understanding or our normal utilitarian use—even exploitation—of nature could possibly provide. I hope that those who possess the talent will add an aesthetic dimension, a moral dimension, and in the end an ontological dimension—by means of art, literature, ethics, and philosophy—to this initial attempt to discriminate and articulate the religious dimension of our human experience of nature.

Part 1

Reality, Science, and Religion

1

Issues of Language and Truth

Science and religion are essential aspects of our common life, necessary for that life and for each other. At one time, such an assertion seemed debatable with regard to science; more recently it has been so with regard to religion. Nevertheless, the radical reappearance in power of religion—and of its surrogate, ideology—indicates that both science and religion are likely to persist. The ways in which they interact are of importance because historically they have cooperated under all sorts of unexpected, bizarre conditions, as they did in Shinto Japan, Nazi Germany, and Stalin's Russia.[1]

Science is utterly basic for our understanding and knowledge of the world and for our control, such as it is, over the forces in this world. Because culture is, in significant part, composed of the ways we know and the ways we have used our world, science dominates our cultural life: politics, industry, medicine, self-defense, and education. That we live in an age of science is not an issue.[2]

But that religion in the broadest sense is also necessary is equally not an issue. Every community, even a scientific one, lives in and from its general understanding of the reality that surrounds the community. Every community, therefore, shares a set of symbols common to the community that describes the whole of this reality and the whole of experience. And each community's understanding of the whole of things is and must be penetrated with or intertwined with some scheme of meaning, some vision of fulfillment that resolves the pressing dilemmas, tragedies, and evils inherent in existence and that gives realistic direction to our choices, moral and otherwise, and hope to our life. In both our existence and our action, we participate in reality through our deepest symbolic understanding of it, of the truth about it and the values within it. Such visions of the whole and of our place in it—generally of our community's place in it—are "religious" in character, although they may not be lodged in a particular religion.[3] They are articulated in symbols that shape the whole; they are adhered to by assent; and they give meaning and direction to our common and individual life.

Further, knowing raises questions of its use; power creates fearful dilemmas. We now realize that, surprisingly, the more we know, the more ambiguous and yet the more crucial our action is in the future. Knowledge as power drives toward ethical dilemmas, and both knowledge and power drive toward searing questions of meaning. Knowledge may be directed at truth; but, as Francis Bacon said, knowledge leads also to power, the power to do what we will to do. Doing necessarily involves choosing, in this case choosing the better rather than the worse use of our new power. Knowledge here does not tell us what to do; rather, it makes it possible for us to do what we think we want to do and tells us the consequences of the alternatives now made possible. In the present we must choose as deciders and actors, not as knowers. It is simply insane to think that every new development made possible by new knowledge represents a wise or better choice. It is also insane to think that the merely profitable decision, the kind of decisions that our culture makes somewhat automatically, will necessarily add to the common good or lead to more security or well-being in the future, even if only for ourselves. Thus science, in creating this vast new power, leads to an endless array of new ethical dilemmas, especially choices about the application of knowledge to its many new uses, for instance, in medicine, in biological developments, in industrial techniques, and in the development of weapons.

Use raises a problem for judgment, in this case for ethical judgment. Is this course better or worse? And on what grounds, that is, what *is* better or worse? Here appear questions of ethics: of what constitutes values, of what values are real values and hence of judgments between competing values, and, ultimately, of the grounds for these judgments about values. All of these questions inescapably arise. No amount of knowledge will settle these issues: they are ethical or moral issues. We either reflect on them or are dependent on "folklore," conventional wisdom, traditional piety and mores—and probably the American variety of moral folklore is not a great deal better than many other sets of tribal obligations and taboos. Unconsidered judgments here—even those by doctors or by scientists—are no better than are the judgments of the families, the schools, and the suburbs that have helped to produce the physician, the scientist, or the technician. As the creators of all this power and thus of these dilemmas, scientists are deeply involved and cannot, as scientists or as citizens, avoid this obligation to consider their choices. Religion is one of the places—not the only place but probably the principal one—where serious theoretical and practical ethical reflection occurs.

At the deepest level, therefore, symbols of *structure* and symbols of *mean-*

ing, symbols of what is the good and thus symbols that guide our action, symbols of fulfillment and hope, all interpenetrate one another to form some coherent whole. This is true even in a so-called secular society, as the Marxist vision, on the one hand, and the liberal progressivist vision (adhered to by most scientists), on the other, both show. Such global visions of the whole, of which Marxism and the progressivist vision are modern examples, are essential for human existence. In the broadest sense they are "religious" visions, though the classical tradition of philosophy has shared them. Both are transscientific and yet central to science. Both of these combine a vision of the structure of the whole with a clear affirmation of its meaning.

In any case, for both science and religion as so understood, the question of the relation of each to reality, of the truth each holds, is crucial—for both essentially represent a relation to reality that is cognitive or believed to be so. And thus, because science and religion are mutually interdependent, the issues of the truth of science and the truth of religion and of the relations between these sorts of truth represent fundamental concerns for each. It is these issues of knowledge and so of truth that we first address.

The question of the relation of either science or religion to truth is raised negatively from both sides in our day; on each side there are those who would eliminate or silence the other side. Consequently, any real resolution of the problem, any definitive movement toward mutual understanding and cooperation, can come only when each side is able to deal creatively and per-suasively with the "negators" in its own group.

Those religious adherents who deny the truth or the relevance of a scientific knowledge of nature—the so-called creationists—are, unfortunately, on the increase. Regarding religious knowledge as omnicompetent formally and in content extending far into the domains of scientific and historical knowledge, they flatly deny that scientific knowledge, where it contradicts their own so-called knowledge, is valid. At this point, science is to them a hidden form of religious knowledge—it is essentially atheism. Unfortu-nately, these views are important politically and sociologically (especially when the "creationists" claim their religious knowledge to be "scientific"), even though theoretically, from either a scientific or a theological viewpoint, they may not be so important.

For the creationists, the first chapters of the Hebrew Scriptures—espe-cially Genesis—represent an infallible "report," divinely inspired, of the cos-mic and historical events with which our universe began, a kind of biblical equivalent to a contemporary cosmology book about the "big bang" and the early history of hominids. Creationism, therefore, represents a religious real-ism not unlike scientific realism, a positivism of revelation similar to a

positivism of scientific inquiry.[4] Here the religious symbol of creation, crucial for all Christian belief, is taken as containing indubitable religious
information, including a complete "biblical" cosmology, given to us in toto
by revelation, instead of one derived by scientific inquiry—and thus a cosmology in competition with and in contrast to any cosmology produced by
contemporary science. As a consequence, God is pictured in creationism as a
cause among other causes, a being acting in space and time, from "above"
and over six days, to create and to affect other entities that share with God
the same space–time manifold.

By being thus made part of the physical cosmos, God is, incidentally,
reduced to the status of a finite creature. This God creates at a first moment
and continues to create over six days. Further, these founding events happened at a specifiable date in the recent past, and at that date the present
forms of matter, that is, of earth and of life here on the earth, were
produced. From this scenario results the creation-science cosmology, a cosmos once revealed by divine communication in Scripture and therefore
unchanging since. Unlike a scientific cosmology, this cosmology is unaffected
by our changing experience, the changing forms of our consciousness, and
our changing fundamental notions. It appeared with Moses when the Pen-
tateuch was written, and it remains just as valid today as it was then.

The error here—that is, the theological–philosophical error—is to regard
religious knowledge as identical or even similar to scientific knowledge, as
theoretical information about both material and historical matters of fact. It
is a matter-of-fact knowledge without the probability inherent in all such
knowledge, even in scientific knowledge. As we noted, it regards God as a
being among other beings and a cause among other causes, and hence it sees
religious speech as similar in form and function to ordinary speech about
ordinary objects around us—except that this literal speech about the cosmos
has been divinely revealed. Even science cannot think of itself in this absolutist, literal, and realistic way—although much of scientific realism tries to!

An absolutist and literal understanding of religion consequently sees itself
as able to provide us with a revealed astronomy, geology, biology, and
botany, if not also a revealed physics and chemistry. The irony is that those
who on these grounds counter the hypotheses of genuine science with their
own pseudo-science support and, in fact, encourage the medical, industrial,
and military technology that the very science whose validity they deny has
produced. Personally, I want the medicine and the science; they want the
missiles made possible by that science, and they do not disdain the technical
wonders of radio and television, also made possible by science. Creation
taken alone, without cosmos and consciousness, is not quite as intellectually
respectable in our scientific age as is cosmos taken alone, without conscious-

ness or creation—but it presents us with the same abstracted and, therefore, one-sided world.

Like scientism, its opposite number, creationism can become socially dangerous. The theocratic movement, which is very much alive in our culture—the effort to transform us into "Christian America"—is neither a harmless absurdity nor unrelated to the creationism we have described. It represents a rapidly growing religious movement, already manifesting political ambitions and political effects. Its goals are not only to enact so-called Christian laws with regard to evolution, religion in the schools, and abortion but, in the long run, to return our public life to what the theocratic movement believes to have been America's former "Christian" character, a body politic ruled by Christian leaders, dominated by Christian teachings, and even structured by Christian laws. As a picture of our "former" character as a nation, most of this is historical illusion; of this there is little doubt. But a "return" to this mythical past is unquestionably the long-term goal of the creationists. Such a naive yet absolutist form of religion, wedded to a modern technology, represents an authentic future nightmare—as do parallel unions of absolutist religions or ideologies with mature science and technology that have already been evident in our century: in the Shinto Japan of 1930–1945, in the Nazi Germany of 1930–1945, in Stalinist Russia, and in embryonic form recently in Maoist China and Shiite Iran. In all of these, an unreflective religion—creation without either cosmos or consciousness—made union with a philosophically naive and socially irresponsible science—cosmos without creation or consciousness—to form syntheses of religion and science that were unexpected, bizarre, scary, and yet historically very real indeed.

More hopeful, possibly, is the prospect that lies with those scientists who deny the validity and relevance of religious knowledge and so deny that religion contributes anything at all to "truth" about reality. There are also many in modern culture outside of science who feel this way. Among scientists, the dogmatic negation of religion—and one notes that scientists become dogmatic only when they deal with issues bordering on religion—grounds itself in two claims about scientific knowledge. First, scientific knowledge represents the sole cognitive entrance to what is real, the sole source of valid statements about "what is the case." Science alone defines reality for us: "As a scientist, I can make only such statements about what is real as have been established scientifically."[5] Nature, therefore, is as science defines nature, and reality is equivalent to nature as so defined by science. It is widely assumed, in both scientific circles and the wider intellectual community, that when the special sciences of physics, chemistry, astronomy, geology, and biology are put together into a unified picture of the physical universe, a cosmology, one has described all there is in nature and in relevant reality. This is, as Carl Sagan said, "all that there is."[6]

Second, some scientists seek to negate religion by claiming that the knowledge science has gained is knowledge of nature *as it is in itself;* what science describes "is real out there" and, as we noted, all that is real. Further, because science traces out invariable and so, by implication, necessarily determined relations, many in science assume that reality therefore is itself totally determined. As Frank Tipler says, "We are ontological reductionists and determinists because this is what is directly implied by our scientific equations and formulae."[7] Finally, because science neither looks for nor can find purposes in what it studies, science concludes that "science knows that the universe is pointless."[8] What are, in fact, requirements of the method of science in studying nature have become for many the sole constituents of the reality which that method studies, a leap from methodological rules to ontological conclusions.

One finds this naive realism throughout books about science, written by scientists. According to this realistic view, scientific inquiry into nature exhaustively defines reality itself. This is scientific realism or positivism: the special sciences describe what is there, as it is there, as if we held up a mirror to nature. What they find, moreover, is all that is there; hence the special sciences, in defining the nature they study, in effect define all that is included or is to be included in reality.[9] Science knows reality as it is in itself. And empirical science is our only cognitive contact either with nature or with reality; or, put another way, natural science defines our knowledge, and in defining knowledge it defines reality and all of reality. This scientific positivism is mostly assumed, not reflectively argued; yet it remains an important and widely held viewpoint. In the end it is self-contradictory, and, worse, it is fatal both to science itself and to civilization. Our main point here, however, is that such a view of our knowledge of nature is fatal to our understanding of and appreciation for nature.

These two assumptions—(1) that natural science (and, possibly, only physics) alone knows what is real; and (2) that what science knows through its models and formulas is "there," real in itself, the way it all really is— represent pervasive and powerful assumptions in our intellectual world. They are held by many as quite axiomatic, and many people are quite unaware of their radical implications; they are rarely reflectively argued. These assumptions make it difficult to talk importantly and realistically about knowing subjects (and so about scientists) not to mention persons; and any hint of the sacred—of those aspects of experienced reality that lead in the direction of religion—is interpreted exhaustively as a projection onto a real nature, as described via science, by that dubious subject (though who does the projecting in this universe is as mysterious as who does the science!). For this viewpoint, the humanities and religion alike as disciplines trace out only patterns of subjectivity. Correspondingly, the moral ideals and social convictions on which civilization depends, as they bear no reference to reality, represent only the most ephemeral subjective preferences. Although the responsible men and women who share these scientific dogmas are by no means nihilists but, on the contrary, traditional, moral, and humane, the implications of their credo lead inexorably in the direction of nihilism. If one wished to prepare the way for renewed religious dogmatism, scientific dogmatism surely would be the way to do it. In this chapter and the ones that follow, I challenge this understanding of science, not primarily because of its views of morals or religion but rather because of its misunderstanding of science and, through that, its even more important misunderstanding of nature, of reality as a whole, and of the sacred latent in nature and in reality.

Science is our most reliable and, on one level, our most fruitful way of knowing. It is a wondrous power and creation of the human spirit or mind. As one consequence, what it knows—its picture of the universe, the cosmos it describes—is itself in part a construction of mind. Necessarily, as another consequence, scientific inquiry leaves out the subject doing science, the scientific mind that helps to construct what is known,[10] or, when it studies the subject—for instance, in the physiological or neurological sciences—science turns the scientific subject into another object, an object for yet another subject, another scientist, to study! Hence scientific inquiry represents an abstraction from all that is there, from the richness of the nature it seeks to know. It abstracts, therefore, from the richness of reality, from the whole, for the full reality, which is nature in itself, also manifests itself through the subject; through the self-awareness, consciousness, and self-consciousness of the subject; through the other as person; and, finally, through the deep intuitions of the whole that accompany and structure all of experience, including scientific experience.

Therefore, when science speaks of the whole—of what "is really there" or of "all that there is"—it is, strictly speaking, no longer science, though a scientist may well be doing the speaking. At this point the inquiry has turned itself into philosophy and, in my mind, not a very complete or coherent philosophy at that; for it has taken an abstracted though important aspect of reality as a whole, namely, its objective, physical side, that part known through the senses (which themselves translate what they know), and taken it as *the* whole, as the concrete actuality that necessarily includes the sensing, experiencing, and thinking subject. It commits, as Alfred Whitehead said, the "fallacy of misplaced concreteness,"[11] mistaking the abstraction of careful inquiry for the whole of experienced reality. In scientific realism as a worldview, the knowing subject is reduced to a known object, consciousness to neurology, the ordered cosmos of science to a system of inert parts, all without the organizing mind of the scientists, the genius of the neurologists, the creativity of the knowing subjects—who, incidentally, are performing the reduction.

Not only is there an error in this view; there is also implicit in it a danger. In leaving consciousness out, this view omits the human subject from being part of what is taken to be truly real; and with that omission, most of what makes organized inquiry (science) and communal social life a possibility and human life meaningful is rendered merely subjective, evanescent, fleeting, a matter merely of preference. All that is human, all that creates science—the organizing and theoretical creativity of mind, the responsibility and commitment of will, the active self-constitution and self-direction of being a person, the participation through mind and will in cooperative community—is "scientifically" unknowable and thus, for this view, unreal. In an objective world of inert and determined objects, subjects (and with them, persons) vanish; and with them, all values and meanings—that on which civilization, including science, depends—vanish too.

This has not yet happened in our liberal culture. Our traditional belief in the reality of persons and hence in the value of personal identity and autonomy has prevented this denouement. But wherever in a culture this liberal belief ceases to hold, science radically changes its character and becomes the dangerous instrument of an ideology. Scientific realism provides no theoretical basis for the continuation of this important belief and of the social values based on it. We speak easily in academic life of "a free society"; but without the objective reality of persons, of consciousness and of autonomy, there is little theoretical basis for this confidence in and commitment to persons and to freedom as the foundation of civilization. Because science is dependent on a matrix of civilized life built on the foundation of intellectual freedom, autonomous community, and the humane quest for truth, science is dependent on extra-scientific modes of awareness and knowledge. Cosmos alone, without consciousness and ultimately without creation, is self-contradictory, and therefore it can hardly be self-sufficient or self-perpetuating.

2

Changes in Two Ways of Knowing

Not only has there emerged a fascinating parallel in the recent changes in the understanding of religious truth and of scientific truth, but also, in both wider communities, a failure to keep pace with these parallel changes can be identified. The changes in the conception of religious truth came earlier and were, if anything, even more dramatic than the later changes in the understanding of science. The understanding of religious doctrines as including literal statements of matters of fact, frequently in areas covered by scientific inquiry and historical research, has changed slowly over the last two centuries. What has replaced it is an understanding of that truth as *symbolic,* as disclosing deeper, often obscure, but ultimately important levels of experience—levels so important that they are constitutive of our existence and our powers.

Whatever doctrinal or religious truth was considered to be before the advent of empirical science, it was thought by all—clerics, theologians, scholars, artists, philosophers, even scientists—to include "facts" about the age of the world, about how the world came to be, about early events (such as the Fall), and about the early history of the human race. To be sure, accompanying these stories of origins and early history were "religious truths" about God, about human possibilities and destiny, about divine acts and promises. These truths formed, more than the facts that accompanied them, the fundamental elements of the gospel, the religious message of Christian faith. Great theologians concentrated on these deeper dimensions of truth and articulated views of human origins, the Fall, and redemption through God's power and grace. Nonetheless, these symbols of revelation, creation, Fall, and redemption were thought to correspond directly to facts about the universe and its history. Thus, for example, the religious truth that God created all things was intertwined with the belief—on a quite different level—that this act took place over six days roughly six thousand years ago and that an event labeled "the Fall" followed almost immediately on these acts of creation.[1] It is this intertwining of symbol and fact that has come unraveled in our time, the symbolic truth about God and human destiny having been separated from the factual accompaniment of dates, places, concrete events, and so on.[2] Our question is: What "cause" effected that change?—a dramatic change, surely, and one almost defining what is now meant by liberal or modern religion.

The thesis here is that, roughly since 1800, it has been largely under the pressure of developments in science that the understanding of religious truth has changed its form. What religious truth has become remains, of course, a matter of wide debate. But I think it is safe to describe it at present as representing a symbolic but limited—and yet, crucial—perspective on the real; a disclosure of who we are in the totality of things; a symbolic "knowing" of ourselves, of the divine, and of the whole of things, and not a factual knowledge of the world around us. This is taken for granted—and has been for 150 years—by those who reflect on religion, that is, by theological, scriptural, historical, and ethical scholarship alike. And it is this understanding of religious truth that fundamentalism repudiates.

The thesis here is that it is because of developments in the natural sciences in the eighteenth and early nineteenth centuries that this shift in the conception of religious truth took place and thus that the form of modern theology familiar to us appeared on the scene. Just as scientists are loath to admit the presence of important presuppositions of modern science that stem from the Hebrew and Christian inheritance, theologians (even historical theologians) are loath to admit such an influence of science on theology; they prefer to talk about "in-house" influences, such as new interpretations of Scripture or new modes of religious experience. But the evidence in both cases is very strong, and it is healthy to admit and celebrate our mutual interdependence.[3]

Interestingly, the development of classical physics and astronomy with Galileo Galilei in the early seventeenth century (1564–1642) and the completion of these disciplines by Isaac Newton's work in the early eighteenth century (1642–1727), despite radical effects on other matters, did not directly challenge the Genesis account of creation in its literal form. To be sure, classical physics created an entirely new view of outer space and of the workings of moving bodies within outer space. But it did not deeply affect the understanding of time, of the *history* of stars and of the earth, and it did not challenge the assumptions that the present forms of things around us— of the earth and its botanical and biological life—went right back to the beginning. This view of nature as a wonderfully harmonious "machine" did seem to require an intelligent and purposive maker, and so, for a brief period, science and Christian theology enjoyed a mutually enriching, if brief, "affair."[4]

Toward the end of the eighteenth century, however, other sciences came into prominence, and this happy relationship began to be troubled. These were, interestingly, the historical sciences—geology, paleontology, and biology—and they spelled out a significantly different history than did the Hebrew Scriptures. In 1795, James Hutton, the early Scottish geologist, remarked: "We find no vestige of a beginning—no prospect of an end."[5] He also declared that geological science assumed about time exactly what classical physics had presupposed about space, namely, the uniformitarian principle that the same laws as governed events in our present applied right back to the beginning.[6] As a consequence, geology by 1830 (cf. Charles Lyell's *Principles of Geology*) assumed that the changes in the earth's history had taken place over vast eons of time, that they represented changes literally unrecognizable to us, and that they were changes that were the result of *natural* causes and not of divine intervention or specific planning—as, for example, in the "Great Flood." During that same decade, strange, fearsome bones were uncovered in Western Virginia; Ohio; and, later, Illinois—as well as in Russia. These were bones of creatures quite unknown in the present world: giant sloths and tigers; mastodons; and, later, dinosaurs. Clearly, these weird and unfamiliar species, even though once created, had since become extinct—and, even more to the point, they were species that Adam had not named and the ark had not carried![7] The history of the earth and of its forms of life that was uncovered here was vastly different from the one presented by a literal, historical reading of the Bible. As a consequence, anyone interested in and respectful of the new developments in science—as most university and many seminary theologians were—could not do otherwise but begin to rethink what the nature of the religious truth that they found in Scripture, and which they continued to affirm, might be. The Bible contained truth, of that they were sure; but apparently it could no longer be literal, factual truth, of a scientific or a historical sort: truth about the origin of the heavens, about the age and beginnings of the earth, about the appearance of forms of life, or even about the early history of humans and of their cultures. If, then, religious truth did not include factual, "scientific," or "historical" types of truth, what sort of truth was it?

Friedrich Schleiermacher provided the first systematic answer to this new problem. First in 1799 and then in 1821–22, he redefined religious truth, stripping away its factual scientific and historical components. Religious truth is, he said, not scientific or philosophical or even ethical truth;[8] it is rather truth located in and so confined to religious experience, the experience of the infinite in and through the finite, the experience of absolute dependence.[9] The truths of religion are, therefore, articulations in human and hence historically conditioned language of this most fundamental and constitutive of all human experiences.[10] Later, Albrecht Ritschl and the neo-Kantians said religious truth was constituted by value judgments, that is, judgments about the world based on the experience of moral values and of commitment to them. In our century this tradition has continued: religious truth has been defined as existential truth, truth as personal encounter, truth referent to our ultimate concern, or truth relevant to liberation.

In all of these redefinitions, religious truth is strictly circumscribed. In none is religious truth said to include authoritative factual knowledge or information—geological, astronomical, biological, or botanical truth. There is no longer a professor of biblical botany at Oxford; nor does a contemporary critical or theological study of the Hebrew Scriptures embrace the geography or astronomy presented in those Scriptures. We recognize these matters to be illustrative of the "worldview" of the seventh through the fourth centuries B.C.E. and not authoritative statements relevant to our own geographical and astronomical knowledge. Rather, we speak of the religion of the Old Testament,[11] the theology of the Old Testament,[12] the Word of God there, the Word of God contained in and through the words[13]—that is, the religious content, the gestalt of religious symbols and so of religious teachings contained in these texts.

Truth—and with it, revelation—is therefore a *disclosure* expressed in symbols; a disclosure of the divine presence, the divine judgment, the divine promise, and the divine call; a disclosure that appears through events and the human witness to them. For no point of view belonging to the modern scene is religious truth a disclosure of matter-of-fact information. And the articulation of that religious disclosure is not through factual propositions but by means of symbols: in narrative, metaphors, and analogies; in symbols that signal a "doctrine," for example, creation, providence, revelation, incarnation, and so on. Most important, these are symbolic or analogical descriptions of the divine in relation to the world, to history, and to ourselves, not factual or theoretical knowledge of the world in itself. These symbolic modes are, therefore, human ways of speaking that are appropriate to their divine referent.

On the one hand, religious truth has become symbolic and analogical, not a literal description of God or of the cosmos. On the other hand, it has been recognized as human, historically and culturally conditioned, representative of its own time and place: it is the human witness to the divine presence and call. This general view we take for granted in present theological study and reflection; and this new view was, I maintain, largely the result of science. One can hardly imagine a more dramatic change to our understanding of religious truth than this or a more fundamental influence of one discipline upon another.

As is evident at once, the same scientific developments effected changes in the substance of theological doctrines as well as in their forms. The symbols expressive of God's relation to the world and to us in the world, the symbols of creation and providence, remained; however, the ways these symbols were articulated and conceived—and thus the way *God* was conceived—underwent a great transformation in the light of the new scientific understanding of the past. A sudden and recent creation of all things as they now are was no longer credible; or at least such language was transmuted into very symbolic language. To see this, one may recall the creation-science view of creation as just such a sudden event taking six days, ten thousand or so years ago. In its place "creation" is now understood as referring to a long, slow process of change in which new forms developed slowly out of older forms, the whole manifesting the same order of invariant relations ("laws," we call them) evident in our present world.

There were two immediate theological effects of these new scientific concepts. First, if God is creator and ruler of this slowly developing process—as Christians surely continued to believe—then the immanent working of God in and through these processes of change replaces God's originating action on the world: a transcendent act of creation at the beginning by a God originally separate from the world is replaced in dominance by an immanent action of the divine power and intention, over time, on and in the process, as Schleiermacher showed. Put another way, the action of God as creator becomes difficult to distinguish from the creative work of God as providential orderer, as, again, Schleiermacher argued.[14] The symbol of creation remains, I believe, as an expression of the absolute dependence of all beings on the divine power and intention; but an absolute first moment becomes not only dubious but irrelevant, even to the idea of creation so interpreted. Neo-orthodoxy shied away from these conclusions—I ought to know, for I did precisely that![15]—but only at the expense of virtually ignoring God's relation to cosmology and nature, on the one hand, and confining its attention to history and the inward soul, on the other hand. Now that ignoring nature has itself proved nearly fatal, the implications of the immanence of God have begun to return throughout theological discourse.

The second effect of the new, progressive, evolutionist understanding of nature—full-blown by the end of the nineteenth century—had to do with understanding the divine purposes within creation, that is, with the meaning of the divine providence. If the whole world had appeared all at once in its present forms as the purposive work of a transcendent creator, then the marvelous adaptation of things to one another—of codfish eye to salt water, for example[16]—showed clearly enough this divine artisanship and these divine purposes at work. But if all this harmonious adaptation is the result of slow, natural, and so apparently unintended changes, and if the forms of life come into being in the first place and remain in being *because* they are adapted to their environment, then where is the purpose in creation? A harmony among developing forms seems to be a requirement of these forms existing at all; why, then, should we speak of God's purposes here, and what does it mean when we speak of them? Not only was the older teleological argument, based on the sudden act of creation, now apparently defunct, but, more important, it seemed to make no sense to speak of divine purposes in the changes of nature at all. First, these were changes according to natural law (that is, they were apparently blind and random); and, second, adaptation (and therefore relative harmony) appeared as a constituent and necessary aspect of any set of changing forms. If the cod exists at all, then, ipso facto, its eyes must be such that, if the cod can see, it can see in salt water.

An answer to these questions appeared during the latter part of the nineteenth century in what was called "the wider teleology": a divine purpose shaping the entire process of change over time, as opposed to a purpose harmonizing things to one another at the purported beginning. This wider view of divine purpose was of a purpose directing changes of form over the entire process, thus "explaining," or giving grounds for, the long development of the universe into more excellent forms—an evolutionary development or "progress" that was assumed throughout the latter part of the nineteenth century. This understanding of providence became common among theologians at the end of the nineteenth century, especially in the light of the theory of evolution: the "ascent" of forms in the process as a whole manifests and so requires the divine immanent purpose. One sees this view illustrated in the work of Henry Drummond, Lyman Abbott, Lloyd Morgan, Henri-Louis Bergson, and Samuel Alexander, culminating perhaps in the writings of A. N. Whitehead, F. R. Tennant, and, later still, Pierre Teilhard de Chardin. Moreover, as the recent debate over the "anthropic principle" shows, the question of the wider teleology is by no means dead, having been resurrected by certain speculative astrophysicists. This development resurfaces frequently in the following chapters.

The changes in theology in response to scientific developments—both in the form and in the substance of religious propositions or doctrines—are even more evident when we turn from the developing creation of nature to the creation of human beings, especially to their purported "Fall." Here issues close to the very center of the Christian gospel seem to be at stake. It should be noted that it is primarily to preserve as inviolate the actual,

temporal Fall of Adam, the Fall as a literal, historical event, that the creationists hold stubbornly onto a literal interpretation of Genesis; for, as
Henry Morris and Duane Gish write, only if there has been a literal Fall can
there be grounds for the Blood Atonement of Christ.[17] This point aside, the
felt necessity to preserve intact the special creation of human beings and
thus a credible articulation of their uniqueness as moral, religious, and so
potentially immortal beings—all centered on the concept of a divinely given
soul—accounts for most of the resistance to Charles Darwin's views that
religious groups continued to express in the nineteenth century.

Characteristically, the liberal theology of the nineteenth and early twentieth centuries concentrated on the divine creation of humanity through the
long development of ascending forms of life and ignored the "old-fashioned,"
even "medieval" assertion of the Fall. Equally characteristically, twentieth-
century neo-orthodoxy concentrated on the symbol of the Fall and ignored
or dodged the problem of how God had created human beings through the
evolutionary process. Had they talked in any detail about this issue, the neo-
orthodox theologians would almost certainly have had to provide an evolutionary account of God's creation of human beings. In each case, however,
in neo-orthodoxy as in liberalism, the biblical story of creation and of the
subsequent Fall is taken as a figurative account, "disclosing" through its
narrative (myths) and its symbols a deep religious truth: in short, it is taken
as a symbolic story, expressive of the divine in its relation to the developing
world and to human beings. Creation here is, at least implicitly, a symbol
expressing the divine action of bringing the human into being out of
preceding forms of life, while the Fall is presented as a symbolic narrative
that discloses our undeniably universal but nevertheless puzzling alienation,
or estrangement, from our divine ground, from our real selves, and from
one another.[18]

Because this new understanding of the symbol of the Fall has been so
thoroughly explored and articulated in our time in this new version by
Reinhold Niebuhr, Paul Tillich, and Paul Ricouer,[19] to name a few, I turn
here to the symbol of God's creation of human beings. Do we mean by this
a special divine intervention in the agelong process of cosmic development
and evolutionary change? If we do not—and most theologians, if they talk
at all about this, most likely would not like to talk about intervention—then
we have to go "whole hog" and talk about creation *through* all the factors
within the evolutionary process of development. These factors are described,
in their own way, by the sciences dealing with biogenesis, microbiology,
evolutionary biology, paleontology, and genetics and by the sciences dealing
with the evolutionary development of culture, particularly physical anthropology, sociobiology, and anthropology. These sciences present us with a

picture, admittedly incomplete and speculative, of changes of life forms or "species," ending with the early hominids; and they further begin to fill in a picture of cultural development (to call it evolution is perhaps to prejudice the case) up to the clear appearance of agriculture, of towns, of writing, and so of what we have always called "history." This is apparently the way God created human beings: through natural and social processes of development.

In explicating these processes, such categories as mutations, random mutations, combination and recombination, natural selection (that is, the elimination of the unfit), genetic inheritance and programming, and kin selection are used. As both biologists and cultural evolutionists reiterate tirelessly, none of these categories implies a "divine hand" in creation; in fact, an undeniable implication of these "scientific" categories is that any sort of external and purposive explanation of these processes which theology might offer is precisely excluded in scientific explanations.[20]

A theologian might respond in a number of ways; for instance:

1. These categories also omit and, by implication, exclude the influence of freedom and "spirit" on the later developments of culture—elements that must be brought back in at some point if science itself is to be understood.

2. These categories represent perspectives on the real process, certain dimensions of that process and not necessarily all of the factors that are there—though most scientists are loath to admit such a seemingly limiting description of what they know.

3. These categories do not explain the remarkable—in fact, "miraculous"—*story* involved in the initial cosmic process and then in the development of life and its species, a story in which, against almost infinite odds, the process led to an environment where life is possible and thence to the development of forms of life of greater size and of remarkable complexity—even, as the astrophysicists have noted, forms of life capable of astrophysics![21] This is the fascinating question pointed to by the Anthropic Principle and hovering over present scientific inquiry into origins, one denied vehemently by biologists and debated by physicists. It arises as a question for theology as soon as it is recognized that this scientific story is a part of the theological story of creation.

Meanwhile, latent in the scientific account of the process of creation are many fascinating implications about matter and its potentialities for life, psyche, and spirit; about nature as our divine source and ground; about the biological and sociobiological origins of life and of the spirit: of customs, of morals, of law, of religion, not to mention of science itself. Of course, all these "human" things, even science, morals, and religion, are genetically and biologically prepared—if God creates *through* the natural process. Again, this is a mammoth change in theological understanding.

It is interesting that there was a change in the understanding of scientific truth that parallels the change that we have just described. This change in the view of scientific truth occurred with the developments of the new physics around the turn of the last century. I can only in a very amateurish way summarize some of the developments:

1. A new and puzzling indeterminism of the objects studied by physics has appeared. No absolute prediction of the behavior of the quantum was possible, and this has been seen to represent an *essential* limit, a limitation on our knowing that cannot be overcome. Whether this indeterminism is instrumental, epistemological, or ontological could not definitely be known. Reality as portrayed has seemed to proceed or, at least, to reveal itself in "jumps," which was bizarre and subversive of the mechanical, totally "caused," deterministic understanding of reality that preceded the new science.

2. All observations manifest themselves as radically observer-dependent. At the micro level, we cannot perceive and know things as they are in themselves but only as they are in relation to us, the observer. Our knowledge here is not only limited (if not inadequate) but relative, a perspective, and in part therefore a construction—and again, this has seemed an essential and not an accidental limit.

3. What we know has seemed impossible to be as clearly and coherently conceived as had been, for instance, the atom. Smallest particles have been infinitely elusive and seemed to exist in "jumps"; "fields" of force appeared; waves and particles seemed to dance along together; matter seemed to fuse into energy and back out again. As Niels Bohr and Werner Heisenberg agreed, our models and concepts, taken from ordinary experience, no longer apply; only our mathematics applies.[22]

What are "jumps," at this level; "fields" without dirt; "waves" without an ether; how can we conceive a convertible matter and energy? Is all that is a "dynamic force" without substance, a force made up of "events" without matter? It would seem so. We are now dealing with analogies but, further, with analogies or models that do not seem to apply on the ordinary level of sensible experience—that theory in fact denies as soon as it asserts them. No wonder it is hard for the ordinary citizen to understand modern physics![23] It has seemed impossible any longer precisely to specify the nature of nature.

The referents of our microcosmic theories are no longer available to us, either phenomenally or conceptually. The more we know of the fundamental structure of nature, the clearer it is that nature in itself has become a mystery.

These developments in science have proved in our century to be as radical as those in religion nearly a hundred years earlier. The primary qualities of classical physics—mass, velocity, position, and distance, the matter in motion once believed to be "out there" and "real"—have become in effect secondary qualities dependent on the observer; and what is "out there" has only partially disclosed itself in our cognitive relation to it within scientific inquiry. As scientific knowledge has shown itself—now here is a mystery!—as more and more trustworthy, its relation to its real object has become less and less clear. As many scientists have reiterated, "nature as a phenomenal object has gone" and "the new truth about nature is our epistemological distance from nature."[24] Science seems to translate the nature it experiences and charts into symbols that are validly expressive in some deep way of the contours of the real but by no means into literal copies or mirrors of the real or into anything exhaustive of nature's richness. Both nature and reality have in principle again become mysteries, that is, they are again not to be fully known "in themselves" by science.

It is no surprise that not long after the development of the new physics, the reflective understanding of science itself—the philosophy of science— also began to change dramatically. Previously, scientific method had been only logically interpreted: as induction of a hypothesis from data, as deduction toward an experimental situation, and then as verification in light of the new data. The subject here represented only a logical thought process— though where the subject was in the universe was left out![25] In the light of the new science, it made sense to focus anew on the scientific subject: the observer who was now seen as contributing so much to the results of science; the observer as a historical being, on the one hand, and as an experiencing, knowing, evaluating, and projecting being, on the other. E. A. Burtt, R. G. Collingwood, Herbert Butterfield, and Thomas Kuhn[26] showed the influence of cultural and historical presuppositions and paradigms not only on the development of empirical science but on each of its changing epochs; here science as observer-dependent became science as culture-dependent. In turn, Michael Polanyi, N. R. Hanson, Bernard Lonergan, Paul Feyerabend, and now Harold Brown have shown in various ways the contribution of the experiencing and knowing subject[27] to the conclusions of science. In this interpretation we are a long way from the concept of the scientific method as carried on only by a logical and not by a human subject.

The new philosophy of science thus has emphasized the contribution of the scientist as knower and as person to the knowledge that constitutes science and so to the historical developments of science. All scientific inquiry is, as these philosophers say, "theory-laden." The old picture of scientific inquiry as the objective, theory-free gathering of pure data and then the marshaling from those data of an induction, which is finally tested, represents (according to this new view) not science as it actually presents, but a sheer logical abstraction, the product of after-the-fact analysis. In actual practice, on the contrary, significant data appear only to trained minds out of the infinite welter of experienced facts, and these minds have already been prepared by largely unconscious presuppositions and a host of important conscious assumptions. Such prepared minds, moreover, come with prior questions to their data; they are bothered by crucial questions or puzzles that preceding theory has disregarded and which these "significant" data can illumine and the new hypothesis perhaps can resolve. Data appear in relation only to preunderstanding; and preunderstanding is possible only if an entire prior structuring of the world is presumed, and if a part of that assumed structure is being placed under challenge by a new, hypothetical restructuring. Correspondingly, it takes training and expertise, insight and art, to read the data so as to see in them not only the illustration and validation of theory but also a problem to present theory. Science is thus a *hermeneutical* art, a disclosure of new meaning through the data—a meaning others may well at this point not see.[28]

Even more, scientific insight takes a leap of imagination to perceive what is not there—namely, a new answer—and to recognize a new constellation of facts as a confirmation or a refutation of that new answer. Inquiry, whether it be to validate or to challenge existing conclusions, is as much a matter of layers of presuppositions and assumptions; of tacit knowing; of intuition, imagination, and flashes of personal insight as it is of logical procedure or brilliance of thought. Science is here strangely like diagnostic medicine or the appreciation of a painting, more an art than a science. In any case, the imaginative and intuitive subject, the personal being of the scientist, has become crucial.

The doing of science, however, requires not only the intuitive, imaginative, intellectual subject but also, as Polanyi has shown,[29] a communal, moral, and so responsible and committed subject. To be a scientist is to be brought into—in fact, to be trained and inducted into—a moral as well as a social *community* of expertise, in effect, a guild. In graduate school and in the laboratory, one learns how to do science by imitating those who already do it.[30] This "absorption of techniques" is hardly "objective," impersonal learning; it is more like the communal, tacit, person-to-person relation of an apprentice to the master artisan and an intern to the head resident, an initiation into a guild and absorption through practice of a communal art and the "moves" and intuitions of that art. Moreover, the apprentice–scientist thereby also absorbs the standards and expectations of the community she is entering, the "spiritual requirements" for this role: major ideals, commitments, tacit rules, fundamental do's and don'ts. Without this "moral" learning, there can be no scientific community and so no science.

Finally—and here Tillich is particularly clear—there must be in each scientist an ultimate concern if science is to be possible; "objectivity" is a moral and a spiritual achievement, a triumph of an intense and impassioned subjectivity, an existential commitment of the self. Objectivity does not come either with a diploma or with a white coat; it is the result of passionate personal attachment to the truth, as Polanyi put it, or of ultimate concern for uncovering the truth, as Tillich perceived it. Without this personal dedication, this requirement of spiritual inwardness, the scientist can be "bought" by the lure of fame and grants and in the end find himself fiddling with the data, falsifying evidence, and plagiarizing.[31] Just as money and power nearly destroyed the church, so these same two can and do lure science away from itself.

The scientific subject, then, is of necessity both an intellectual, imaginative subject and a communal and moral subject. She is also, as Collingwood, Kuhn, and Stephen Toulmin have emphasized, a historical subject. The preunderstanding that shapes a scientist's mind as she conceives and creates an experimental situation is constituted by the many-layered presuppositions about the world that have come to her from her culture's history and which she therefore shares with the contemporary scientific community. Hence most scientists from other cultures must be "converted" to these (historically Western) assumptions in order to do science. Many of these presuppositions are subconscious; as *pre*suppositions they are not continual objects of our conscious reflection. Many go far back in cultural history—in the case of empirical science, in part to the Greek tradition and in part to the Hebrew tradition. Science would have been quite impossible without their presence in the culture in which empirical science arose. These presuppositions include assumptions about what is real (for example, that the material world around us is real) and about how experience signals that reality to us (for example, through the senses). They also include very general presuppositions about the continuities of experience over space and time, that is, about universal order and of what sort that order is as well as about more particular paradigms or forms of order that have dominated the epoch of empirical scientific theorizing.[32] These general metaphysical assumptions are not discovered inductively from the data; rather, they represent the necessary conditions of there being organized data at all and of there being these sorts of data—and so of there being the possibility of induction.

The scientist's preunderstanding is also constituted by models and images common in the wider culture and borrowed for use in scientific conceptuality, for example, the model of the early industrial machine, so important for science from Newton to William Paley; the model of population increase and the mortal struggle for survival, so important for Darwin; the model of computers and programming, so crucial for modern genetic biology. These imaginatively conceived cultural phenomena provide analogous (and note *how* analogous) conceptualities for scientific innovations. As is the case with religious metaphors, once these analogous models are established, their metaphorical character is forgotten and they become simply and literally "what is there."

Thus science is subject-dependent. And because the knowing subject is himself culturally and historically dependent, science—that is, the theoretical structures of science—has become (like the symbolic constructs of religion) in part a function of wider cultural and historical change, not the self-sufficient and steady accumulation of objective knowledge it once thought itself to be. Just as theology suffered a rude shock and had to reassess itself when, in the early nineteenth century, it was no longer able to consider its contents as directly revealed and so infallible and changeless, so contemporary, late twentieth-century science is having to face the uncomfortable fact of its own cultural and historical relativity. And this is perhaps one reason that this new philosophy of science is so unpopular—that, in fact, it is ignored, except by humanists.

I have herein traced a path from the naive realism of nineteenth-century science and of many contemporary scientists back almost (but not quite) to the constructionism of Immanuel Kant.[33] As this description of the new understanding of science implies, science is a *human* endeavor, a part of culture and thus of historical time, a creative and imaginative construction by human subjects, by knowers. The theoretical structure of science, therefore—its theories and formulas and hence its own conclusions (its "cosmology")—is deeply dependent on the instrumentality of that human knower: on her mechanics of perception and so her sense organs; on the nervous system and brain that characterize such a complex organism; and above all on the forms of consciousness, of thought, and the modes of self-consciousness of the knower.

In short, what is known and, in being known, is shaped into a theory and then used and tested is a magnificent creation of *spirit*, of mind, unifying and organizing its data with equal amounts of precision, intellectual clarity, imaginative wildness, and fidelity. As experience creates an organized world out of the senses, so spirit, through naming, imagination, and reflective logic, creates the systematic world of scientific cosmology. Out of the environment, the self as spirit creates a "world," an ordered, unified cosmos over against the observing self. This is a cosmos laced with the theoretical rationality, the mathematics, and the language characteristic of the self and thus a world organized and understood and offering potential for the technical use of the self. As there are, in our experience, no organisms without an environment and no selves without a world (and no spirits without bodily organisms, minds without brains), so there is no world, no ordered cosmos, no scientific cosmology without self and spirit. Therefore nature, as science defines it and technology uses it, is not merely "nature in itself" but also in part a magnificent construction of embodied spirit; not so much a construction incited by our sensory contacts with nature as it is one organized and reflectively known by our minds. As a complex body of theory, science represents and signals in part, and yet clearly, our distance as minds over against nature as reality; that is, it represents the translation of that reality into the terms of our minds. It discloses our distance as much as it represents in its conclusions our dependence on and participation in nature.

It is ironic that the scientists (and here I cite especially the cosmologists and the sociobiologists) who present us with a magnificent vision of nature as science sees it, in effect a wonderfully accurate edifice of scientific theory, should find in that vision of the whole no apparent place for the scientist, for the scientific subject who, through dependence on communal tradition, training, inquiry, imagination, commitment, and testing, has created that very "subjectless" cosmos. In its wonder at the objects spread out before the gaze of its inquiries and at its own brilliant theoretical understanding of that system of objects, science has tended to forget, as Kant reiterated, that the entire vision is in part a creation of the scientific observer. As Holmes Rolston has said, "The most astounding entity in the universe which an astronomer surveys lies just back of the eyes looking into the telescope."[34]

The changes in the understanding of truth both in theology and in natural science have indeed been dramatic; but it is not at all clear that these changes have penetrated widely through either the religious or the scientific communities. In both communities, literal, realistic interpretations of their own truth remain; and these inherited and uncriticized viewpoints from both sides wreak havoc with efforts to bring the reflections and the attitudes of the two communities closer into cognitive harmony—while precisely such cooperation is now possible, as well as called for.

In this discussion of the new interpretation of religion and the new philosophy of science, certain parallels have appeared that were both unexpected and important.

First, in both, the role of symbols is crucial; the expression of what is known appears in metaphors, models, and analogies rather than in literal, univocal descriptions. In each case, there is the sharp awareness that the metaphor or symbol is not precise: that waves and fields in physics are not like "ordinary" waves and fields, and that religious language about what transcends ordinary experience of things and persons around us is analogical and not literal language. To be sure, both science and religion proceed on the assumption, or "faith," that their discourse and so their knowing is a response to what is real; but both recognize the inadequacy, the perspectival character of their articulations—and the consequent mystery of the object of their knowing. Interestingly, at both the microcosmic level of physical science and the macrocosmic level of ontology and theological language about the whole, a symbolic discourse becomes inevitable. No mode of discourse, therefore, encompasses all of human reality as it is. Each mode represents a perspective—relatively valid, to be sure—on what is there; none is a simple mirror of what is. Symbols, perspectives, and mystery characterize, in different ways and on different levels, the two ways of knowing we have discussed.

Second, it has become evident that, in each mode of knowing, the subject of knowledge, the knower, plays an essential role in the knowing process. Each mode of symbolism, religious or scientific, is in a sense a construct of consciousness in response to a disclosure of what is real. This constructionist view of knowing has long been recognized with regard to religious affirmations: fundamental religious symbols in every culture articulate the disclosures on which they are founded not only in "human" language and human terms but even more in the categories and symbols central to the particular cultural life surrounding that religion. In this sense, religion is a part of cultural history, dependent on that history as well partly creative of it, as are the other aspects of culture: science, art, political theories, moral values, and philosophy. One unexpected element in the new philosophy of science is the recognition of a similar cultural dependence on the part of scientific developments: a dependence of science on the metaphysical presuppositions of its culture and so on the culture's most fundamental ontological and religious symbols; a dependence on presuppositions about order, change, and novelty in that particular cultural and historical life; and, finally, direct dependence on models and paradigms crucial to that cultural time and place. In each case, the human response to the reality encountered is structured, conceived, and articulated in a human and hence a cultural mode of symbolic discourse. The response is in that sense relative, a perspective on what is there, a responding construction of consciousness or spirit. In the case of both "creation" as a religious symbol and "cosmos" as a product of science, the creative role of consciousness is essential and crucial—and so the mystery of divine being, of being as a whole, and of nature, being around and in us, remains.

Third, if both scientific and religious knowing represent symbolic constructions of experience and responses to disclosive encounters with the reality in us and around us, then it follows that they are, in ways neither one has fully recognized, mutually dependent on each other. What we have termed "religious" symbols articulate, in metaphors drawn from ordinary language, the experienced relation of our existence to the whole of things: that is, to the reality of the whole, its order, its fundamental processes and issues, and its goals and meaning. It is on the basis of such a symbolic vision of the whole that the fundamental character of natural and historical processes and our relation to each of them as knowers and doers are articulated. And as does all else in culture, science draws *its* presuppositions, presuppositions necessary for the inquiries and the conclusions of science, from these common cultural presuppositions. There can be no science such as ours in a world structured by a significantly different set of presuppositions. Further, from the moral context of its culture science draws the necessities of its own communal life and thus makes possible its own stringent requirements. Without these two bases, these cultural and moral presuppositions, science is impossible. Science is thus dependent on what Tillich called "the religious substance" of its culture, that most fundamental vision of reality, truth, and value that animates that culture's life.

Religious symbols are just as dependent, only in the reverse mode. To be intelligible to us and thus adequate for our inner assent, religious symbols must make reflective contact with our world, that is, the world as it is structured and organized in our cultural existence. Religious interpretations of the possibilities of our individual existence, of our society, of our sin, of spiritual rescue and fulfillment, of history's meaning, and finally of nature's relation to us can only have meaning for us if they are in our cultural idioms. I am convinced that such religious interpretations provide by far the most profound and ultimately the most valid understanding of these important matters. But in order to realize the depth of our experience and to provide creative guidance to our actions, such religious symbols must make contact with and relate to all else we know in our ordinary dealings: about society, about human waywardness, about the psyche, and so about one another, about history, and especially about nature. Hence religious symbols, dependent on their own autonomous disclosure (in revelation) and structured by human analogies, must be filled out by, correlated with, and related to the "knowledge" gained, first, in ordinary personal and social experience and, second (for theological reflection), in the historical, the physical, and the social sciences. If doctrines are religious symbols, responsive to divine disclosure but structured in human language and expressive of our experience of our own existence in the world, then an important part of their meaning lies in what is known by ordinary experience—and so by inquiry into ordinary experience—of nature, history, and ourselves. In the same way, part of the meaning of any scientific articulation lies in the wider presuppositions on which that articulation depends. Thus, as symbolic constructions by the culturally and historically relative human subject, science and religion are mutually dependent. Each is a creation of the one spirit in response to the mystery of reality around and in that spirit.

3

The Nonscientific Bases of Science

In science, knowing is dependent on the subject as well as on the object known. That subject, I have maintained, is a perceiving, experiencing, unifying, categorizing, theorizing, imagining, and projecting subject, practiced in its art and loyal to its commitments. It is intellectual, imaginative, communal, moral, and projecting, free to follow its own hunches and decisions in manipulating the given in new experiments, free to project hopes for future testing, and, above all, free to assent on rational grounds alone to the probable validity of new hypotheses. Nothing in this process is experienced or could be experienced as determined. Rather, the subject is aware of itself as deliberating, guessing, assessing, and finally reflectively judging the relevance of its data, the probability of its hypothesis, and the validity of the conclusions of its inquiry. Science is clearly an operation of consciousness or mind as well as a sensory encounter with external reality. There are, then, two interacting, mutually dependent factors, cosmos and consciousness—not cosmos alone. This chapter explores further this interdependence and what it might mean for our understanding of both factors and possibly for our understanding of the true nature of nature.

In principle, one could start with cosmos (or "nature"), consciousness, or creation in working toward a synthesis of the three into a unified whole; for, as I have steadily implied, each of these implies the other two: cosmos entailing consciousness and implying creation, and creation entailing both the cosmos that is created and the consciousness that symbolizes that religious affirmation. Nonetheless, the term *consciousness*—or *spirit*—is perhaps the most illuminating of the three with which to begin. Consciousness necessitates an objective world to which it responds in experiencing and in knowing and which, in turn, it reshapes in all it does; and consciousness, as I ultimately seek to show, implies creation as the sole intelligible ground of its own late appearance in the cosmos. If taken alone, however, consciousness ends in idealism; and that one-sided view of all things as produced out of the minds of subjects lost the battle with the vast material universe and

with natural science a century and a half ago. So in examining consciousness, the first question to ask is: How does it mediate between cosmos and
creation?

As was revealed in Chapter 2, human consciousness in sensing and experiencing the material reality that surrounds it and that works within its body
is not merely a passive recorder or mirror of what is there, as if it simply
"looked at" things in themselves. On the contrary, consciousness constructs
its world in perceiving and knowing it. As George Santayana said, sensations
are human cries in response to external stimuli. The manifold or panorama
of sense experience, as Galileo insisted, is constituted by secondary qualities:
colors; shapes; sounds; perspectives; and, before and after, characteristics
provided by the receiving sensory instruments, by the memory, and by the
unifying drive of the human receiver. Finally, the theoretical organization of
experience into a coherent order made up of objects (substances) in systematic relation (causality) represents an environment named, unified, and
ordered by mind into a "world."

All of this process of experiencing and knowing is a *responding construction:*
a creative response of mind in relation to the nature around it, the "environment." Out of environment, spirit creates an ordered world or cosmos. This
is the main theme of critical realism, namely, the constructive work of
consciousness in cognition and so in the appearance of knowledge—that
very knowledge represented by the cosmology of the special sciences—and
this theme runs through modern philosophy as its most consistent thread. It
has, however, been steadily ignored by most of the scientific community,
which remains insistent upon a naive realism—and which encounters the
self-contradictions and dilemmas outlined in the preceding chapters. The
cosmos as known by science is not all there is: there is necessarily consciousness, the observer (Carl Sagan as scientist, for instance, organizing, constructing, and pondering his environment and so creating the world known
by science and described in innumerable fascinating books). Cosmos needs
consciousness as much as consciousness needs the environment. (This also
means that natural science needs philosophy and even, perhaps, philosophical theology if it would speak intelligibly of "all there is," of "reality.")

There are two conclusions to be reached from this obvious but frequently
unheeded philosophical truth. The first is that knowledge is in part a construction of mind and that, as a result, what is known—the experienced and
theoretically organized cosmos of science—is not identical with the actual
environment to which experience and cognition respond. Nature in itself is
not the same as nature known by scientific inquiry. Nonetheless, nature in
itself, the "thing in itself," is known dependably and so is in part validly
known; pragmatic testing shows us that it is certainly not falsely known. But

as a construction of our experiencing and knowing, our knowledge is couched in *our* terms: in the language of our senses, in the symbols of our creative imagination, and in the structures of our modes of thinking. The "thing in itself" therefore lies beyond our cognitive grasp, because this process of translation or transposition inevitably occurs. The reality encountered, in itself and for itself, remains a relative mystery, even to our scientific inquiry with its human formulas, models, and theorems. Nature in itself is not the same as nature "for us," nature reshaped by inquiry through hypothesis and experiment, and nature as experienced in technological reshaping. The world known by science is an abstraction, by means of sense, reflection, and reshaping, from the actuality that is encountered. Being in itself is different from being as it is known and manipulated, from being "for us."

The second conclusion is that this process of sensing and theoretical organizing, ending in judgment, is itself dependent on cognitive relations to reality other than those generated through the senses and through theoretical reflection. Scientific inquiry, science's experience of its world, is set within wider, more constant, and so more fundamental human relations to reality that make existence itself, life, and even science possible. This is obvious enough, if we think about it: we do not ourselves first become real or first experience either our own reality or external reality when we enter the laboratory. The important point is that these other relations to reality are also, in their own way, *cognitive*: they represent experienced encounters with reality that result in knowing something of what is encountered. They are cognitive encounters, which support and structure our more formalized, abstract intellectual and scientific inquiries into our world.

We are aware of ourselves in a real environment, in a community of persons, and in a world that moves in temporal process but is nonetheless structured, held in place in a certain orderly way. And we know all this long before we become scientists. Moreover, this fundamental, generic awareness is cognitive.[1] From it comes our certainty of the reality of world, self, other persons, and their necessary interconnections. Of none of these can the assurance of objective reality be established through sensations, as David Hume noted,[2] but such assurance accompanies all scientific inquiry as its deepest presupposition.

A major primordial part of this general awareness is our self-awareness. Self-awareness (self-consciousness) is as broad as it is fundamental. It is essential to any scientific procedure. Our inner certainty that we are experiencing data and what they are, that we are reflecting on those data and what they mean, that we are making judgments about them, and that those judgments are falsified or validated by an adequate experimental event—all of these inner certainties constitute the basic steps of scientific procedure.[3]

Because we are self-aware, and so aware inwardly not only of what we are doing but also of what that series of operations means, we can conduct a procedure that is logical, a methodological progression constituted by steps that bear a logical relation to one another. Without self-awareness there is no meaning or consciousness of meaning; and without meaning there can be no such logical, methodological, scientific procedure—even a scientific procedure that traces in someone else the neural processes that were doing the procedure. Self-awareness, knowledge by the subject from the inside of her own experiencing, reflecting, and judging—that is, from the inside of her knowing and the meanings she knows—is as constitutive of science as are sensations and measurements. In fact, without self-awareness there can be neither of those!

An equally primordial element is the awareness of the other as person and so of community as human community. Through this primordial knowledge of the other as other and as person comes our awareness of the vital role of the community (in this case, of the community of other scientists) for our participation in scientific procedures. Through this intuitive awareness of other persons as persons and so as moral persons, we know the standards and expectations of this community, its procedures and habits; through this awareness we become conscious of our obligations within that community and of its values—and so of our own participation and commitment to those values. Participation in a community's life depends on knowledge of others in this community as persons, that is, on "moral knowledge."[4] Knowledge of the procedures, standards, and goals of the scientific community is as essential to doing science as are the laboratories, technical equipment, and theories of science. This knowledge also is acquired in a nonscientific mode of awareness, probably as a tacit aspect of graduate apprenticeship, wherein an apprentice observes, copies, and reduplicates the procedures, habits, and obligations of a master. This knowledge of community as community also forms a part of the nonscientific, cognitive basis of science.

Finally, the assumption of an order spanning all of space and time is essential to all modern scientific thinking and inquiry. This assumption is unprovable because it is the basis of all proof. Without it there are no data at all, data from yesterday in time or from somewhere else in space; and without data there is no empirical proof. As Alfred North Whitehead put it, that yardsticks used to measure distances yesterday in Cambridge should hold good today in New Haven is a faith based on general intuition and not provable by any use, however ingenious, of yardsticks. This faith in order, Whitehead continued to explain, is not only basic to science but also to all human (he said "civilized") life.[5]

Immanuel Kant thought these forms of our thinking—this faith in order—to be provided by the subject. In contrast, one of the naive realist cosmologists examined herein, Heinz Pagels, called the presence of universal order an "absurd but given fact," apparently one simply discovered by scientific inquiry. To me, the histories of religion and philosophy show these forms to be general and pervasive intuitions, first of nature and then of reality as a whole, as old as human culture, expressed in each religion, and appearing in explicit form in all early philosophy. These intuitions or disclosures of order, rationality, and value take a different form in each culture. In the development of modern culture, because of its Greek, Hebrew, and Christian roots, they took the particular form needed for modern empirical science to develop. These cultural roots therefore form the necessary preconditions in cultural history for the development of modern science.

All of these intuitions represent cognitive relations of consciousness to reality, which are at once foundational for science and yet themselves nonscientific. I suspect they can be validated, if at all, by religious and philosophical arguments. For this reason a positivist account of science, which finds meaningless all such extra-scientific arguments, is self-contradictory. Without this level of cognition, science is impossible, as impossible as it is without self-awareness.

Science, then, represents a construction of sense experience, intellectual reflection, and cognitive judgment (that is, consciousness or spirit). And what is constructed is, on the one hand, different from the objective reality cognitively encountered and, on the other hand, dependent on other cognitive relations to reality: relations to the inward self, to others, and to the whole in which consciousness resides. The *objective* reality of nature is thus richer and more mysterious than even the scientific models and theoretical pictures of it created by science. And the cognitive manifolds of human beings, and so their knowledge of reality, are at once much wider and more varied than is the systematic knowledge, however intricate and accurate, offered by scientific inquiry. Not all that we know is science, lest there be no possibility of science.

If all this is true of consciousness in its cognitive encounter with the reality around it and in it, then two more implications follow. First, it follows that all our knowledge is symbolic, that it consists of human signs or words uttered in response to this encounter. Contemporary philosophy of science has arrived, by a quite different route, at this same conclusion. Surely our sense data are such signs. Even more evidently, our theoretical categories and judgments—formulas, laws, models (molecules, atoms, neutrinos, genes that program, etc.; the entire set of constituents of our theories)—are constructs, symbols for events and processes, to which events and processes are related but from which they are very different.[6] Our symbolic constructs for the most complex of entities—for organisms and persons, for social processes and history, and for the "whole" itself—represent a further mode of understanding, symbols that are less precise but perhaps more fundamental and certainly more important for our total experience. Mind or consciousness is not a mirror of reality; at best it is a faithful tabulator in another, more "homey," tongue. What we know is made up of human symbols or signs; it is not a duplication of what is known.

Second, this analysis has made plain that cognition takes place at different levels, levels that are mutually distinguishable but nevertheless mutually dependent. I have distinguished, as different modes or levels of knowing, sense data; self-awareness; awareness of another, of community; and, finally, general intuitions of the whole, as reality, as process, as order, as related to value. Each of these levels is represented in our experience and reflection by different sorts of symbolisms, different sorts of language games. These are in turn composed of models, drawn from different areas of experience, with which we organize, judge, and communicate our experience and in terms of which we respond in decision and action. These different levels interpenetrate to form one experience. Self-awareness, knowledge of the other, and intuitions of the reality and order of the whole unite with sense data and theoretical judgments to form scientific theory: the cosmos with which we began. In turn, cosmological experience and knowledge, our understanding of nature and history, join with self-awareness and our intuitions of the whole to create our fundamental symbolisms of self, of society, and of history. And involved with all of those levels as intrinsic to their possibility are our intuitions of reality as a whole and of the sacred, symbolisms necessary to each level of culture and of civilization.

It is through a mediating synthesis of these different levels that our three terms—cosmos, consciousness, and creation—can be brought together in some intelligible and coherent harmony, rather than be left separate and distinct in isolated self-contradiction. Only if we recognize these wider areas of cognition, the symbolic character of all knowing, and the different levels necessary for any knowledge at all is such a synthesis possible. Our common civilization, being dependent on all these levels, therefore relies on the achievement of such a synthesis.

In summary, I have emphasized the importance to science of the subject, the knower who constitutes and creates science and who thus forms the central precondition of science. This subject very early distances himself in distinction from "world" and looks at the world in wonder and curiosity. This is the perceiving, organizing, naming, wondering, thinking, understanding, and judging subject, who remembers and ponders past experience and imagines what is not yet, who manipulates the given in experience, and who projects future hypotheses and future uses of knowledge; who is aware—and self-aware—of each of these steps or methods; and who is committed, or could be, and so perseveres in pursuit of truth and the good. It is to this subject in science and of science that the words spirit, freedom, and self-transcendence, as well as mind and reason, have been applied. Science is the result of such embodied spirit and mind.[7]

Appropriately, therefore, the *results* of science, its theories, are not "explained" by its genetic, physiological, and neurological conditions or causes—all of which are there as "causes," to be sure. On the contrary, scientific theories are judged, or assessed, as true or false by empirical and logical warrants, by the correlation of these theories with experimental evidence, by their coherence with other theory, and by their fruitfulness. In this sense, science is not understood when it is explained by all the causal factors that produce it; no scientist would recognize a Marxist economic or Freudian psychological explanation of physics as providing a satisfactory understanding of the theorems of that science, though they might say it illustrated the needs and urges that led particular scientists to uncover those truths. After all, the neuroses of practicing analysts do not invalidate the theoretical structures they use in their practice. Science is understood when its theories are understood on their own terms and in the light of their own evidence, and those theories are then assented to as (probably) true or rejected as false. The same mode of assessment should be (but is not) the case with regard to philosophy and religion. Currently, philosophy and religion are thought by most intellectuals and scientists to be explained and hence understood through the genetic, biological, neurological, psychological, or sociological factors that have helped to produce them—as these same factors helped to produce science and these very theories about philosophy and religion! No scientist or social scientist applies exhaustively this mode of explanatory understanding to her own theories.

In any case, it is clear that science as an operation demonstrates the reality and the effectiveness of spirit: of mind, freedom, and commitment; of the transcendence of spirit over past, present, and future; and of the power of spirit to project plans into the future. Despite this, many scientists say they cannot find any sign of spirit among the objects they investigate. Of course they cannot; what they investigate are objects, and all objects of inquiry lack inwardness, as all such objects also already lie in the past of the observer. Spirit is known only by intuitive awareness, by disclosures, of self and of others, not by inquiry into objects. This is one important reason for why scientific knowledge cannot represent all we know: it leaves out the creative subject of science, the scientist, and thus has only half the story. The subject must be added to reality in any full account of nature. The cosmos thus is not all there is; there is also the scientific observer looking at nature and constructing his or her cosmos. Not only is the subject as consciousness fundamental to our scientific understanding of nature, but the subject as spirit also provides, as an unexpected product of nature and therefore as an example of nature's richness, a clue to the mystery of nature that is fully as significant as all we can know objectively of nature.

4

Whatever Happened to Immanuel Kant?

This chapter traverses with greater care the general area I have so far been delineating, namely, the scientific positivism or naive realism of much current science. A more specific study of this area is necessary because of the widespread character of this understanding of science; its devastating implications for the humanities and so for many fundamental elements of our common civilization; and its even more negative implications for religion, for religious symbolism, and so for the rational articulation of the deepest symbolic bases of our common life. Most important of all here is the effect of this positivistic realism on our understanding of nature: if science is our only cognitive avenue into nature's reality, and if that reality is defined by empirical science alone, then nature is—and will be—for us only a useful object or system of objects, without inherent value in itself and so only there "for us." Scientific realism leads to a pragmatic understanding of nature and hence, if we are greedy enough, to exploitation. Strangely, scientific positivism turns out to be the most anthropocentric view of nature of all.

The area to be considered, then, is that of current cosmologies, of which I present a few representative and widely read samples.[1] The questions I raise about these cosmologies are neither scientific nor theological but philosophical in character; and because I am really not a professional in either cosmology or current philosophy, this will be at best an amateur effort. But perhaps in this day of specialization and therefore of uninhabited and unpatrolled "no person's lands" between fields, an amateur may, in his or her innocence, raise some useful questions. Readers familiar with my thoughts on science may expect religious or theological criticisms of science: for its intellectual or spiritual hubris, its dogmatism, its unawareness of its status as "established," its naive mythologies, its utopianism, and so forth. Such criticisms, instructive as they may be, do not appear here.[2] I am interested (as I was in most of *Religion and the Scientific Future*) in the points where both science and religion meet on a philosophical common ground, or should do so: namely, in the necessary epistemological and ontological or metaphysical middle ground between scientific theory and theology. Having gone through a goodly number of cosmologies, I am now assured that it is in what might be called the "philosophical middle wasteland" that many, though not all, of the misunderstandings and problems in the relation between science and religion lie. In any case, I am convinced that both sides—the scientific and the religious—can in our day only profit by more exposure to the issues and principles lurking in this currently deserted philosophical middle ground.

This came, I admit, as a surprise. Having done some of my homework in current philosophy of science, I was as aware as anyone not only of the demise in philosophy of science of logical positivism and even of "scientific empiricism" but also of the birth of what has been welcomed as the "new philosophy of science."[3] What is more, it was evident that those philosophers of science who presided over the heir's recent birth were also conscious of the new relevance to the understanding of science of *hermeneutics,* a mode of philosophical understanding appropriate not only to the humanities—its "home ground"—but even more to religious understanding. In principle, therefore, the philosophical problems of the interrelation of scientific theory and theology, and so of scientific knowledge and religious disclosures, seemed resolved.

On the level of philosophical discussion, this rapprochement is no illusion. Nevertheless, from my limited reading of scientific cosmologies, it appears that word of this breakthrough in the philosophy of science has not reached most of the "working cosmologists." In a sense, then, this chapter represents elements of that new philosophy of science's viewpoint, now applied critically to selected cosmologies; however, my references are more inclusive than that, for I am interested in the relation of modern cosmology to that rich, varied (but perhaps now forgotten) philosophical tradition, from Immanuel Kant to our time, known as *critical philosophy.*

This is not to say that contemporary cosmologies are not exceedingly impressive works. I have found Heinz Pagels, Carl Sagan, Steven Weinberg, Richard Dawkins, and John Barrow and Frank Tipler learned, intelligent, enthralling, and surprisingly charming. They appear (to a layperson) to know exactly what they are talking about—even if much of it remains incomprehensible to me—and each is astoundingly able to synthesize clearly and helpfully (if in quite different ways) very disparate realms of scientific theory. And what contemporary science can legitimately claim to "know" about the vast physical universe is a source of continuing astonishment, even "wonder," to an amateur such as myself.

What I did find, however, is that none of these cosmologists seems to be conscious of the important epistemological and metaphysical problems that inevitably hover in the background of their work. It was as if these questions concerning the possibility and status of our knowledge, even of our scientific knowledge, were simply not there; or, although these authors were aware that such questions had once been raised in a quite different cultural matrix than our present one, still it was as if for some reason or another these questions did not now apply. If they had heard of these questions (and many referred to Alfred North Whitehead, even to Kant), these authors did not seem to think that these puzzles from the tradition were relevant in any way to what their scientific colleagues were saying or to the "up-to-date" cosmologies that they themselves were writing. Apparently, therefore, the relevance of philosophical questions and discussions to the possibilities, the limits, and the validity of cosmology never occurred to these authors, even though these philosophical issues are crucial to the intelligibility of what they are writing.

One can only suggest that a "cultural atmosphere," "a plausibility structure" (to use Peter Berger's phrase), of positivism—that is, an idea that no philosophy is necessary or relevant to any of the special sciences—has engulfed the scientific (and the academic?) communities to the extent that this irrelevance of philosophy has become an assumed and not an argued subject of our intellectual life. I wish to be clear that it is about the philosophy of science implicit in these cosmologies, not about the science with which these books explicitly deal, that I am raising questions. The question "Whatever happened to Kant?" has occurred to me before, but only with these cosmologies has the critical problem moved center stage in my mind. What is it about these cosmologies that makes me think that they have forgotten the tradition of critical philosophy—and have forgotten, along with that tradition, most of the points emphasized in the "new philosophy of science"?

There are four propositions about science and its knowledge that seem to be assumed by these cosmologies. It is not irrelevant that these four propositions are characteristic of an older (in fact, nineteenth-century), now frequently repudiated, "objectivist" understanding of science and therefore challenge directly the new understanding of science. On most important issues these propositions also represent the kind of naive realism, "the fallacy of misplaced concreteness,"[4] that critical philosophy from David Hume through Kant to Whitehead and Michael Polanyi (not to mention Bernard Lonergan and Paul Tillich) has sought to challenge.

The first proposition is that science—in this case, physics—is about to answer satisfactorily its own most important questions, resolve fully its deepest puzzles, and thus in effect bring about, through this virtual apotheosis, its own end. Not all scientific cosmologies utter these surprising, almost "eschatological" predictions; but Pagels's book is full of them, and he quotes some impressive authorities for this view. Early on he asserts that "today scientists confront the universe as a puzzle with scattered clues to its solution. Challenging as it is, many believe they will solve it some day. That day may be closer than many people think." At a later point he expands on this: "Some day . . . the physical origin and the dynamics of the entire universe will be as well understood as we now understand the stars. The existence of the universe will hold no more mystery for those who choose to understand it than the existence of the sun. Steven Hawking (in his Plumean lecture) . . . said that the major problems of the universe may be solved in several decades." Therefore "the end is in sight for theoretical physics."[5]

Quotations such as these from pre-quantum physics are frequently cited in current philosophies of science (much as medieval or Reformation dogmatic statements are cited in liberal theological histories) to illustrate the kind of objectivist realism that was familiar at the end of the last century in "classical" physics, before the revolution of quantum and relativity theory. With that "revolution"—so current philosophy of science assures us—there was evident a new sense of the mystery of the objects of physical science; of the perspectival character of every inquiry, even new ones; of the consequently symbolic character of human conceptuality; and so of the non-identity of our concepts with actuality.[6] It had also become evident that observations depended on observers and were affected by them, so that the results of inquiry were always "infected" by the aims, assumptions, instruments, and loci of the inquirers.

Recent philosophy of science, then, has increased the weight of the perspectival, relative aspect of inquiry. It was therefore a great surprise to encounter in Pagels these assertions, with their undeniably objectivist assumptions. To predict that the deepest puzzles of actuality will soon be "solved" and therefore that the inquiry on that level may well cease is (1) to regard actuality and theory as potentially completely congruent, if not identical, so that actuality is completely "available" to theory; (2) to deny any perspectival or relativistic aspects of theory; and (3) as a consequence to regard theory as in principle totally ahistorical, almost "eschatological" in character. The second proposition intensifies this interpretation of science.

The second proposition is that there are no effective presuppositions to scientific inquiry and so to adequate scientific judgments; such judgments, on the contrary, are purely empirical, based on objective evidence alone, and thus are influenced not at all by the locus, perspective, or preunderstanding of the inquirer. One of the major thrusts of the new understanding of science has been the emphasis on science's theory-laden character. Evidence and facts, many philosophers of science now argue, take shape only as a result of prior theories; arguments in scientific disputes hinge on the "paradigms" (Thomas Kuhn), the "ideals of natural order" (Stephen Toulmin), that current science assumes; and, finally, every scientific inquiry and scientific conclusion makes sense against a "background of order," a "metaphysical world view," or an "idea of nature" (R. G. Collingwood) that only metaphysics can elaborate (Whitehead).[7] The conceptions of "presuppositionless" facts or evidence and of scientific judgments based only on objective induction from that evidence are for this viewpoint a vast abstraction, a utopian dream of empiricism, an illusion of logic, in contrast to the actuality of the perspectival, theory-laden, and so historically and intellectually relative character of the mind's cognitive power.

Throughout the cosmologies I read, the objectivist, empiricist view of science was assumed. Barrow and Tipler, for example, assert that "whereas philosophies and theologies appear to possess an emotional attachment to their theories and ideas which requires them to believe them, scientists tend to regard their ideas differently. They are interested in formulating many logically consistent possibilities, leaving any judgment regarding their truth to observation." They further suggest that "in modern science models and descriptions of natural phenomena are taken up and discarded solely according to their transient usefulness, whereas for early scientists they represented not just the model but the very essence of the Universe, the 'thing in itself.' "[8] The sense of the empirical, pragmatic objectivity in these passages is clear: no cultural or epochal presuppositions or paradigms (not to mention any ideological undertow!) undergird, shape, or deflect the empirical knowing of science. Other attempts to know may be weighed down by all manner of subjective needs and biases, but not contemporary empirical science. Hence Pagels welcomes the fact that cosmology—by which he means the inquiry that addresses itself to most of Kant's antinomies—is now "an empirical science" and thus can look forward to exploring once and for all the age-old questions about ultimate origins, the "very origin" even of space, time, and matter itself, as a manageable, empirical discipline.[9]

The third proposition is that scientific criteria of the meaning, the validity, or the "usefulness" of a theory or notion are the only criteria of any interest at all to science or to the understanding of science. This is a most interesting proposition, seemingly innocuous enough—in fact, almost a trivial tautology—and yet redolent with epistemological and metaphysical assumptions relevant to our larger subject.

If there are no presuppositions to scientific inquiry; no ontological or metaphysical—and so epistemological or transcendental—assumptions on which it depends; and not any relevant sociological, psychological, historical, or existential bases of science, then science stands purely on itself: on given "facts" that are unambiguously indicative of the actuality they represent and on the objective perceptual and logical power of the inquiring human mind.[10] If that understanding of science is valid, then this third proposition makes good sense, for then there are no propositions outside the limits of such empirical inquiry, except questions of logic and of mathematics, which are relevant to the interpretation and understanding of any given body of science. But by the same token, if there are presuppositions on which inquiry is dependent; if the inquirer—even with tenure—is a historical, sociological, psychological, and even metaphysical being; and if facts are always in correlation with cultural and historical paradigms or theories, then propositions about these matters not only are extra-science, that is, "beyond the limits of science" (because they have to do with the conditions or possibility of science), but also are important to the interpretation and understanding of science.

This issue—and the distinction between these two views of science—was not discussed in any of these cosmological works. Why should it be, when each assumed that science was self-sufficient, based on evidence, instruments, its own tradition, and logic alone? No prolegomenon dealing with these "conditions" of empirical science was therefore needed or possible. Hence the philosophical questions about the modes of validity and of adequacy and about the testing of the presuppositions of science, that is, testing for extra-scientific "truth," were, as unasked and unintelligible, left quite unexplored. And for this reason this third proposition was implied but never stated.

Evidence that this proposition was in fact affirmed—that scientific modes of validation were regarded as the only modes of validation—did appear, however, in indirect ways. Several examples can be found in *The Anthropic Cosmological Principle,* by Barrow and Tipler. These are interesting because to all intents and purposes they involve philosophical questions of teleology, of ontological reductionism, and of ontological determinism (at least these questions have been so regarded historically). That these had been philosophical issues is recognized but dismissed without argument: the only criteria cited as relevant are scientific criteria, "scientific evidence." I suspect that if the question "How do we know that these metaphysical assumptions necessary for science are true?" were pressed, the same sort of empirical criteria (scientific success or fruitfulness) would be cited for, among others, assumptions of a universal order, of universal causality, of temporal and spatial homogeneity, and of the relevance of logic to the exploration of actuality. Apparently, to Barrow and Tipler, these various "metaphysical presuppositions of modern empirical science"[11] are themselves inductions from scientific inquiry, rather than the necessary bases of that inquiry. Not only is Kant forgotten, Hume is as well. But to my quotations:

The rather violent hostility with which most scientists regard teleology is partly due to the failure of teleological arguments to account for adaptation in living beings . . . but it is also due to the paucity of significant scientific advances derived from teleological arguments.[12]

Both Peacocke and Mascall . . . defend cosmic teleology by arguing that the continuing operation of physical laws needs some teleological justification. . . . This sort of argument is so general that it would be consistent with *any* scientific result. And so, although interesting, it is completely useless.[13]

The clearest example comes, however, in Barrow and Tipler's discussion of "ontological reductionism" and "ontological determinism" (a topic examined further with relation to the fourth proposition). Although the authors are well aware of the history of philosophical disputes about ontological determinism and ontological reductionism—that is, about the physical and deterministic character of actuality "out there"—they do not mention these disputes. On the contrary, the assumptions of science, the methodological rules of its inquiries, and the consequent character of its theoretical formulations—that is, empirical science's *heuristic* principles—are taken as quite sufficient to determine the ontological character of the referents of scientific inquiry in actuality. Quite without thought to the non sequitur involved, the rules of scientific method are assumed to determine and validate ontological judgments.

Although the final constituents of the world have changed with each successive scientific revolution [?], the fundamental evolution equations for these entities have always been deterministic. Thus there is no evidence whatsoever that the fundamental equations are not deterministic; in fact, to the extent that we believe the fundamental equations to be true, we are forced by the evidence to be ontological determinists.[14]

In short, scientific inquiry assumes as a fundamental heuristic principle the determining patterns of cause and effect. There is and can be, therefore, no scientific evidence that is not determined. Because science alone adjudicates the ultimate character of reality or actuality (ontological determinism), "the evidence establishes" that actuality itself is determined. The same argument is applied to reductionism or physicalism. In this strangely circular argument, there is presupposed, on the one hand, an identity of science and its heuristic presuppositions with all truth about reality (i.e., with the ontological) and, on the other hand, an identity between the entities investigated by science and the concepts with which science thinks those objects. In other words, methodological rules or canons have become ontological assertions; hence however convoluted and circular these arguments may be, questions about the founding assumptions of science are regarded as scientific and not philosophical questions and so are to be determined by scientific evidence alone.

The fourth proposition is that of identity between the concepts, formulas, and models of science and the ontological objects to which scientific inquiry directs itself—what is, to use Lonergan's phrase, "already out there real," or the *Ding an sich* to Kant. Scientific theory thus describes reality directly, immediately, and "as it is"; and for many that description, now in principle and soon in fact, can become so accurate, so isomorphic, that no further descriptions are necessary.

As was noted, this realistic identification of objective ontological entities (e.g., the atom) with the concepts and models of physics was frequently exemplified in classical physics. Although this realism (naive realism) is repudiated widely in much of the literature of current philosophy of science, nevertheless it reappears in cosmological literature and is, I suspect, assumed widely throughout the scientific community; one wonders if it was ever seriously questioned in that community on a wide scale (much as recent changes in religious understanding to a "symbolic" rather than a "literal" interpretation of doctrines may not be so widely assented to among clergy and laity as once was thought). Of all the assumptions herein delineated, this naive realism is the most fundamental and the most significant for the relation of science and religion. This assumption represents the height of anthropomorphism, of the radical "humanizing" of nature; for here the rules and codes of human thinking are without argument assumed to set and limit the characteristics of natural reality.[15]

The assumption of the identity of scientific models and concepts with ontological objects is the fundamental presupposition of Carl Sagan's widely read book *Cosmos*. Sagan's book begins: "The Cosmos is all that is or ever was or ever will be." He proceeds then to tell us how well our race through science is penetrating the mystery of the cosmos: "In the last few millennia we have made the most astounding and unexpected discoveries about the Cosmos and our place within it, explorations that are exhilarating to consider."[16] The cosmology that follows, learnedly and charmingly written, delineates that exploration through scientific inquiry. There is not the slightest hint that there is any other modality by which humans might explore this mystery. The cosmos is what is real, and the cosmos is described without ambiguity by scientific inquiry.

Naive realism assumes (1) that ontological entity and scientific explanation are isomorphic; (2) that this explanation uncovers the entire "mystery" of the object, so that no other explanation is either necessary or possible;

and (3) that any alternative explanations, or modes of inquiry, are competing explanations on the same plane, unequivocally false, and thus cancelled out by the "correct" explanation. Were there genuine distance between object and scientific explanation and thus mystery in actuality—for example, if scientific explanations represented "constructions" or "abstractions" from the fullness of experience—then an alternative explanation (metaphysical or religious) could be complementary or supplementary and not contradictory. Therefore to state that scientific explanations rule out as "false" metaphysical or religious explanations is to espouse—although perhaps unknowingly—a naive realist position concerning established scientific theories. This is what Dawkins does in *The Blind Watchmaker:*

> The only thing he [William Paley] got wrong—admittedly quite a big thing—was the explanation itself. He gave the traditional religious answer to the riddle. . . . the true explanation is utterly different, and it had to wait for one of the truly revolutionary thinkers of all time, Charles Darwin. . . . Paley's argument is made with passionate sincerity and is informed by the best biological scholarship of his day, but it is wrong, gloriously and utterly wrong. . . . Natural selection, the blind, unconscious, automatic process which Darwin discovered, and which we know now is the explanation for the existence and apparently purposeful form of all life, has no purpose in mind.[17]

Another example of this utter certainty about the whole of the universe—about ontological statements—on the basis of the results of scientific inquiry (in short, about the identification of the two sorts of questions) comes at the end of Pagels's book, when he expresses his approval of a conclusion by prominent scientist and cosmologist Steven Weinberg:

> Weinberg, therefore, spoke for many scientists when he wrote . . . "The more we know about the universe the more it is evident that it is pointless and meaningless." . . . This is not the conclusion of pessimistic religion or the raving of an unhappy philosopher, but the only rational inference that emerges from our scientific view of the cosmos.[18]

Because science describes exhaustively and accurately the structure of the "real" world, and because science is such that it can find no meaning or purpose in the objects of its inquiries, the universe as a whole—when known by science—is known to have no meaning or purpose.

All of the cosmologies discussed herein manifest what can only be called an "unyielding dogmatism" on issues relevant to teleology and religion, that is, on ontological or metaphysical issues. Here the characteristic tentativeness of scientific statements, which each author well represents when scientific theories are under discussion, ceases, and utter certainty enters the scene: William Paley is portrayed as "utterly wrong," for instance. This certainly is unexpected in writings that intend to be "scientific"; however, it is not at all surprising when one realizes that such claims have transcended science and have moved, quite unknown to the claimants, out of the range of scientific—and so of empirical and probabilistic—judgments and into the realm of ontological and even theological judgments, where dogmatism (as these authors are very well aware) finds itself quite at home! One of the problems with the unphilosophical consciousness of many scientists (as can also be the case with theologians) is that these scientists become as rigid and dogmatic as have religionists on subjects that transcend science and so are essentially unprovable and yet, thinking they are still speaking in the discourse of science, claim the authority of science—in fact, much more authority than real science ever claims![19]

Naive realism identifies unequivocally the ontological object with the scientific explanation or description of that object. One of the clearest cases of this is found in the interesting and rather radically unconventional volume on the anthropic principle by Barrow and Tipler. The book is unconventional in its insistence on a fundamental correlation between cosmos and mind, and it sets out to explore—within the parameters of the assumptions delineated herein—that fundamental correlation. Nevertheless, Barrow and Tipler also make an unequivocal affirmation of naive realism in their discussion of "ontological reductionism" and "ontological determinism":

> *Ontological reductionism* claims that the "stuff" comprising the world can be reduced ultimately to the particles and forces studied by physics; the vast majority of biologists (and we ourselves) are ontological reductionists. . . .
> *Ontological determinism* claims that the evolution equations which govern the time development of the ultimate constituents of the world are deterministic; that is, the state of those constituents at a given time in the future is determined uniquely by the state of those constituents now [shades of Pierre-Simon Laplace!]. All theories of physics which have ever been proposed as fundamental . . . even quantum mechanics—all of these are ontologically deterministic theories. . . . In fact, to the extent we believe the fundamental equations to be true, we are forced by the evidence to be ontological determinists.[20]

Equations and entities are here radically identified; if the first are deterministic, so are the ontological entities. This is the essence of realism.

There is little question in this quotation, first, that it is the "ultimate" constituents of the real world that are being referred to and, second, that it is assumed that scientific descriptions give an accurate, univocal, and exhaustive account of these constituents. What is known through physics, in all its characteristics as delineated by Barrow and Tipler, is what is real ontologically—though how this squares with the vast changes in physics that are mentioned is not clarified.

This appears to be precisely the error that Whitehead, in describing the understanding of classical physics after Isaac Newton, characterized as "the fallacy of misplaced concreteness": the error of taking the conclusions of science—its models, entities, and theorems—as indicating directly and unambiguously the real constituents of actuality.[21] Not only does this fail to recognize (in fact, it denies) that there may be other modes through which actuality is experienced and "known"—for instance, self-awareness (causal efficacy) or moral, aesthetic, or religious experience—but, even more, it identifies an abstraction (because all knowledge abstracts in order to become knowledge) with the richness and mystery of what is concretely actual. Because of the naive realism of these cosmologists, the role of philosophy as "the critic of abstractions" is left unrecognized; in fact, the idea that philosophy—or anything else—might have that role never even surfaces. Science is adequate, and it is self-sufficient.

The definitive example of naive realism in connection with scientific inquiry appears in Pagels's book. Pagels is understandably excited with the prospect, imminent in his view, that scientific inquiry can at last answer all the traditional puzzles about the coming to be of things, what he calls "the very origin" of the universe.[22] He is aware of all the strange questions—What happened before time? Where did matter come from? and so forth—that have accompanied this issue since Augustine; and he is sure that cosmology as an "empirical science" is now equipped—with the help of Einsteinian relativity theory and new instruments—to answer these questions. I will not here go into the details of his argument that empirical science can now trace out "the origin of all things from nothing," but I cite it as the clearest example of the belief in the omnicompetence of science for all important questions about reality and of the realistic assumption that empirical science describes all of reality as it is "out there." One cannot help but notice also that this project assumes a "rule of law," a universal order, that precedes actuality and ushers it from nonbeing to being. Such an unconscious, Platonic assumption of an order separate from actuality (because originative of it) poses any number of puzzling metaphysical questions.[23]

Aristotle made sense when he said that, as far as *empirical* inquiry is concerned, "nothing can come from nothing."[24] Empiricism must always assume that there is *something* already given in order for inquiry to begin.[25] Pagels, however, seems to think that modern science can trace the derivation of something from "nothing" or at least from a "vacuum,"[26] even though in science a vacuum is not nothing. To me, however, it seems that Augustine was right (as was Whitehead, who denies the possibility of these questions in legitimate philosophical discourse)[27] that questions about the origin of the space–time continuum (the very origin of the universe) are structurally different from questions presupposing that the space–time system is already there and working.

Pagels's optimism about the capacities of empirical science to answer all questions about actuality illustrates his view (1) that science represents the only way that all questions about actuality can be asked or answered and (2) that scientific theory can now, in principle, and will ultimately, in fact, trace out the principles and the dynamics of every aspect of actuality, even of its origin. No more clear case of unqualified realism is, I think, possible than this claim to describe in empirical terms what has been called "the ultimate ontological question," namely, Why is there something rather than nothing?

This perusal of selected cosmologies uncovers clear and significant difficulties for religious understanding in science *so interpreted,* and certainly for any religious understanding based on or associated with a metaphysical interpretation of reality. The strongest difficulties for religion lie in two points.

First, scientific inquiry represents the only relevant avenue to truth about what is real, with the result that any proposition, whether religious or metaphysical, that is based on grounds other than those provided by empirical science is merely "subjective."[28] Thus alternative views are considered to be false, the result of projected "needs and wishes," rather than objective evidence, and representative of "closed minds."[29] When reality is exhaustively and adequately defined by physical science—and is therefore only physical, determined, and "meaningless"—there is little place for any credible referent for religious language or belief.

The view that scientific and religious affirmations are equivalent and so are rivals (the former, in most scientific and several other circles, being true and the latter false) is also shared by the creationists. For the creationists, of course, the religious doctrine of creation is true and its equivalent, the cosmology of modern science, false. Given this connection, one notes that the investigation herein of modern scientific cosmologies—though not of the scientific theorems on which they are built—tends to justify the creationist complaint that many, if not most, explications of scientific theory bring inescapably with them assumptions about the universe as a whole that have definite "religious," in fact "naturalistic" or atheistic, anti-religious overtones, namely, the assertion that all that is arose blindly and pointlessly from material, deterministic origins. The cosmologists I have read would probably assent to this description of the direct naturalistic implications of modern science.

The problem is that when the theories of science are interwoven as closely as they are in these cases with a materialistic, deterministic cosmology—as if the two were one—the teaching of science as so understood is the teaching of atheism. Moreover, this, among other things, "breeds creationism" as a reaction.[30] Thus the sorts of cosmologies here described represent part of the cause of creationism; for these cosmologists are more sure of, and so more categorical about, the ontological conclusions they see in the theories of science than they are about the theories themselves.

Second, it also seems evident that this understanding of science renders ambiguous—in fact, practically undiscussable—a number of assertions important to science and yet not amenable to scientific inquiry itself. Each of the scientists cited in this chapter refers to the assumption of *order* as an ingredient in all scientific inquiry, in fact, as necessary to it. Pagels goes so far as to affirm that this rule of scientific law holds even "in the void" and "prior to space and time"[31]—although it is hard to know what such apparent Platonism might mean to him. And all of these scientists recognize that the uniformitarian principle, namely, that events in the past and in the farthest reaches of space exhibit the same orderly processes as do observable or traceable events around us, is the necessary basis of every scientific theory about origins, proximate or ultimate.[32]

Not surprisingly, the cosmologies here analyzed do not recognize this principle of order as extending out into space, back into time, and forward into every relevant future as a metaphysical insight. Such metaphysical principles, as Whitehead saw, are unprovable because they represent the presupposed grounds of all proof; they therefore are based on fundamental intuition and held by what Whitehead terms "faith," a faith peculiar to some cultures and not to others.[33] For this reason the questions of the historical origins (in past culture) and the rational grounds (in philosophy) of such a faith necessary for science become significant. These questions lie not in science itself but in the history of ideas, in epistemology, and in ontology and metaphysics. All this, however, does not arise in these cosmologies, where "knowledge" is strictly confined to scientific knowledge. Because universal order is not seen as a principle, a view of things that develops historically; as thus historically contingent; or as a principle that might be questioned (or wondered at), it appears in these cosmologies simply as a fact about the universe like any other fact, a fact presumably not known before science but now known through scientific inquiry.

Pagels states it as if it were both obvious and uncontroversial: "Since these properties are universal"; "Physical law is universal—it is a fact, never controverted by any observation"; "The fact that the entire universe is governed by simple natural laws is remarkable, profound and on the face of it, absurd."[34] To me this understanding of a presupposed principle of order as an empirical datum represents a serious intellectual confusion and is, accordingly, intellectually vulnerable to criticism. Such confusion about the status and grounds of the fundamental presuppositions of science is another result of the naive realism and the positivism of such cosmologies.

One final, minor point in this chapter: it is both natural and yet ironic that the books examined herein are filled with wonder at science. This wonder is natural because the capacity to do science is surely one of the most extraordinary of human powers and because the knowledge science brings is of the greatest value to us all. And those who practice science well are particularly aware of these "virtues" and so of the "high" nature of their own calling as scientists. This awareness of the importance, even the "glory," of what one does is hardly new: holy men, priests, and monks have always regarded (even taken for granted) the religious capacities of humanity as the most sublime of our gifts or of the gifts of grace; correspondingly, philosophers (except, perhaps, John Dewey) always regarded philosophical rationality and wisdom as the crown of human achievement and the essence of what is uniquely human. At this point, therefore, modern cosmologists find themselves in a long and distinguished tradition.

Carl Sagan is particulary rapturous about the human and even the cosmic meaning of his profession. He is, he says, proud of and confident in our species. And, to be sure, there are various grounds for this pride; humanity possesses a host of "excellences." The only one, however, of which he seems to be aware is the ability to know and to know the cosmos: that is, physical science.

> And yet our species is young and curious and brave and shows much promise. In the last few millennia we have made the most astounding and unexpected discoveries about the Cosmos and our place within it, explanations that are exhilarating to consider. They remind us that humans have evolved to wonder, that understanding is a joy, that knowledge is prerequisite to survival. I believe our future depends on how well we know this Cosmos.[35]

All this is understandable, if a bit exclusivist, as if to know the cosmos were the paradigmatic human gift. The rapture becomes fairly heavy, however, when he tells us that if there were no changes in our world, "there would be no impetus for science," and if things were utterly unpredictable, "again there would be no such thing as science"[36]—as if *life* would have been possible under these conditions! Not unnaturally, it is the capacity to observe the cosmos and so to understand it scientifically that motivates interest in what is called the anthropic principle: to address the question "How is it that the entire universe developed in such a way as to make possible and to produce a being capable of science?"

All this is, I agree, a wonder. It might be even more of a wonder, however, if scientists wondered at a universe that brought forth an unusually loving mother, an artist, a dependable and responsible colleague, a courageous act of self-sacrifice, an unexpected capacity to love what is unlovable! One gets the sense from these undialectical effusions about science that, as for far too many of the religious saints and wise men of the past, all of these other "virtues" of humanity are regarded as somewhat lower than the ability to know—now epitomized in the community of scientists. This is ironic, because the religious person's identification of human religiousness with the center and purpose of the cosmos is considered by these scientists to be, as Dawkins put it, "conceited" and "small-minded."[37]

In any case, I now turn to the constructive task of addressing the question: What is wrong with the understanding of scientific knowing and so of the world it describes in these cosmologies, and how can we provide a better interpretation of science, its conditions, and its role than these works provide?

5

Science, Philosophy, and Theology

In the preceding investigation of a selected number of modern cosmologies, they were found to represent the same objective scientific empiricism, positivism, or "naive realism" that was analyzed in Chapters 1 and 2. As in the late nineteenth century, such a positivistic view of physical science today presents a world within which any mode of religion makes little or no sense. In such a world, if it be the real world, religious experience cannot have any conceivable referent and so cannot be understood except as a human projection grounded in ignorance, fear, and fundamental alienation; a projection that can only dissipate as scientific knowledge and reliable techniques advance. There are a number of arguments against this position: it represents a misunderstanding of religion; it is a challenge to the status and value of the humanities and so to the important aspects of life they represent, as well as a challenge to religion; it is based on and reflects a false estimate of the existential and historical human situation.

The most relevant and fruitful, however, seem to me to be arguments claiming that this positivistic view of scientific knowledge and of its cosmological results represents a misinterpretation of the character of the knowing process and thus a misunderstanding of scientific knowledge itself. This is a critique of the philosophy of science that these positivistic cosmologies assume and so of the physicalist ontology they proclaim as science; it is not a criticism of the science on which these cosmologies are based. Such a line of argument is philosophical in character; it proposes in effect a different philosophy of science, and in principle it would develop an understanding of scientific knowing that would lead into the beginnings of a more encompassing epistemology, ontology, or metaphysics. Its aim would be that of establishing, by means of epistemology and ontology, the kind of philosophical theology that, in its own way and on its own grounds, could encompass the otherwise excluded sphere of religion. In this chapter I suggest a beginning of such a movement of thought. The argument is neither new nor particularly original, except that to my knowledge it has not heretofore been aimed in the direction of contemporary cosmologies such as those of Carl Sagan, Heinz Pagels, and Richard Dawkins. I begin with a summary of the discussion of the new understanding of science as was outlined in Chapters 2 and 3.

It is one of the main themes of the new philosophy of science that all knowing involves a preunderstanding, that all inquiry is theory-laden,[1] and that therefore natural science is "kin" to the discipline known as hermeneutics. There are no facts or data in and of themselves; nor, as a consequence, are valid theories based solely on objective induction from self-standing evidence. On the contrary, aspects of the manifold of experience become facts or data only when they are discriminated as important, as "clues," from the whole welter of experience; and that discrimination arises only because prior theory (hypothesis) has joined to prior habitual familiarity (long experience) to organize or order experience in a certain way. Only with such prior organization does experience yield data; only in such an ordered world is it possible to conceive and then to test a hypothesis. Theories, paradigms, and other "forms of order" accompany the investigation of experience from beginning to end. Without experience, such forms of order are empty, but without them experience is blind.

The experience into which the scientist inquires, out of which she shapes her new hypothesis, and in relation to which she tests it is therefore already organized by more fundamental forms of order; hence the picture of each hypothesis as simply induced from "pure" data and tested "objectively" is false. Thus the reality known by the scientist, explicated and organized in and through her structure of theories, is a reality in part shaped by and even constructed in terms of the intellectual tradition of the scientific community, the preunderstanding of the scientist herself, and the particular hypothesis she is testing. Granted another intellectual tradition, another set of paradigms and forms of order, and therefore different questions asking for different answers, different sorts of facts and data would arise—and, accordingly, tests with different consequences would ensue. This is the point so forcefully argued by Thomas Kuhn with his theory of "paradigms" and "paradigm shifts," by Stephen Toulmin with his varying "forms of order," and by R. G. Collingwood in his discrimination of different "ideas of nature" in the intellectual tradition of Western science.[2] Because these differing forms of preunderstanding have been themselves influenced and shaped by their cultural matrix, the world created by science is not simply already "out there," objective to human perceiving, knowing, and evaluating. On the contrary, the world described by science is in part always a historical construct, differing as the cultural "minds" of different epochs and places differ. Science itself has a history, and the world created by science is itself a function of that cultural history. Reality, whatever it may be, and "scientific reality" are therefore not identical: science is not a mirror of nature.[3]

The findings of science—and so the cosmologies science produces—are therefore *historical* documents, molded in part by the paradigms of their time and place. This insight into the influence of cultural and historical forces on even the most objective sort of thinking, which was delineated in Chapter 3, is itself grounded in an even deeper influence on inquiry and on thinking. I refer to the essential and inescapable role that sensible and intellectual consciousness, that is, perception and thought, play with regard to the knowing process. Here the constructive role of consciousness itself in the creation of the "world" that is known—the world both as perceived by the senses and as "known" by the cognitive power of mind—comes itself to full consciousness. The thoughts humans think and the inquiries they make are historical, because human consciousness helps to construct the world that is experienced and thought, and human consciousness is itself historical.

Ironically, this modern sense of what the perceiving self adds to experience began with Galileo, who showed that the "secondary qualities" of experience were not attributable to the quantitative, mechanical world that physics studied, to "primary qualities";[4] thus these secondary qualities (e.g., color and sound) were added by the experiencing mind. This critical analysis was pushed further by George Berkeley and David Hume, who proposed that all knowledge, primary and secondary qualities alike, is based on sense impressions; therefore no form of our knowing can penetrate through and beyond this screen of impressions to "reality." Immanuel Kant formalized and ordered this critical view: the manifold of experience is shaped originally by the forms of intuition (space and time), and it is unified and ordered by the categories of understanding (causality and substance). Thus the entire manifold of experience possesses its universal order, thus it is amenable to inquiry by means of mathematical physics, thus it is characterized by an omnipresent determinism: modern "empirical" physical science in this way becomes possible. Nevertheless, that world of ordered sequences governed by necessary law is only the *phenomenal* world, a construct by human sense and by the human mind out of the given. As a consequence, the world so constructed, the world even of science, is not the "real" world, the "thing in itself" or *noumenon*—which (and here another tradition gets its start) we know directly only from the inside in moral experience.[5] Critical philosophy did not completely sunder scientific knowledge and "reality," but it surely distinguished them—and led many to think that the naive realism of pre-Kantian philosophy was at an end.

As is evident from the preceding chapter, however, the traditions of critical philosophy, first formulated in the philosophy of Kant, have apparently had an effect on only a few current writers of scientific cosmologies, such as Paul Davies. To the unaffected majority, the world known by scientific theory is simply the real, "ontological" world, uncovered or discovered (seen) by means of objective scientific inquiry based solely on observations, hypotheses, and experimental testing. If our senses are congruent with the real shapes of the world and our minds characterized by the real world's forms of order, this is for modern cosmology not (as Kant had said) because the known world is a construct by our cognitive faculties but because the forms of our experiencing and thinking have (according to tested biological theory) arisen out of the ordered processes of the precedent world. Far from the world of science being an effect of mind, mind itself is simply an effect of the precedent and objective order of the world. As Pagels said wonderingly, "The universality of law is simply a fact," and those laws characterized even the void before the world began—so "already out there real" are they. The "human" sensible shape and the "human" rational order of the world out there pose no problems for modern cosmology; it is simply that these anthropomorphic characteristics of actuality are the way the world really is in itself. This deep gulf of ignorance between critical philosophy and the spokespersons for modern science begs for an explanation. Why is it that modern cosmologies are not so much in disagreement with this major philosophical tradition as seemingly so assured of its irrelevance?[6]

The tradition of critical philosophy has continued in much important philosophy into our own day. Hence it has, like science, been significantly transformed. For this reason my mention of Kant, as representing this tradition's most distinguished formulation, does not signal either full agreement with Kantianism or any effort to argue his case in our day. Two very creative philosophers from the first half of the twentieth century, George Santayana and Alfred North Whitehead, elaborated and, I would say, each in his own way improved on Kant; that is, they reformulated in more intelligible terms the Kantian distinction between the world of appearance and so of scientific theory, on the one hand, and the ontologically real world, the *Ding an sich,* on the other hand—"the realm of matter" for Santayana and "concrete actuality" for Whitehead. Edmund Husserl, Martin Heidegger, and Paul Tillich each represented a parallel mode of distinguishing the world of science from what Husserl called the primordial life world. And in current philosophy, Richard Rórty and Richard Bernstein continue these motifs. In the following elaboration of the tradition of critical philosophy in its application to the question of scientific knowledge, appeal is first made to Whitehead, then to Tillich, and off and on to Santayana, as giving strong reasons why the naive realism of current cosmologies lacks philosophical credibility.

Whitehead is impressed with what he likes to call the "abstract" character of the cosmos as described by modern science. By this he means that the cosmos of modern science, the world of "vacuous entities" blindly following determined causes, does not fit with and so cannot be thought to undergird important and pervasive areas of common experience: social relations, courts of law, literature and art, commerce, morality, and so on. As he remarks, it presents us with a world that is "quite unbelievable."[7] Moreover, none of the presuppositions of science—that an order obtains throughout experience; that entities "over there" are real; that there is unity of effect between past, present, and future—what are in philosophy the "categories" of existence, is experienced or known (and certainly they are not to be established) either by means of the experiments of science or in the sensory experience (Presentational Immediacy) on which science is based. "The categories are manifested elsewhere."[8]

The wide variety within experience and the possibility of science itself show, therefore, that the two sensationalist dogmas that *only* through sense data is reality known and that science *alone*, therefore, gives indication of what is real, are false. There are other, more fundamental modes of experiencing, which are more directly in touch with actuality. These nonsensory perceptions are multiple. Principally, they are the sense of "withness with the body" through which we are self-aware, or "know" ourselves as an organic unity; the sense of continuous and pervasive passage and yet of continuity with—in fact, conformation to—the immediate past; and the sense of aims and of intentions for the immediate future.[9] Here actuality is itself experienced through our own participation in being the organic society we are, and this level of experience is rich in metaphysical implications. It is therefore through nonsensory experience that the reality, the "processing," the interconnectedness, and the order of experience in time are known; and it is this level of experience that, while beyond science (nonsensory), provides the bases or presuppositions of science. This Whitehead labels "experience in the mode of causal efficacy," and it is by metaphysical, not scientific, inquiry that these modes can be explored and concrete actuality more directly known.

Thus metaphysics provides the theoretical framework (the "rationality") for science, which science by itself lacks; or, put another way, it articulates into a coherent system the presuppositions necessary for the special sciences. It provides a clearer, less abstract, more concrete, and more direct delineation of what is real and so the basis of our knowledge of the real. As "the critic of abstractions," metaphysics can assess the cognitive value of each special mode of experiencing and knowing: the physical sciences, art, psychology, religion. Above all, it can give a credible account of those factors crucial to all of experience that the sciences, by abstracting from them, tend to overlook, ignore, or even deny: the universality of change, the pervasiveness of order, the continuity within time, the appearance of novelty, the importance of aims and values, the reality of purposes and responsibility, the grounds for hope—and the trust that value characterizes even the farthest depths of actuality. These pervasive traits of experience, always present, can never be seen by the empirical method, for they are assumed and so are not noticed: "Experience never takes a holiday from them."[10] And because of their pervasiveness throughout *all* experience, expressive statements about these traits (metaphysical statements) cannot be falsified, there being no conceivable experience that does not illustrate them.

Civilization is utterly dependent on this faith in persuasive order and in value amid transience. If there were not credible grounds or rational articulation for this faith, that confidence would become precarious—even though science must be based on that confidence to flourish. For Whitehead, then, while metaphysics will temper and limit the claims of the sciences described in these cosmologies, it will also provide the rational grounding that science needs; for metaphysics alone can ponder and articulate the structure of the whole, that unity of objects and subjects, of structure and meaning, of inquiring and the values of inquiry on which the sciences depend.

Many of these same themes appear in Tillich—in fact, the ontologies of Tillich and Whitehead are remarkably similar. For both thinkers, science represents an abstraction from actuality (from "finite being" in Tillich), of remarkable, if only relative, validity. Thus science, if understood correctly in its validity and its limitations, is of vast use to civilization. Again, only ontological inquiry can uncover and recover the full structure of finite being from which science (technical reason) has abstracted and thus give a more accurate and inclusive account of what is real.[11]

Tillich begins, as had the whole critical tradition and as had Whitehead, with the influence of the experiencing self on the creation of its "world." Self and world, he says, represent a mutually dependent *polarity*; the one is essential to the appearance and reality of the other. This applies to all finite being everywhere.[12] Through modern empirical science we have become aware of how the self arises out of and is dependent on its world. The self arises as a part of nature out of nature. Its social character is a function of the habits and traditions of its community, its psychological contents come to it entirely from its material and social environment, and its personal character (as "spirit") comes to it in communion with others.[13] This dependence of consciousness and self-consciousness on "world" is assumed and delineated in all the modern sciences. But self and world are polar, mutually dependent; thus world, as experienced and known by rational selves—by the sciences—is throughout dependent on the self as "reason" and as "spirit."

With the introduction of reason or spirit, says Tillich, what was a mere environment to the organism becomes a world to it: a potentially ordered unity, with patterns of similarity and difference, continuity and discontinuity; a potential whole with potentially discriminable parts. Therefore, as the self was in effect a creation of its world, so in a different way this world, experienced and subsequently known by mind, is also a creation or a construction of the self. As Sagan implied, there could be neither the possibility for nor the impulse toward science were the manifold of experience, the world, not so constituted as a whole of potentially identifiable elements.

Tillich's defense of his view is brief but interesting.[14] The shift from environment to world presupposes "distance," a separation of the self from its world so that the latter becomes an object. The objectification of world into a realm to be "looked at" is the work of consciousness. Further, in order for judgments about that world to be possible—this is this and not that—negation is necessary (see a similar theme in Whitehead: "The negative judgement is the peak of mentality"),[15] which involves even more distance, not only so that objects appear but so that novel possibilities—what is not yet—are objects of consciousness. In all this, the self "stands out" from its world, so that the world is "over against" the observer; thus can self or mind look at its world—and also at itself. Self transcends world and itself, and thus it can make both world and self objects of itself—which for Tillich is the first sign of the infinite dimension of self, its relation in experience and cognition to "the infinite ground of reason."[16]

Finally, in its experience of the world as objectified and of the self as self-conscious, the self brings order to each. It has the capacity for language and so for universals; thus it can "grasp" reality in cognition, and it can remake its world in artistic expression. Consequently, it is capable of proposals and projects for its own action in the world, and it can "shape" as well as grasp reality cognitively—the two great capacities of reason. Thus the world is "named": patterns of order and continuities are seen (metaphysical visions, paradigms, and so on) and discriminations, identifications, and definitions are made—and science begins. The self also shapes reality through its projects and on the basis of the order it has discriminated there: language and *techne* are the first fruits of reason, of the active constructing and reconstructing of its world. In modern life these are in part represented by empirical science and technology; both are dependent on world as constituted by the rational self, by spirit.

For both Tillich and Whitehead, the rise of "world" and of sciences of the world (or, in Whitehead's terms, of the appearance of presentational immediacy as an abstraction from causal efficacy) represents in human form the pervasive ontological or metaphysical structure characteristic of all reality everywhere. The conditions for our experiencing and especially for our knowing our environment are for us clues to the fundamental structure of reality, of "being." An analysis of the conditions for epistemology leads to the possibility of metaphysics or ontology. The self–world correlation (experienced "inside" by us) represents, for Tillich, the universal structure of finite being; and for Whitehead, the felt internal relations of entities with one another, experienced by us in causal efficacy by means of what White-head terms an entity's feelings or *prehensions* of another entity, represent the most fundamental structure of all actuality. Thus, for Tillich, all of finite being represents an *analogous edition* of world and self, of order balanced by spontaneity; and finite being elsewhere illustrates analogous forms of the other polarities characteristic of the self in the world: individuation and participation, dynamics and form, and freedom and destiny. Similarly, the categories of space, time, causality, and substance that are experienced by us (from the inside) in our own being in the world are found, again analo-gously, to characterize finite being everywhere.[17] Correspondingly, for Whitehead the internal relations of prehension or feeling, the inner experi-ences of conformation to our past and of new aims for future novelty, which can appear in us in conscious and intentional form, are analogously repre-sented in all of actuality—in fact, in "the most trivial puff of existence in far off empty space."[18]

Although the structure of finite being—the real world "behind" the scientific cosmology—differs in each of these ontologies on many counts, still there are significant conceptual parallels. Above all, to each ontology science, while within its own limits valid and exceedingly reliable, represents an abstraction—in part, a construct—because it is a product of sense, of consciousness, and of self-consciousness. Hence in order to delineate the structure of actuality, we must pass through and beyond, without denying, the objectified world of the physical sciences into the richer, "thicker," more mysterious actuality that lives within our widest experience. For Tillich, this task is accomplished by "ontological reason" and carried through as the work of ontology, philosophy's major task; for Whitehead, it is accomplished by "speculative reason," an analogue of science but one that deals with the whole of experience. For both, this metaphysical or ontological task is to seek for pervasive and universal structures that characterize all that is, insofar as it is.[19] In proposing that the sensed and human world (and so the science based on that world) is a "construct" and not the "thing in itself," a construct in correlation with a given that is "prehended" or felt, both are in the Kantian tradition; in affirming that a metaphysical analysis is nevertheless possible beyond the range of scientific empirical inquiry, both are non-Kantian.

The most important conclusion of this discussion is that world and mind are inextricably correlated or mutually dependent. World does not originate from mind, as idealism had stated; by the same token, however, the world as it is known by science is not independent of mind—*a se,* so to speak—but is itself in part a product of mind. That scientific world—abstracted, mindless, vacuous, determined—cannot, therefore, be the mindless origin of mind, as naturalistic philosophy argues; rather, the origin of mind and hence of scientific cosmology is a far richer, more mysterious reality than any abstracted cosmology, based on the special sciences, can possibly picture.

This correlation of self and world, of mind and universe, has fascinated religious, philosophical, and scientific thought since the beginning, as is illustrated in myths, in early philosophical speculation, and in the science that has supplanted this speculation. For the Greeks, nature was permeated with mind; and for early modern science, mind—the divine intellect— preceded nature's mechanism as its necessary designer and engineer. For modern cosmologies, however, mind has largely been removed from the cosmos, which is regarded as governed throughout by necessary and determining law and is in principle capable of being reduced to the objects of the inquiries of physics. The arguments here are part of a process of challenging this exclusion of mind: mind is there in the creation or construction of that cosmological world, the world as it is *viewed* by science.

Interestingly, the cosmologists seem to sense this; they rejoice in the observer who inquires and understands. But the weighty contribution of that observer in the construction of the world as it is known by their research is overlooked—and no grounds are given for that omission. This is one reason the appearance of speculation and debate about the so-called anthropic principle is so fascinating; for "this principle has sought to relate mind and observership to the phenomena traditionally within the encompassment of the physical sciences," and "the Anthropic Principle seeks to liken aspects of the global and local structure of the Universe to those conditions necessary for the existence of living observers."[20] This stubborn reappearance of the role of mind within modern cosmology is interesting and reassuring. There is, however, a legitimate question about the way mind is here being brought back in. As I understand it, the propounders of the anthropic principle accept a reductionist and determinist ontology, and they therefore depend entirely on scientific data, scientific evidence, and scientific theorems to establish and describe the "link" between the world of science and the observing mind that they seek to find.

The argument herein has been that mind is correlated to the universe prior to scientific inquiry, as the precondition of such inquiry. Thus mind actively reshapes the "given" in the construction of cosmology, in the interpretation of the developing physical process as science understands and pictures that process. If this is so, the role of mind—the link between mind and the universe—must be uncovered by epistemological, ontological, or metaphysical analysis, by the analysis of a "reality" that is more concrete and so more full than the abstracted material sequences of physics. For Whitehead and Tillich, it is in that richer actuality—an actuality unavailable to abstracting scientific inquiry—that mind, purpose, aims, and novelty reside, and thus it is only through ontology that both the possibility of spirit and the role of teleology are to be understood and interpreted. Here mind and purpose appear as conditions for science itself as a human capacity, not merely as conclusions of scientific investigation. Hence science and its conclusions, as the *results* of mind and purpose (i.e., of the scientist or observer himself), can hardly exclude either mind or purpose from the "real" world.

If, on the contrary, the world that science portrays is taken as primordial, real, and self-sufficient—*a se,* in the classic sense—and if scientific inquiry is taken as the only mode of knowing what is real, then neither mind nor purpose (nor the conditions of science) can appear for reflection at all. In such a situation, mind and purpose are invariably understood as only epiphenomenal products of a process void of both; and if the role of each is established and tested by scientific criteria alone, neither one will or can be found in that process. The method of the physical sciences rightly excludes consciousness, self-consciousness, and purposes from the objects it recognizes; this is its genius and should not be challenged (even though some, such as Eugene Wigner and John Archibald Wheeler, have mounted the challenge). By the canons or rules of its method, its world is reductionist and determined. The mistake, as Whitehead said, is to take that world not as a construction of sense and of mind—and therefore as an abstraction—but as itself the only real world. And this mistake is continued in the current discussions of the anthropic principle. These discussions seek to establish the link between mind and universe *scientifically,* as an inference from scientific data and as implied by scientific theories and formulas; they look to the conclusions of science for that link, rather than to the conditions of science. Unconsciously, a movement has been made from a *methodological* requirement to an *ontological* affirmation. The argument I put forward is that, granted the heuristic requirements of physical science as reductionist and deterministic, the link between mind and cosmos can be established only by an analysis of the characters of experiencing, of consciousness, and of teleology, an analysis that must be carried deeper by metaphysics and ontology if it is to be carried out at all. What is then uncovered about the conditions of knowing can be correlated with what is found by the scientific inferences thus made possible, and a fuller view of "nature," and so of reality as a whole, begins to come into view.

In my argument I have espoused a modified or, perhaps, "soft" critical philosophy, emphasizing the role of mind or spirit in providing some of the essential conditions of science and thus in actually structuring the picture of reality that science presents to us. One important consequence of this constructive role of mind is that "reality," what is really there, remains obscure at best and quite unknown at worst. A view that rejects naive realism and stresses the constructive activity of mind faces the dangers of relativism and skepticism; and specifically, in limiting the absolutist claims of science, it seems to put itself in danger of ultimately granting no validity to scientific knowledge at all. But this is impossible for members of modern culture (not least myself), who consistently in practice, if not in theory, assent to the results of science as valid; for instance, I travel by air and check with my physician with moderate regularity. In a scientific and technological culture, where we all participate in the results of science (willingly or unwillingly), it is hypocritical and inconsistent to think about our knowing process in such a way as to leave to science no validity. One thing the continually accurate and reliable results of science in advanced technology, medicine, and agronomy (to name only a few) show is that science, in its effort to know "reality," is somehow on the right track. The only question raised here in each case is whether the pictures, models, theorems, and formulas of the special sciences give us either the entire or the final knowledge of what is there. How, then, are we to understand the positive relation of our knowing to the realities that are known, if the simple positivist or naive realist picture is denied?

If sensory experience and the science based on it are not isomorphic with the actualities so experienced and known, then at the least they can be said to be analogical. Sense experience, as Whitehead reminds us, abstracts from the real relations and the internal dynamics of actuality; it objectifies those relations into necessary, determined, and external relations, and it ignores the inward spontaneity of what it observes. (After all, Whitehead notes, sensory experience presents to us a past world and so an objectified one, a reality shorn of its immediacy, its inwardness, its subjectivity.)[21] Hence the objects of science represent an invariant, determined pattern of physical relations, a sequence of material events that are "vacuous and empty" and so subject to the exact formulas and equations of mathematical science. That this is not *identical* with the "ontological character" of process, with actuality, with the concreteness of actual reality, the rest of our experience affirms—as Whitehead says, "it [this picture] is unbelievable"—and science so understood cannot account even for itself. But that this abstracted account is *analogical* to the reality it portrays, the success of science more than verifies. And that success has taken two quite specific forms, which have given to science its prestige far beyond the bounds of the scientific community and which would make it quite inane for us to question the general reliability and validity of science.

The first successful form is science's power of *prediction,* well illustrated in the physical sciences. The ability to predict on the basis of a hypothesis does not indicate that all that can be known is known; another factor might regularly be at work. Nevertheless, prediction necessarily entails that aspects of invariant relations are known and therefore that the hypothesis in question is probable. It shows, at the least, an analogous reading of reality that is reliable for practice, a reading that encourages further inquiry into possibly fruitful directions; for one consequence of our understanding of science as abstracted is that no formulas or theories at a given time are final. Thus there is always "more" in the mystery from which the abstraction has been made to be uncovered—or to disclose itself.[22]

The second form, closely linked to prediction, is the power to reshape reality: the power of *technology.* Knowledge implies, said John Dewey, a plan of action, a program of planned activity that will resolve a perceived problem; and knowledge is validated when that plan of action "works."[23] Technology reshapes the reality within which we live, and it does so by building instruments and tools and applying them to the environment around us. Knowledge here is the power to manipulate through understanding the forces that control us and that control our environment, by redirecting those forces as our aims dictate. Insofar as knowledge results in such power and such consequent redirection, that knowledge is tested and validated. (The deepest ambiguities of technology arise from the aims that direct it, rather than the fallibility of the knowledge it uses.) Again, validation is not complete; pragmatic success indicates only that we have understood and controlled aspects of the mystery of dynamic actuality. Nevertheless, the steady success of technology in achieving our aims in relation to the actualities within and around us qualifies radically the relativism and the skepticism inherent in a critical view of scientific knowledge.

In this discussion Santayana's "critical realism" is helpful. To use Santayana's metaphor: sense reproduces in our own "local" language the movements of matter outside of us; our sounds are not its motions but a translation into another tongue. But the translations work—"they are not misleading as signs."[24]

Sense experience and science, then, are analogical. Sense experience is "the babble of our innocent organs under the stimulus of things"; and as Santayana asserts, "A sensation or a theory, no matter how arbitrary its terms (and all language is perfectly arbitrary), will be true of its object, if it expresses some true relation in which that object stands to the self, so that these terms are not misleading as signs, however poetical they may be as sounds or pictures." Santayana further explains that "the terms of astronomy are essences no less human and visionary than those of mythology; but they are the fruit of a better focussed, more chastened, and more prolonged attention to what actually occurs."[25]

These analogies or signs translated in human vocabulary, then, are checked and subsequently refashioned or improved, according to their predictive power and their technological or practical fruitfulness, into signs that are "less and less misleading." (Note the interesting relation to Karl Popper's insistence on falsification.) This seems enough. Nevertheless, our "acquaintance with reality," our sense of participation in knowing and so in truth, and our confidence in our knowledge—and in science—seem to be more deeply and more firmly grounded than this practical, manipulative, instrumental interpretation of signs would warrant, were it all we have. To uncover that firmer grounding, it is helpful to consider what these critical realists can say positively about our "knowledge" of the reality, which eludes even the inquiries of science. Here the critical philosophies that have been cited in this chapter depart from Kant to explore, by way of an "analogical metaphysics," the actuality from which science has abstracted signs.

The common methodological thread that guides Whitehead, Tillich, and Santayana out of the subjectivity of the Kantian maze is the notion of "participation." We know reality through the senses and through science "from the outside," as an object "over there"; this is inescapably the perspective of science, and it results in the objectifying abstractions of science, in the "signs" of which Santayana speaks. But this external relation through the senses to the process that constitutes reality is not our only relation to that process. The process manifests itself in us, as well as in those objects "outside" of us. Further, this manifestation in us kindles our self-awareness: we are aware of our participation in existing, in being "real," in "being there," and in being immersed in change; and we are aware of our awareness, our consciousness. In us, "being" comes to self-awareness and self-consciousness (Tillich); prehensions change to *ap*prehensions, consciousness, and intellection (Whitehead); the rush of matter becomes the awareness of spirit (Santayana). As Tillich puts it, "We know a tree from the outside, but we do not know what it means to be a tree. We do, however, know what it means to be ourselves and to be human. We are aware of our own being *from the inside*. Hence human being is the gateway to being."[26]

As we have seen, Whitehead proceeds to explore "participation," our self-awareness of our actuality in time, through an analysis of the nonsensory experience that he terms "causal efficacy": the inner, powerful experiences of being conformed to and united with the immediate past; the experience of "withness" with the body; and the experience of being lured by the possibilities of the future. These inner experiences of being real and in process, of being in essential relation to a world in our past and to possibilities in our future, can themselves become an object of reflection and articulation, of imaginative, speculative inquiry. The result is the possibility of a metaphysical discrimination of the structure of actuality as actuality appears in us, which can provide the essential foundations for science, for culture, and for an intelligent and confident praxis.

Santayana also concentrates on the experience of existing as a vulnerable, temporal, and mortal being in a surging world, an experience again of our own reality from the inside; and on the basis of what he terms "animal faith," he can discriminate the structures of our real world and provide a basis not only for the understanding of science but also for all the needs of "spirit."[27] In the work of these thinkers, a modest metaphysical analysis discloses and articulates an order in experience that corresponds to, is an analogue of, and so provides grounding for the more abstract, quantitative, and necessitating order of science. It shows us how we can know that we know.

I pursue this matter further with the help of Tillich, partly because his thought on this question has not been as well known as that of Whitehead and Santayana. The question posed is why we can be assured that the order that we uncover in and through our scientific inquiries is an order also characteristic of actuality, if our minds do—as they do—contribute that order to our knowing. Whitehead names this ground of assurance "faith," a faith in the rationality of things that grounds all civilized life as well as all science. Tillich's answer is more interesting because it makes use of a tradition with which Whitehead was not familiar, namely, the "existentialist" tradition.

Tillich notes, as does Whitehead, that we participate from the inside in the same structure of being that scientific inquiry examines from the outside. Thus however external, abstractive, and "distant" scientific inquiry may be and however lacking in direct grounding its (unconscious) assumptions of order and of continuity may be, we can have confidence in that inquiry because we know that the order perceived by our minds is the same as the "order" experienced inwardly in our own being. And we know that because the order of our understanding, of our inquiring mind (of our "subjectivity"), is experienced as correlated with the order of actuality (of "objective being"), as the latter manifests itself directly in our participation in actuality in and through our awareness of our own being. In our self-awareness of our own being—a being that is an example of objective being—we experience in ourselves the same order or logos in being that we find present in our minds (in our subjectivity) when we inquire and know, a correlation of objective and subjective logos.[28]

We are, says Tillich, aware of our finitude "from the inside," as anxiety, on the one hand, and as courage, on the other. This awareness appears in us in and through the forms of our finitude, through the categories of space, time, causality, and substance. Not only do we therefore know these forms or categories as the modes of our thinking about objects in our "world" (as in Kant) and so as the intellectual presuppositions of our science, ordering the "world" science knows, but even more we know them "existentially" and therefore directly as the forms of our own existence. In our awareness of our temporality (of having to die), of our being caused (of our vulnerability), and of our being a cause (of our power), we possess an inner understanding of those external relations of temporality, of "being an effect," and of causality that appear as the categories of actuality within us and yet as also the categories that order the phenomenal world of external and sensory experience.

Whitehead says about sensory experience and science alike that "the categories are derived elsewhere," as are the rational grounding of science in a universal order and the basis of our certainty of that order. This derivation comes through our inner participation in the same existence that externally we are investigating through our "participatory experience" ("causal efficacy," "animal faith," "self-awareness of finitude"); and this correlation of inner and outer participation provides a point of unity between our subjectivity and the external, "objective" world, between self and world, between subjective and objective logos, which science alone cannot provide. Knowledge is participation in the object known as well as distance from it, inner accord as well as external manipulation, a "knowing that we know" as well as an objective observing and checking of data. Without these inner participatory elements, known by self-awareness—elements that unite both the subject knowing and the actuality known—what we know either is an exclusive totality of objects that eliminates all subjects or is vulnerable to radical skepticism from the side of the triumphant subject.

My argument thus far has been that science is inconsistent and its self-understanding incredible, if it seeks to understand itself merely in terms of itself and, as a consequence, paints itself as a purely empiricist enterprise and its conclusions as an unequivocally realistic portrayal of reality "out there."

This is precisely the way a number of current cosmologists (see Chapter 4) present science and the cosmology, the "world," that science has constructed. An analysis of knowing, however, indicates that, far from being a self-sufficient mode of knowing reality "as it is," science is in significant part a construct of a historical community of sensing observers and human knowers. The possibilities of empirical inquiry, intellectual understanding, and theoretical judgment lie within the power of mind or spirit; correspondingly, the world disclosed by empirical study and described by science is a world constructed by the sense organs, the theoretical powers, and the intellectual categories of human experience and thinking. It is a realm of human symbols analogous to and so relevant to reality as human signs of reality; it is not a mirror of that reality as it is.

The examination herein of critical philosophy in relation to this argument has posed the questions: Is reality then quite unknown? How are we to understand the validity of science, which we all recognize and affirm, and also the many activities of cultural life that are founded on a confidence that we know something—and something dependable—of what is going on? The examples in this chapter have been of epistemological and ontological or metaphysical analyses of experience that enable us to understand those basic aspects of experience that imply a valid cognitive ability and that give us a direct "acquaintance" with reality sufficient to undergird the inquiries of science.

If the arguments put forth in this chapter, and those that preceded them, are sound, then I have shown that an intelligent and self-consistent science points beyond itself to an ontological or metaphysical ground, to an analysis of actuality as inclusive of self and world, subjectivity and objectivity, purposes and causation. Such an analysis depends on extrasensory and so extrascientific experience: the self-awareness of our participation in actuality as existing, thinking, and willing beings; the awareness of "the other" as persons in community with ourselves as subjects; and the awareness of actuality as real, in process and yet in a continuity of orderly process. Such an analysis can provide a theoretical bridge between the significant activities of science and the cognizing subject of science: the existing, experiencing, willing, and thinking scientist and the community of scientists (who otherwise are quite omitted from the cosmological picture). It can also provide the necessary theoretical point of unity between the cognitive disciplines and the other important aspects of human communal life that are now subordinated to, if not excluded from, the universe as it is pictured by scientific realism. The unity of the intellectual disciplines and the unity of these disciplines with the actualities of life itself—not to mention the unity of human existence with nature—can be achieved only if an ontological base is provided, which begins with the human as subject as well as with the "world" as object and thus is enabled to provide concepts that unite self, culture, and world into an intelligible whole.

There is, however, another result of this line of argument. It has been noted that scientific empiricism and scientific realism create a world within which there is even less room for religion—or any relevant objects of religious worship, experience, and knowing—than there is for science itself and for the humanistic activities of culture. The possibility of ontological analysis—a "knowing" of some sort beyond science—does not guarantee a universe in which religion is credible; Santayana's "naturalism" manifests this point. But it does provide the possibility of such credibility. As both White-head and Tillich show, an ontological analysis of actuality in which self and world represent participant polarities presupposes that actuality (or "being") possesses, or can possess, the mystery, the richness, and the "thickness" requisite for religion. If cognition is limited to the terms of scientific inquiry, then religion either in principle expires altogether or separates itself intellectually entirely from science. In the latter case, when religion (or faith) seeks to interpret itself entirely in terms of itself, faith misunderstands itself by its attempts to portray itself as self-sufficient. But if the reality that reveals itself to us and in us—to our senses, in and through our existence and our cognitive powers, in and through nature, in the sequences and events of history—is a "mystery" as well as an intelligible order, if it transcends our understanding as well as gives order and meaning to our existence, then a religious as well as an ontological analysis of it becomes possible. And religion as a response to reality as well as a human construction (as science is a response as well as a construction) becomes intelligible—and a philosophical theology is well underway.

In sum, I suggest that our cognitive life be conceived as composed of three interlocking but distinct hermeneutical inquiries: science, philosophy (ontology or metaphysics), and (philosophical) theology. Each differs from the others in the kinds of data or evidence in experience to which it appeals and in the areas of experience in which it works. Each differs in the kind of intelligibility it seeks, the kinds of "explanation" it finds appropriate. Each differs in the sorts of authority—or the interweaving of sorts of authority—to which it appeals. And finally each differs in the sorts of symbols it finds significant and useful.

Briefly put, science seeks (on the basis of some preunderstanding) the invariant structures of specific ontic processes, and it appeals to sensory, quantitative data for both its materials and its forms of validation. Philosophy seeks (from some chosen perspective) the universal structures of all that is, and it appeals to the entire width of experience; philosophy thus criticizes, formulates, and reformulates the principles presupposed in science and in all the arts. Theology, on the basis of one perspective on existence, seeks the meaning of the structures provided by the sciences and envisioned by philosophy. Its fundamental symbols are drawn from its own religious tradition, in dialogue with other traditions as well as with all else in cultural life; but its explication of these symbols is in terms of the sciences, the philosophies, and the theologies of its time and place (i.e., in terms of the structure of existence as that is then understood).

These disciplines are hermeneutical in the sense each searches in its own way for the meaning of the experiences in which it originates. They are distinct in that they search in significantly different ways for different sorts or levels of meaning; and they are mutually interdependent and mutually corrective, as has been indicated above. Science depends on philosophy for its most fundamental principles inclusive of self and of world—both of which are involved in cognition. Correspondingly, any philosophical interpretation of the structure of existence and any theological interpretation of the meaning of that structure will be vastly dependent on what science knows that ontic structure to be. Further discussion of the mutual distinction and yet mutual dependence of philosophy and theology—a subject thoroughly elaborated from a hundred perspectives in our own century—appears later in this book.[29]

Part 2

Nature, Science, and Religion

6

Nature and Nature's Power

This part deals with the character of nature, that is, with the human understanding of and attitude toward nature. It can probably be agreed that our modern relations to nature, and behind them our attitudes toward and understanding of nature, have disclosed themselves as disasters. Also it can be said that at fault are at once our Western religious traditions as they have been interpreted and the modern scientific understanding of nature. Both together made possible, even resulted in, our industrial and technological use of nature and so, in the end, the exploitation and despoliation of nature. All this is familiar territory.

My concern at this point is to pursue a new understanding of nature, one that not only assumes a scientific understanding but also explores other ways in which we as humans relate to nature and so can be said to "know" nature. We must perceive nature differently than we have in the recent past if we are to achieve a more creative relation to nature.

Our actions toward other realities, even toward ourselves, are in part determined by our attitudes toward them. If we feel deep respect for other people, especially people different from ourselves, we are likely to treat them with the openness, courtesy, and tolerance that is their due. In turn, our attitudes toward them are determined in large part by our understanding of who and what they are: in this case, that they are human beings, persons, and that as persons they possess an inner integrity, a self-determination, a capacity for free and spiritual activity that we also sense in ourselves—that their reality or being includes "spirit," a spiritual dimension, as does our own. It is such self-understanding applied to the other that can become the foundation for treating other persons as "ends" and not as means, as Immanuel Kant stipulates, and that can in large part provide the inner basis for an outward social order characterized by equal rights, justice, and mutual respect and accommodation. A humane society—in fact, civilization—depends on a mutual recognition of the other as person, of their "reality" as spirit. Thus actions toward other beings depend on our attitudes toward those beings, and, in turn, those attitudes depend directly on our understanding of the reality of those beings, what we "know" them to be. Because of this interrelation or interdependence of action, attitude, and understanding or "knowing" the other's reality, a reductionist or depersonalizing view of reality, if that view stipulates that it encompasses all that reality is, endangers the civilization on which science itself depends when that view is taken as truth.

Given this interdependence of action, attitude, and understanding, our attitudes and our subsequent actions toward nature will depend on our understanding of nature, on what we take nature's reality to be. I reiterate here that knowledge and reality are always correlated: what we believe we know is always taken by us to be what is real and not illusion; whatever we believe we know about anything is what we know to be real about it. Contemporary scientific positivism has regarded the "scientific knowledge of nature," the knowledge of the special sciences, as providing the only knowledge of nature and, as a consequence, as telling us exhaustively what nature's reality in itself is. My effort here is to explore other ways of perceiving nature, other kinds of knowing of nature's reality that might enrich, thicken, deepen our understanding of nature.

One of the most important and certainly the longest lasting of the now vanished alternative intuitions of nature is that represented by the primal or archaic religions. Nature to them was infinitely mysterious, awesome, and terrifying, teeming with sacred and demonic powers humanity could barely understand, much less control. And as these religions were well aware, it was on this infinitely rich, utterly omnipotent, and mysterious reality that humans were utterly dependent. This sense of nature, while genuinely human, is the reverse of our contemporary understanding, in which nature's reality is understood as there for our use, nature's powers are believed to be almost entirely under our control, and our dependence, if remembered at all, reaches consciousness only at abnormal moments.

I am, therefore, interested in exploring further this archaic religious apprehension of nature and setting it into juxtaposition with our scientific, technological, and industrial apprehension. What contemporary science "knows" is what we call nature. The same natural environment was also the object of the deepest and oldest religious intuitions of humankind. How are these two related? Can they be fruitfully thought about together? How may they enrich each other?

This is not to relinquish or replace the scientific view of nature. This investigation accepts scientific inquiry and what it knows as one of the most remarkable and useful of human achievements. The scientific view is a form of knowing that is, on its own terms, valid and that provides an amazingly accurate and useful path to the understanding and control of natural forces—

as long as we can control ourselves! What is denied here is that science tells us all there is to know of nature; that it knows exhaustively the reality of nature; or that it represents the only human mode of understanding, knowing, and defining nature's reality. In this argument against science's exclusivity, other ways of knowing nature—for example, self-awareness, the knowledge of the other, and the general intuitions of nature—have already been delineated in Part 1.

This effort to reinterpret archaic religions' view of nature in juxtaposition to a scientific understanding of nature does not represent, therefore, a natural theology, at least at this point; at this juncture I do not seek to move through nature to some divine reality beyond or within it. It is rather an attempt to rethink our relation to nature in the light of another sort of human relation, that of archaic religion; and then perhaps to begin to reinterpret archaic religion in the modern context. This is not yet constructive theology, the development of a theological view of God and of God's creation. However, in exploring nature through the eyes of archaic religion (in the sense of nonscientific or prescientific religion), perhaps we can, although we are modern people, discern there traces of the sacred that may well in another context be of great constructive theological interest.

In this articulation of the knowledge of nature latent in archaic religion and modern science, it should be remembered that for neither one is the category "nature" the central concept. Science studies nature, to be sure. But science is itself divided into distinct disciplines, the special sciences—physics, astrophysics, chemistry, biology, geology, and so on—each of which has innumerable subdisciplines; and each of these special sciences has its own report to make. A coherent unification of these disciplines is itself an elusive achievement in our day; this unification bears the title "cosmology," and it is rare that it is even attempted at all![1] Generally, what unified voice about nature there is among the sciences is the result of a process of reductionism: the reduction, in the first instance, of all human knowing of nature to what scientific inquiry reveals of nature and in the second instance, the reduction of all other sciences to physics and to the account that physics gives of nature. Correspondingly, early religion is constituted by myths, rituals, rites, sacred objects, obligations, taboos, and so on; and each intermingles in a baffling way what we distinguish as human and as cultural—as society and its history—with what we now call nature.

Nature, as we use this word, therefore has as its referent a duality that is not easy to synthesize: (1) the entire physical environment over against us, which is the object of scientific inquiry and of industrial use; and (2) the basic system of natural entities out of which we arise, which provides our own most fundamental physical being and thus appears *in* us as well as *over against* us. Nature is both the object of our knowledge and use and the source of all of our powers, including knowing and using. Nature is therefore a strange, ambiguous word, loaded with diverse meanings and nuances and of transcendent importance in our contemporary world. To uncover "nature" and what we can think nature to be—a perilous but inescapable task—we must, on the one hand, put the sciences together into a proto-cosmology and, on the other, abstract aspects of the archaic religions.

It is helpful to enlarge a bit further on the ambiguity of the category "nature" as it appears at the edge, so to speak, of both the sciences and the archaic religions. In both, nature tends to have two meanings and to slide from one meaning to the other. First, it refers to the all-encompassing source, ground, and effective determiner of all we can talk about, including ourselves. In this sense, nature appears as the widest environment outside us and also as the physical, psychic reality within us. Since Charles Darwin, this role of nature as source or "whole" has been very clear as the implication of most scientific discussion of the place of humans in the scheme of things, and this meaning comes to clear philosophical expression in modern "naturalism."[2] This same implication is present in early religion, where nature's forces represent the source, ground, and power behind and within all life, including human life. In archaic religion, *all* is nature; there is no supernatural world beyond nature; and human existence, personal and social, is embedded in nature as one of its products and examples.

Second, nature represents an objective world or cosmos over against the human who lives in and from nature but is clearly distinguished from it. In this sense, which is as old as the Greek and the Hebrew traditions, nature provides the background or stage for civilization and so for history, for the system of artifacts and the human arts—that is, for a human world lived in and from nature and yet clearly different from it. At this point, science as theory about the objects of inquiry becomes part of culture and of history and not simply part of nature. It is subject now to norms of validity and its use to norms of ethics. Thus, despite nature's role within the sciences as the source of the scientist herself, nature in the special sciences is objectified over against the perceiving sense and the inquiring mind of the scientist. In sum, nature as source is, for our reflection, a philosophical construction out of nature as the object of the special sciences. This "jump" from special science to philosophical construction represents precisely the confusion of science and philosophy that has been criticized in the previous chapters, namely, that in its discussion of nature as a material system of objects, scientific positivism thinks it speaks of "nature as a whole" and yet has omitted the subject undertaking the inquiry and hence the real meaning of "nature as a whole": nature as source of both objects and subjects, of both the system of objects science portrays and the science that portrays them.[3]

This duality came to expression in the history of religions, when self-consciousness appeared and a distinction of the self ("soul") from the physical body was made. Along with that distinction, nature was distinguished from "art" and thence from society and history; and, finally, nature was distinguished even from "supernature," time and change from eternity.[4] In what Karl Jaspers has called the "Axial Period," a new understanding of the human in relation to nature appears:[5] psyche is distinguished from body, soul from flesh, spiritual substances from material substances, and so on. These important distinctions were as much the result of the discovery of thinking and of cultural creativity as they were the result of religious pressure. In any case, these two meanings of nature—as all-encompassing source of both objects and subjects, on the one hand, and as object or system of objects distinct from human inquiry and use, on the other—run through all human relations to nature. Both represent valid perspectives; but both also challenge reflective thought to construct a more coherent and useful picture than the simple, undialectical monism of scientific positivism.

In our day, science tells us about nature and defines it intellectually for us. Most people, including most scientists, take these descriptions as realistic, as describing what is there objectively, what nature really is; hence nature as encompassing source would be (unconsciously) constructed out of the objective system of external objects described by science. To the so-called new philosophy of science, however, these special sciences represent an ascending series of abstractions, accurate, provisionally valid, and trustworthy but themselves in part constructs of mind and so representing relative perspectives. They are abstractions from the scientist, the inquiring subject, and so abstractions from the whole realm of consciousness and experience that surrounds, constitutes, and orders scientific inquiry as a coherent and tested body of theory in relation to experienced data. Inevitably, in inquiry "reality" is sundered into objects over against and studied by subjects. Consequently, as a description of nature science provides us solely with a system of objects, a construct experienced, organized, known, and tested by subjects. Science cannot speak of all of being; nor can it, ironically, speak of that all-encompassing source implied clearly by evolutionary and naturalistic philosophy, except through its own abstractions.

There are further abstractions. The realm of objects before us is seen and articulated by the various sciences, each from its own point of view and with regard to particular and limiting aspects of that realm. Physics is the most abstract and so the most universal of the empirical sciences: all objects are articulated with regard only to their mass, force, velocity, and direction.

Chemistry approaches this universality for the same reason: all objects, here on a more complex level of organization, are articulated with regard only to their constitutive elements (though physics can claim to provide the fundamental understanding of those constitutive elements). As Alfred North Whitehead points out, the dominant error of our time is to understand these abstractions from the richness of actuality (as actuality is experienced elsewhere) as a series approaching *reality*, so that the most abstract of the empirical sciences is taken to refer to the most real of entities; this is what he called "the fallacy of misplaced concreteness."[6]

Biology, physiology, sociology, and psychology deal with entities of vastly increased organic complexity and hence by no means with all entities; these life sciences do not claim universality. (The differential separating "organic" entities from inorganic ones is dealt with later in this book.) Whether or not the so-called physical sciences, physics and chemistry, provide all the principles needed to explain or comprehend the data of the life sciences is a most important question—a question, among scientists, of "reductionism." In any case, it seems that, in these life sciences, biological events, as Holmes Rolston says, superintend physical events; the laws of physics and of chemistry are obeyed, but these patterns are now used in new ways and for new purposes.[7] The physical sciences are thus abstracting inquiries. They present us with a limited, if very accurate, view of nature, of reality: they abstract from the objects of the other, more complex sciences; from the greater complexity of the human being (psychological, social, cultural, and historical); and finally from the perceiving, intelligent, and cognitive subject of science.

It should be kept in mind that the accuracy and reliability of science, of the results of its careful and controlled method, are directly dependent on this limiting, abstracting character of scientific inquiry into nature. Without these limitations, the sciences would not be as trustworthy as they are. But by the same token, these limits make the claim to describe "reality" or the whole of things a travesty of science.

This brief survey of the hierarchy of the sciences—physical, life, psychological, social, historical, culminating in the interpretation of the subject of all these inquiries—helps to clarify an important issue of misunderstanding, even of conflict, between scientific explanations, logical explanations, and humanistic interpretations. Each discipline—possibly because each human— has hidden imperialistic aims; theology exercised these for generations! Each discipline, therefore, seeks to provide the sole explanation for the subject matter of other disciplines—and, in doing so, not only to render the other modes of understanding subservient to or dependent on their own but even more to leave them as modes of understanding shorn of independence, autonomy, and so real explanatory power—as when a psychological or sociological analysis (Freudian or Marxist) "explains" a moral commitment, a philosophical position, or a religious belief. To take more recent examples: Can a biological theory about genes "explain" the moral standards, the moral and immoral actions, and the religions of human groups? Does science—as cosmology, evolution, genetics, sociobiology, anthropology, sociology, and psychology—essentially define morality and religion and their doctrines, as some maintain, as well as reshape them? If so, does it therefore explain religion and explain it exhaustively? Are morals and religion then, as this implies, epiphenomena, not merely conditioned but caused by factors that have little to do with moral judgments or religion? Are morals and religion merely pious, credulous reeditions or representations of what is known of our world by science? So many scientists—as well as others—believe.

Interestingly, it is presumably also the case that all these "causes" (biological, genetic, psychological, or sociological) of such cultural concerns as morals and religion are fully as much the necessary conditions or causes, for example, of the science of genetics; thus, on the face of it, these causes seem also to explain that science, or explain it away as a function of genetic determinism. No geneticist, however, thinks this "genetic" explanation provides the exhaustive understanding of or the only grounds for the assessment for his own theories in genetics. The theories of genetics, he would severely remind us, represent "empirical science." Hence they are cognitive and either true or false, valid or invalid; they are to be understood and assessed on entirely different grounds from morals or religion in terms of their causes, that is, on logical grounds: the grounds provided by the empirical evidence for each theory shown to us, that theory's rational coherence with other accepted theories, its "elegance," and its fruitfulness. We do not *explain* the genetic hypotheses or theories of that science; on the contrary, we seek to understand their meaning and their consequences and then test them, that is, we assent to them or we falsify and reject them.

The same sorts of genetic, sociobiological, sociological, and psychological causes lie behind the sciences as lie behind and so explain morals and religion—and explain these away. Generally, however, the scientific explanation does not include the scientific subject who is conducting the inquiry and thereby making the explanation. In almost all cases that scientific enterprise is excluded from the range of objects to be explained—as when an anthropologist is tempted to "explain" everything in a given culture as a function of that culture's determination, except for its science and especially its anthropology. Correspondingly, sociobiologists explain everyone's morals except those of the sociobiologist who writes the treatise on morals.[8] Each discipline tends to abstract itself from the determination it sees in other disciplines. This is necessary, because assessments of truth and falsehood are logical assessments, not explanations in terms of causes. They thus appeal to empirical evidence and coherence; to an elegance, harmony, and fruitfulness; and to nothing else. An explanation of the genetic, physical, or psychological causes of the ideas and propositions of genetics, physics, or psychology is to science irrelevant—as positivists say, these are issues of *discovery*, not issues of *justification*, and they have nothing to do with the logic of science.

That sword is, however, double-edged: if sociological, psychological, and biographical explanations are irrelevant to the assessment of scientific assertions (though of possible interest in scientific discovery and so to scientific biography), then the same applies to moral judgments, philosophical affirmations, and religious convictions. That is, the truth of these latter affirmations represents a different issue from their genetic, physical, or neurological (to name but a few) causes—unless a priori one holds these affirmations to be epiphenomenal and so to possess no theoretical or truth value.[9] (Such a position, however, is not based on the positivist argument detailed herein but on other, probably also biographical, grounds.)[10] The least the biological interpreter of morals is required to do is to understand his own philosophical opinions and moral judgments in terms coherent with his biological interpretation of the moral opinions of others. This, however, is a philosophical endeavor, uniting two disparate sorts of experience: (1) the scientific experience of biological inquiry and (2) the internal and social experience of one's own moral affirmations and actions.

It is important to note that in the case of those disciplines or modes of inquiry and reflection that we hold to be cognitive, we do not explain their cognitive theories in terms of the causes of these theories but rather we seek to understand the meaning and to assess the validity of these theories. And scientists do that not in terms of the standards of other disciplines but in terms of the self-set standards for justification of the discipline in question.[11] No one discipline possesses the entire truth about reality; rather, in our contemporary pluralism, the nature of cognition and hence of what is known to be real results only from a coherent synthesis of differing perspectives—and that is a philosophical and not a scientific task.

This book assumes ways other than empirical science of knowing what is real: through interior self-awareness, through personal and communal awareness of the other, and through intuitions of external reality that are much wider and deeper than either sensory experience or inquiry based on sensory experience. In other words, it assumes manifestations of reality to us and in us other than those through the five senses. These wider forms of knowing long antedate natural science; they have resulted in myths, philosophy, and theology, and they provide the commonsense presuppositions necessary for all of communal life, for civilization, and for science itself. They represent perspectives on reality in which the latter discloses itself in all its richness and depth. They occur through participating intuition and recognition on our side and through disclosure on nature's side. Only thus is the unity of reality, in itself and with us, brought to expression, that sense of the whole and of our relation to it necessary for every level of cognitive existence. Religion is the most concentrated response to these encounters with what is real; but every aspect of civilization and all its philosophical articulations are also based here. To recover these nearly lost rich and varied human interpretations of nature, one must not only take them seriously and listen to them but also revise them, that is, translate this archaic religious apprehension of nature in relation to a modern scientific understanding. This section begins such an effort in recovery and translation, and in this effort I am especially and vastly indebted to Mircea Eliade, Lawrence Sullivan, and, for modern science, Holmes Rolston III.[12]

I suggest that there are four major categories in terms of which nature has been and is experienced and known, and, interestingly, these appear prominently both in modern science and in archaic religion: nature as *power*, nature as *life*; nature as *order*, and finally, in one difficult to name, nature as manifesting a *redemptive unity*.[13] These are characteristics of nature and of a richer apprehension of nature both as our source and as the surrounding reality over against us. These four categories also represent "traces" or "signs" of the sacred within nature; to archaic religion these were direct manifestations, what Mircea Eliade called hierophanies, and in them nature was named as sacred. To us they are indirect traces at best.

What does science tell us of nature? What does its perspective indicate that other perspectives must take into account? From roughly 1600 to 1900, the scientific picture of nature was Galilean and Newtonian: nature was a vast, harmonious machine of matter in motion,[14] whose parts were all obedient to absolute and changeless laws. Only efficient and material, that is, physical causes are here at work; no internal purposes, conscious or unconscious, and no self-direction are present. And there are here no "real" secondary qualities such as color, sound, heat, and cold. Only primary qualities characterize the objective world: mass, velocity, shape, time, and space (distance). These are "there," and hence they characterize the machine "nature" as it is in itself.

Machines have, however, extrinsic purposes and hence an extrinsic designer; they are constructed for some purpose and hence according to certain definite theoretical and practical principles. For this reason, the inference that an intelligent and purposive designer was involved in the creation of *this* machine made real sense; therefore Deism was a commonly accepted system of thought. Moreover, because this scientific picture also required a scientific thinker to devise and think it, a provisional dualism of mechanical extension and rational thought was implied.[15] Slowly, however, as such "metaphysical" inferences have gone out of fashion, the two inferences of the creator and of the scientific observer and thinker have been quietly dropped, and only the objective "machine" is left as the picture of reality resulting from modern empirical science.

The new physics and, as its consequence, the new philosophy of science appropriate to that physics give us a very different picture of nature. The new philosophy of science, which views science as representing a relative perspective, a hermeneutical inquiry by means of symbols and models into a mystery, has already been discussed. Here I examine what sort of ontic picture contemporary physical science gives of nature.

First, there is now a strange indeterminism in nature as physics describes it. A thoroughgoing causality, an all-encompassing determinism, seems no longer to apply. The grounds for this appear to be twofold. On the one hand, as inquiry penetrates further into the microconstituents of nature, it becomes increasingly difficult to specify just what is there—in fact, Werner Heisenberg thought there was no smallest particle. Is this because such a real particle is beyond the reach of our present instruments? Or is it because the microscopic realm is beyond the possibility of our language and concepts—the latter being attuned to ordinary, "objective" experience? Is the microscopic realm a "wave," a cloud of energy—if not a smallest thing? The mathematical formulas through which physics understands its world still seem to apply, at least statistically; but our conceptual and verbal models seem less and less helpful. They appear to be dealing with an "object" more and more out of their range.

On the other hand, at the smallest level it seems impossible to predict what will happen. We can know precisely where something is or where it is headed, but apparently we cannot know both. Hence reality seems to communicate with us only in "jumps" or spasms—or is actuality itself characterized by "events" and not by some mode of continuing substance? There seems to be no continuing, causal chain, no subsistent determining system of material realities that can be located, much less verified; confidence in the order represented by causality is thus transempirical, an article of faith.[16] What is apparently in existence on the microscopic level is spontaneous, undetermined, open; these are characteristics that appear in more complex form on the biological level as randomness, openness, purposive action, growth, and self-direction. Again, there is no way of establishing whether this "indeterminateness" is the result of an *epistemological* problem of the limits of our instruments and concepts or the result of an *ontic* problem of the indeterminacy of actual nature. In any case, the primary qualities of classical physics, what is "out there," "real," and "effective"—mass, velocity, and space–time distance, obeying a determining system of causality— are gone; all is observer-related; and all that we can cognitively achieve are glimpses of a spontaneous, pulsating, yet statistically orderly cloud of events. At the microcosmic level, the more we know about nature, the more we are aware of the mystery of nature.

The second characteristic of nature as physical science uncovers it is the fusion of matter and energy and, as a result, the fundamental definition of physical reality as power, the energy to effect something—reality as an ordered stream or process of dynamism. In this stream, depending on the intensity and speed, mass and energy are "differentiated out," energy becoming mass and mass energy. Fundamentally, therefore, they are convertible— mass is energy—and together they equal power, literally, the power in all real things, the power of physical things to be and to act. Although humanity now understands that power in such a way as to be able in part to control this power, humans did not create it, just as, much earlier and on another level, humans did not create fire. In summary, then, in the picture contemporary physical sciences gives of nature, primary qualities (mass, velocity, and distance) have disappeared; absolute space and time are gone; quantification and measurements seem precarious, even when derived in a precise mathematical manner; and objectivity, as independence of the observer, has vanished: "We cannot give an objective account of the nature of nature."[17]

Thus microscopically nature discloses itself in this vision as a *process*, a stream constituted by dynamic energy or power, careening into events that can become masses; a process radically temporal, that is, open to the future. It is shaped by its past history, determinate in the present, but indeterminate in its future. At any moment it represents a definite set of possibilities, matrices of indeterminate possibility. Necessity and order, on the one hand, and contingency and openness, on the other hand, seem mysteriously mated and balanced in the stream of process. (One cannot help but note how this description is constituted by analogies from ordinary experience—process, stream, events, energy, power, openness, and so forth—used here precariously, if justifiably, as models for a "reality" clearly as different from as it is the same as the ordinary referents of these words.) Thus the microscopic level seems to prepare the way for the self-direction and the interaction of the organic level and the determinate–indeterminate character of history. This sense of reality as a stream of energy or power, shaping itself into entities and forms and then discarding them, at once creative and destructive, represents (albeit with different analogies) an old and pervasive *religious* intuition.[18]

There are other, possibly more controversial elements to this vision of the physical universe. First, there was apparently an "absolute beginning" to this process, with an initial "expansion into something" that occurred some 15 billion years ago—though whether scientific inquiry can specify an ontological beginning as well as an epistemological limit to our knowledge (a "wall" beyond which our inquiries, based on assumptions of continuity, cannot go) remains in question.[19]

Second, there is a fundamentally temporal character to this process in the sense that its direction over time is irreversible: an explosion that proceeds outward in space as it proceeds onward and forward in time. The entire temporal process may contract in the end, but this will be another, subsequent event that presupposes and so does not reverse the original explosion. Although the time of physics may be multidirectional and hence abstract, apparently the time of actuality, as the time in which process subsists, is monodirectional: there is an "arrow of time."[20]

Third, and most controversial, is the directional character of this process. To all the inquiries of science—from physics and astronomy to biology—this process is radically fortuitous or random. Physical science can uncover only causes and not entelechies or purposes; it is therefore questionable that any statement about purpose or intentionality—immanent or transcendent, unconscious or conscious—could be a part of a scientific statement. Still, this process also exhibits a steady accumulation of forms of greater and greater complexity of structure and of interaction. Atoms, molecules, societies of molecules, and therefore galaxies, stars, and planets appear during the process. The chance of this sort of accumulation (that is, of any "universe") presupposing the presence both of novelty and of continuity of structure is almost zero; and the improbability of a particular accumulation of structure appropriate to our universe is almost infinitely great. Had there been in the beginning of the universe the slightest change—in heat, speed, time, homogeneity, or in any of the other major factors—then the possibility of life and its development would have been utterly eliminated. The "wonder" of the development of life from its simple and rude beginnings— a wonder on which the wider teleology of nineteenth-century evolutionary theory had been based—pales compared to the wonder that a physical universe or cosmos such as ours developed at all. As one physicist said, "Even objectively this is a fine-tuned universe";[21] and as in the case of Isaac Newton's harmonious machine and its purported designer, one cannot but ask about the referent of that "act" of fine-tuning. In a universe where necessities of structure are more than balanced by contingencies of process, the question of the possibility of such an improbable continuity manifesting an even more improbable development must raise the question of meaning, of direction, even of purpose in this process. This is the current puzzle of the anthropic principle.

In this stream or process is resident an awesome and terrible power, the mysterious union of matter and energy: the power of physical things to hold together, to be one, and so to be and to act. Through its ordered power nature has developed itself and us, and through discovery of that ordered power outside of us we have mastered that power over nature and so over ourselves. And in controlling this awesome power, we have paradoxically at the same time experienced its ultimacy, its terrible finality; for we see at once how utterly fundamental it is, how totally destructive it is, and also that we only barely control our control over it. We are hardly the masters of our own mastery over nature's power.

Here again, on a new level, appear for humans as scientists and users of science, on the one hand, determined power in our hands and, on the other, open alternatives before us; and with their appearance comes for the masters an inescapable responsibility and even the possibility of our doom. In modern scientific and technological experience, the freedom implied in moral decision, awesome responsibility, and the destiny of a sort of self-fated doom join together in bizarre juxtaposition, supervening strangely on the determined sequences of nature's power—much as the experience of responsibility and fatedness once did in the most primordial of myths. The creative and destructive, even the ultimate or unconditioned character of this structure of power, this stream of being, is fascinating, puzzling, and terrifying; its strange union of determinateness and indeterminateness, like the consequent new union of modern technological freedom and modern technological fatedness, remains as baffling as it ever was. One is immediately led back to "mythical" thinking to make intelligible and to articulate this dialectic of power and of freedom, of openness and of fate, and also led back to recall the polarity of the sacred and the demonic in all divine power in archaic religious awareness.

Next I turn explicitly to ancient religion, to the human intuition of nature when nature represented the all-encompassing, all-creating, and frequently destroying reality in which early humans existed. Through what we moderns name their religion, they responded to the full reality of nature that they encountered; they recognized and articulated what nature disclosed to them of itself and of their existence; and they felt nature's awesome power around them and in them and so sought to deal as best they could with that power.

These were primal intuitions of the same power that science now describes and scientific technology uses; and these intuitions reflect the same human dependence and the same effort to use that on which we depend. These intuitions of power are today formulated in objectivist, reductionist scientific terms, and this dependence—of which we are barely conscious—is now countered by our awareness of our technological dominance over nature's powers. But can these early, very human, and surely very realistic intuitions be of help to us?

After this introduction, it is not surprising that, according to many students of archaic religion—for instance, E. B. Tylor and many nineteenth-century anthropologists, Gerardus van der Leeuw, Mircea Eliade, and Paul Tillich[22]—the first characteristic of primal religious intuitions of nature and, correspondingly, the first thing sought by all such religion was power. The sacred objects of religious care or concern were "powers," and the goal of religious activity was to share in that varied power (not so much has changed here!). The human complexities and moral ambiguities of any human participation in this power, of human sharing of it, are clear enough in primitive religion and especially in magic. Modernity has been well aware of the authoritarianism, the corruption, and the destructive possibilities latent in the shaman's or the magician's claims to power; in fact, this was to many almost all there was to primal religion! It is therefore ironic that the ambiguity and the corruption of this human use of nature's power has become even clearer now that much more of that power has been gained by men and women through modern science and technology.

These religious manifestations of nature's power, or "hierophanies," are of supreme importance to us. Hierophanies are manifestations or disclosures of reality and so of power through some natural or social entity. For primal religious consciousness, entities such as water, trees, mountains, animals, and earth did not merely manifest themselves; rather, in appearing to us they embodied and communicated an infinite power or, better, an *aspect* of an infinite power on which, in all its various facets, humanity utterly depends.[23] It is therefore through the vast and varied powers of nature that we have been granted the necessary "power" to be born, to continue to be, and to act; on these powers our sustenance, our own powers, our continuance, and so all of our security rest. For this reason archaic religious acts and rites, through which humans participated in these powers, aimed to unite humans with the massive, infinite, inexhaustible powers that bring humans to birth and that surround, support, and threaten humanity. These powers appear in and through special natural forces and objects. Such powers are encountered in both nature and community—moderns distinguish these two, early humans did not—and these powers are multiple.

First, these powers represent the general power within all reality and hence the power to create reality, to bring some entity into being. As a consequence, wherever there are permanence and infinity, life and fertility, health and wholeness, the signs of this sacred power can be found. It follows that rocks, especially massive rocks and mountains; the sun; sea, streams, ponds, and all water; great trees and all plants mediate as well as represent this infinite creative power. Further, nature's sexuality—and ours—both as act and as symbol; animals and birds; chiefs, kings, and shamans all participate in some aspect of this creative power and of the sacred as power; and in that participation they give rise to and use power. Power here is certainly physical; but the physical is a vehicle, a medium, of the deeper power within it and yet transcendent to it. The physical reality of all of these elements and beings is, as Eliade says, a hierophany, a symbol of the inexhaustible power of reality, of energy, of what we term nature.

The meanings or values for human beings that are resident in these structures of power are evident and significant. These are by no means trivial meanings inessential for the important aspects of life; they have been and remain our ultimate concerns: existence, life, family and fertility, food, health, strength, warmth, security, protection, place. The sacred powers that grant all this to us are not at all "subjective." As long as we continue to be, they are clearly there; they disclose themselves by working in and through things and persons. We have not made them up or imagined them; they are there as the presupposition of all humans do and accomplish.[24] At this stage, religion is quite empirical, neither merely conjectural nor argumentative, certainly not the result of mere inference or of metaphysical speculation, and apparently quite necessary for life and for the continuation of life.

Despite its ultimacy, power strangely wanes, weakens, vanishes away; its presence is at once ambiguous and precarious, making our life itself vulnerable and chancy, evanescent as a flame. One thinks, for example, of how exceedingly precarious, in all early human experience, the "values" of health and security, of fertility and crops, of ordered community, and of animals were. And each of these "values" is dependent on some power within the mystery of reality, a power therefore on which humans are utterly dependent. Modern civilization seems to blunt, to disguise, to cover up this continued experience of radical precariousness and dependence—at least for the middle and the privileged classes and when no wars are waged! But when the culture—the immediate society around us, the nation itself—becomes unstable and vulnerable and its existence precarious, this sense of radical loss, this terror, and this angst at basic insecurity come rushing back. And whatever the ups and downs of humanity's unstable history, this loss of power, of the power to be, can be seen continually outside of us in nature's cycles, for example, in the barren quiet of winter; and it can be felt inside ourselves in the inexorable weakening and increasing helplessness of our being in our own late fall and winter years. Evident in all of this is the paradoxically dialectical absence, the *no* as well as the *yes*, of life-giving power: the ambiguity of life; its destructive possibilities; the continual presence of nonbeing amidst this being, of the tragic and the demonic. None of this seems to have vanished or even lessened in the accumulation of knowledge in a scientific age or because of the exponential increases in our technological power.

Two conclusions followed for archaic religion from this continual process of the waning as well as the waxing of power. First, renewal is always necessary. We are separated or alienated from the primal powers; they recede, and it is essential that they return again. This recession is partly a process that takes place outside of us but also partly a process within us; hence we ourselves need to act to restore what has been lost. There is hardly a primordial myth that does not tell this story of lost power, lost security, lost being, and that does not urge upon humans ritual and moral obligations because of that loss.[25]

Second, for this renewal of power—as objective nature itself shows us— apparently suffering is significant, even death. For early religion, nature everywhere sends this message. Seeds must first die in order that there be new growth; in fact, most of nature dies in order to be once again reborn. The sun sets if it is to appear again; the moon regularly disappears in order to become full. Thus throughout the course of nature, death effects and perfects the renewal of life. This obvious pattern in the objective cycles of nature's changes is also recognized and acknowledged inwardly by responding humans. In early religion (and many contemporary religions), consequently, certain acts of suffering are necessary on the part of humans too—sacrifice, purgation, fasting, ascetic self-control, discipline culminating in moral awareness—as almost every religious myth and an infinity of religious rites tell us. The precariousness of ultimate power, the ambiguity of our shared use of it, the need for our responding sacrifice are all "known" clearly in archaic religion's insight into nature. And all this also seems strangely relevant today.

7

Nature as Life

With reflection on the presence and characteristics of life as an aspect of nature, several moves are made: from physical and chemical science to biological science, from inorganic to organic entities, from the story of the cosmos to the story of evolution, from nature as distinct from culture and history to nature as the threshold to culture and history. In religious awareness, this type of move brings into view a significantly different level of the sacred: from the sacred as reality and power to the sacred as life or as the power of life. It is this new level that our scientific, technological, and industrial developments threaten. It is life that is imperiled by our knowledge through physics of nature's power and through chemistry of nature's physical structure.

In what sense, in dealing with life in biology, are we at a different level?[1] To start, there are different data in this science, different sorts of evidence and hence different modes of explanation. The data and evidence concern organisms and hence an organism as a whole and in relation to its environment, and so our modes of explanation vastly increase their scope: they are in a new way organic, holistic, and contextual. In dealing with life in this science, one understands something by understanding its role and function in relation to the organism as a whole, even to what can only be called "purposes" of that whole. Further, organisms are self-maintaining: they grow, they decay, they die, they react to stimuli. They interact—that is, they actively interfere and respond—with their environment at every level, as inorganic entities do not. They reproduce, and they resist dying. Interestingly, organisms draw a sharp line, unconscious or conscious, between themselves and their environment; they assimilate environmental materials according to their needs, they actively affect their environment in return, and they donate their waste to the environment. They have needs: to preserve, maintain, fulfill, and reproduce themselves. And thus they have purposes, unconscious or conscious; a *telos*, an inner directedness that determines all that they are and do. As a consequence, unlike inorganic entities (e.g., a stone), organisms can be characterized as diseased or healthy, living or dead, vulnerable or secure, anxious or serene. Above all, to most modern theoretical biology they represent "information-processing systems," that is, they are self-directing, "self-programmed" (to use the current analogy taken from computers).[2]

Finally, although there are the same elements (physical and chemical) in a biological perspective, set in new combinations, these elements seem to behave differently, to be put to different uses; they have a different praxis and mode of being. They have become "parts" in a new way, functions of a whole with purposes, and there is no understanding of how any part or organ works until it is seen as a function of the organism, of its life and of its values. The parts of a complex artifact, especially of a machine, are also "functions," and their presence and work are to be understood on the macrocosmic level only as parts of the whole. However, in a machine the purposes and the design that create the whole and thus make them "parts" are external, first in the craftsperson and the engineer and then in the design itself. In natural life (as in an acorn becoming an oak), as Aristotle saw, the purposes are internal, resident as "form" in the entity itself and so "directing" it to its goal, its use or fulfillment, or at least its survival. Modern biologists may not wish to follow Aristotle's teleology or his formal/final causality; nevertheless they find DNA—a strangely "directing" sort of "cause" and hence a formal/final one—central to life as its directing agency, and, despite their contortions, they cannot avoid purposive, teleological language in speaking scientifically of the organism and its behavior. Thus the "purposes" of the DNA molecule ("the selfish gene") become the clue to organic growth and behavior, as the purposes of survival provided the clues to organic function in earlier biology and to evolutionary development itself.[3] Although such teleological categories are carefully "laundered out" in theoretical and so in scientific explanations, they seem to recur stubbornly and necessarily. Are these unconscious "purposes" matters of linguistic convenience, of shorthand, or are we speaking of something "there," something to be accounted for by a different level of explanation?[4] In any case, life— and its study, biology—discloses at the least new possibilities, new dimensions (if not new levels), within matter.

What is new here? Is there a material principle of life, one discoverable by scientific inquiry? Probably not. Most current biologists emphasize the "information-processing" and thus the "self-directing" character of life: the principle or gene in each cell that organizes and directs the formation of cells into organisms and sets ordered possibilities before each organism for its life—this is DNA, or the genetic code. Here, if anywhere, is the locus, principle, or vehicle of the sacred in nature, the principle of vitality for life, what a geneticist friend of mine calls the *icon* of the sacred.[5]

As was noted, several polarities necessary for the understanding of the organism appear at the level of life. Although the relations of an inorganic entity to its environment are surely important in understanding, for example, a stone, a planet, or a star, the relations of the organism to its environment become in a quite new way the clues to its behavior, to its being, and so to its explanation. And this level of the organism in relation to its environment is dialectical, polar: the organism sets a boundary between itself and its environment, divides itself off from it, in order to protect, feed, and reproduce itself. But at the same time it relates in much more essential ways to its environment and to others in order to be itself and to survive: for food, for protection, and for reproduction. It is independent (as a stone is not) because it is dependent (as a stone is not); it is newly an individual, and one qua social—and vice versa.

Organisms have had a long history. Not only did they appear when life came out of nonlife; even more, their character as complex wholes has dramatically changed over time. No present form of life, just as no present form of the cosmos, goes back to the beginning. Thus there is a "story" or a "history" of life, as there is one of the cosmos. The story of life is the referent for the word *evolution* as it is generally used. As a "fact" descriptive of developments in the past—of the changes and development of forms of life out of previous forms (note the analogy to historical developments)— evolution seems incontestable. Criticism of evolution in science and in philosophy or theology is therefore directed (1) at how that story is to be understood, that is, what factors seem to be at work in these changes, and (2) at the characteristics of that sequence of changes (gradualism versus punctuated equilibrium). It is the organism (the phenotype) that is the actor in this drama or story; it is this that survives at each level, that reproduces, and that undergoes mutation and natural selection. Hence a biological and not merely a physical–chemical explanation of this story seems necessary in any understanding of life and its development.

The product of evolution, the organism, has immanent if unconscious ends or purposes by which it directs its physical being. Does the process of developing life itself, the story of evolution, have ends or purposes analogous either to the artifact and its external designer or to this immanent telos? Is the process directed in some way? Current biological science replies with a resounding "no": the appearance of life itself out of nonlife, the organic from the inorganic, and the subsequent process of evolutionary change, the transformation of life from the simplest level to the most complex, are for current theory both undirected. The latter is characterized and so understood solely in terms of random mutations of genes, recombination, and the natural selection that preserves (but does not create) these mutations.

Natural selection is, to be sure, "pro-life." It selects for life because the unfit do not last; selection eliminates unfit mutations. But by the same token, natural selection cannot provide the causes for changes in the forms of life and hence for the character of the story of life. First, such words as *random* and *chance* negate rather than provide an explanation. A chance event is by nature an unexplained and hence an "irrational" event. Second, while natural selection selects the fit, present biologists make clear that it does not necessarily select the more complex or the more advanced organisms. Frequently, simpler organisms are more stable and more adaptive. Thus if there is a story, a discernible development toward complexity, it eludes whatever biology has to say. Apparently biology must leave out that story— settling for "steady development through changes to more complex forms" —insofar as that story is there, and so there remains something still to be understood, something that is yet unexplained, something with which present theory cannot deal. Nineteenth-century science—or at least, many who were scientists—thought that science could provide such an explanation; the "wider teleology" inherent in evolution, a "cosmic law of development," was regarded as a legitimate inference from the data of biological evolution. In this century, however, such an expansion of evolutionary theory to include the whole story of life and of the cosmos as a whole has been in disfavor among scientists.

With the question of a "wider teleology," interesting epistemological issues arise. Can a scientific explanation deal with this puzzle? Could science uncover a teleological principle, if such a principle were there? Could science produce a teleological theory, even if it felt compelled to do so? Or does its method, once it understands what that method is about, inevitably objectify what it studies so as to drain out and thus subjectivize all signs of purpose, of story or plot? Is science confined, in Aristotelian terms, to material, efficient causality alone, so that it must eschew any consideration of final causes, inherent or external? And how could a teleological theory be tested, even if it could be derived?

Have we therefore here reached a "limit" of scientific explanation, a point where, if there is something here to be explained, science abstracts from actuality to maintain the integrity of its inquiries and thus leaves to some other mode of knowing what is to be omitted? If so, then what sorts of explanations are possible here, in what disciplines—for example, cosmology, philosophical ontology or metaphysics, or theology? And what sorts of evidence are relevant, what kinds of symbols and language, and above all, what kinds of criteria? What grounds can be given for a legitimate move from a special discipline—in this case, biology—to a further discipline when explanations are not forthcoming from the first discipline—and what discipline adjudicates that discussion?

Clearly, the same sorts of interesting (philosophical) questions of method and of "turf" arise in relation to that cousin to this evolutionary question, namely, the puzzle about teleology in the story of the cosmos. As the current interest in the anthropic principle shows, in the story of the cosmos some sort of further explanation seems required—though there is room for debate about whether this explanation might be scientific, philosophical, or theological. Perhaps, in refusing to consider this question of teleology the biologists are right—as scientists—and not the physicists. If so, then the issue shifts slightly and becomes the one already elaborated, namely, whether science presents a total explanation of natural reality or whether there are cognitive possibilities as well in philosophical understanding and religious reflection—which, as has been argued, alone could provide the cognitive and so the coherent bases for scientific inquiry itself.

Four points have become clear in this discussion, which are not only of interest in themselves but relevant to reflection on religion. First, life is the presupposition, not the effect, of mutations in natural selection, that is, of the process of evolution as delineated in biology. A living organism is necessary for either mutations or natural selection to come into play: there must be reproduction for mutations to occur, and survival to reproduce is a necessary factor for natural selection to operate.[6] Both presuppose a sequence of related organic events over time, over generations, a sequence that can fail to survive; both presuppose life as the condition of procreation. Hence other factors, perhaps analogous but significantly different, must be specified if one is to account for the appearance of organisms out of what was once merely inorganic. Some explanatory "pro-life" principle, force, or set of forces must have been there—unless we are satisfied with no explanation at all. If the rate of breakdown of complex molecules is equal to or, especially, greater than the rate of random assembly, how is it that these newly complex molecules came together and stayed together to begin the process of life? Again, a question seems to remain regarding the boundary of the special sciences, that is, a "limit" question.

Second, we arise from our story, the story of life. In this sense we are more "historical" than even those concentrating on history and tradition have thought. In this story of life, historical tradition has formed us in a new and deeper way, stretching back almost endlessly to the beginnings of life and of the cosmos itself. What we are—all the features and aspects of our being—has developed out of that story; in the process of its developments, forms of life have slowly shifted, complexified, and in our epoch resulted in our characteristic identity as humans.[7] And the same is true of every form of life of which we know. We all come to be over time by a process of slow change into what we are; and this is as true of our minds and spirits; of our ideas, morals, and religions; of our intellectual, moral, and spiritual powers, as it is of our brain, organs, and cells. No more than the psyche or the soma is the "soul" lowered down into a natural, soulless, and so mechanical body. Both soul and body, together and in strange unity, develop out of develop-ing nature, a point with fairly radical implications not only for the human sciences but also for theology and perhaps especially for the philosophy of nature. The influence of this cosmic and evolutionary story—passed on to us through our genes, through DNA—is immense, almost beyond comprehen-sion; and it is not to be denied. In discussions of human beings and of all their works, this historical influence of *nature* must be set down with the historical influence of *cultural traditions* (nation, culture, and community) and the influence of immediate *social environment* (family and community), that is, "nurture," as providing the (creaturely or natural) explanatory factors of what we are and do. All our possibilities, of what we are and what we do alike, are genetic; our physical, psychological, moral, and spiritual similar-ities, as well as all our differences, are patterned here. Thus it is true that our social customs, manners, laws, obligations (morals), as well as our religious rites, myths, and laws, can be traced back—as can our bones and our organs—into the dim recesses of the prehuman past. And biology, medi-cine, and genetics, in fact, the entire corpus of science, can likewise be traced back to those origins.

It seems evident that among the powers—in fact, the necessities—of our human condition and possibly of many forms of life besides ours, we must choose (affirm) and use deliberately these genetic powers and possibilities of our nature; this is also the case with aspects of the cultural, moral, and religious traditions we inherit. The call "to choose ourselves" includes the possibilities of our genetic inheritance as it does the possibilities of our familial, communal, and cultural inheritance. To speak theologically, this is the way the divine creates: in and through this providential story of cosmic and evolutionary development. We have come to accept this influence—not to say determination—historically (with regard to the influence of history) because of the pressure of the modern historical consciousness; we know that each of us is what that person's particular social tradition has fashioned him or her to be. But this is also true of the natural history out of which we arise. The ordered set of possibilities and the élan to live among and through these possibilities, which together help to constitute us, are provided genet-ically, by genetic development and inheritance.

Third, as in the archaic religious understanding of life, there appears out of the biological understanding a mysterious dialectic of living and dying, of death and death's strange unity with the renewal of life. The dying of individuals in the species makes possible the survival, the full flowering, and so the reproductive power of new individuals, of a new generation. Out of this arises—how or why, we do not know—the possibility of mutations, natural selection, and so the gradual evolutionary change of forms. Correspondingly, on a larger scale, the elimination of some species makes room on a finite planet for other species, just as (providentially) the continuation of many forms of life in relatively unchanged form is the condition for the appearance and survival of new and more complex forms of life. At every level—with regard to food, to space, to changes over time—life lives on life and replaces life; more precisely, it lives on the removal, the death, the elimination of other life. How this structural and apparently essential characteristic of life can be creatively wedded to life's obligation to foster rather than eliminate other life remains the major moral issue of existence. How are the need for the survival of life and the necessity in life of moral obligation to the other to be joined? This is an issue at every level of our existence, at the level of ecology, of plants, of fish and animals, of other humans. The interweaving of death with life and with new life is set deep within the most fundamental processes of nature. This interweaving has been immensely illumined by present scientific knowledge, yet it was also universally recognized in archaic religions.[8]

Fourth, life remakes the environment as well as itself. Plants produce oxygen and so help to create the atmosphere; soil is made possible by humus; vegetation prevents destructive runoff of water and so geological erosion. In all of this, even the climate is modified. This interference of life in general with the environment is the preview—in fact, the ontological precondition—of human advances in making human existence more secure within its environment, an interference that John Dewey termed "making more secure, continuing and lasting the merely occasional values that come to us by happenstance."[9] As Dewey did not see so clearly, this interference, granted that humans accumulate knowledge and with it the power to manipulate, is also the precondition of human destruction of its environment—the ironic threat that life, even when developed, educated, and "intelligent," poses to all life generally.[10] From the very beginning, apparently, life uses its environment for its own needs and implicit purposes; it exploits its "world" as best it can for its own ends—and, also from the beginning, distributes its waste in the environment! This side of life does not start with us, but it may well finish there.

This section turns again to archaic or primordial religion, and I reiterate how and why this is being done. First, these are not studies of early or tribal religions; such studies would be done on particular groups by an anthropologist or a historian of religions. I am interested solely in how these religions seem to view and respond to the vast natural world around them, to what we call nature. We are told frequently that these religions manifest a significant, even a superior, relation to nature to that of our modern Western civilization; this is surely credible. Thus they are being examined here for hints of what that relation might have been, that is, what kind of a different knowing of nature is to be found here. My hope is that even though modern humans are participants in a scientific understanding of nature, we may learn from the archaic religions and through them enrich and expand our own modern understanding of nature.

To tribal and archaic religion, nature (to use Mircea Eliade's phrase) was not "natural" in the sense it is to us. That is, nature was not at all "desacralized," shorn of its sacred dimension and thus "on its own" and self-sufficient—and hence secular in its being and its processes. On the contrary, nature's power or powers and its life forces—in fact everything in nature—represented signs or symbols, vehicles, of a transcendent power and order: "hierophanies" of the sacred.[11] The sacred in its many forms was considered to manifest itself through these finite media, the various entities in nature that humans encounter, relate to, and use. Humanity's encounter with these entities and use of them, therefore, represents in each case a *ritual* encounter or action; in dealing with them humans were considered to deal through them with the sacred powers latent within them. In that sense all the activities of culture—farming, hunting, building, cooking, eating, even arranging flowers—are in archaic religion *sacramental*, a manipulation of a visible sign bearing an invisible grace.[12]

As was suggested in Chapter 6, there are four principal aspects to that manifestation of the deeper reality of nature to archaic religion: power, life, order, and redemptive reconciliation. These represented for early humankind four aspects of the deeper mystery of nature as they encountered it. These four are, of course, abstractions, hermeneutically pulled out and reflectively articulated in order that we might relate these materials from our archaic religious heritage to our modern world and so enrich the latter through them.

Considering that nature is today theoretically defined largely in terms of the inorganic, that is, through the models and formulas of physics and chemistry, the priority of life in archaic religion comes as a surprise. It is life that is celebrated here as the most wonderful and precious, because absolutely necessary, gift of the divine and therefore as the central power and characteristic of nature. To *homo religiosus,* nature is teeming with life, infinitely and inexhaustibly fertile. As a result, almost every important natural being is a symbol, a vehicle, of that universal life of nature. In such a vision of nature as, above all, the power of life, nature's reality and our values ("fact" and "value") coalesce and become one. In terms of present scientific inquiries into nature, therefore, it could be said that the clue for archaic human beings to the reality of nature lay in biology and not in physics, in the cell and in DNA rather than in matter and in energy. It is DNA, not the neutrino, that is the icon of the sacred.

The priority of life in archaic religion is well illustrated, as Eliade shows, in the strange career of high gods.[13] Interestingly, the concept of an exalted, transcendent, and supremely powerful creator–sky god is almost universal; almost everywhere there was recognized the existence of—even the necessity for—a supreme, self-sufficient, sovereign power by which and through which all that is around us was established, given its powers, and set in motion. This god represents the presupposition of the existence of all the many beings, not one being among them; hence it is a "high" god.

Interestingly, an examination of archaic religions reveals that these transcendent, creator deities recede in immediate relevance and so seem to vanish from religious attention, which is, after all, existential and practical and not speculative. Like metaphysical structures in a scientific and technological culture, which one may say represent the "hither" legacy of these primordial high gods, such universal presuppositions, however necessary they may be, recede and even vanish from the visible, practical scene. In applying to all things, they fail to apply crucially to any of them, and so (being neither "falsifiable" nor "verifiable") they disappear from sight. As Eliade remarks, frequently the creator gods change into sun gods who have a very different and more immediately significant function, namely, as givers of life, an essential source (cooperating with other forces) of fertility in and on the earth.[14] Further, the sun god, the giver of life who has replaced the original creator, is also the lord over death. Not only are the two, life and death, almost universally interconnected, but here—as elsewhere—nature seems intent to emphasize this interconnection: for each evening the sun clearly dies, descending apparently voluntarily into the realm of darkness; and each morning the sun again rises, unchanged and unscathed, from that polar realm to pour forth once more the priceless power of life. Only the lord of both life and death could perform that daily feat!

An equally universal symbol of the power of life is the moon.[15] Unlike the sun, the moon is subject in its essential being to the familiar cycles of nature; its being as it proceeds across the heavens represents a process of continuing and orderly change, diminishing, disappearing, appearing again, and then gaining to fullness. The moon is the major hierophany for those cyclical realities that govern and make possible all the various powers of life in nature. The moon "controls" (in systematic correlation or in "sync" with) all the becoming of life, those changes that are creative of life in its appearance and reappearance: rains and sun, tides, the seasons, menstruation, the growth of plants and crops, the reappearance of animals. The fertility of all of nature—plants, animals, and human life—is thus subject to the moon, in correlation with the moon's changes. Therefore the moon is associated with all other clear vehicles of fertility: earth as the source of life; woman as the mother of life, and hence the "Great Mother"; snakes (as powerful dwellers within the fertile earth); and all vegetation. Each of these dies and rises again, enters earth and appears again. The moon, in fact, is the first of the dead—the moon dies, the sun does not—and so the moon is the herald of return from the dead.

Nature is here seen, by way of the symbol or hierophany of the moon, as in continual process or change. But this process revealed itself to archaic humans as an orderly sequence of changes, a sequence in which both radical change and regularity are necessary conditions of value and therefore of life. Change here is inescapable, scary, yet in the end dependable. Further, a coherent interlocking system of powers is evident in nature: moon and water, moon and menstruation, moon and the life of crops and of animals, moon and seasonal changes. This entire coherent system of different yet interrelated parts—in the heavens, in our bodies, in the earth and the waters (including snakes and snails)—also bespeaks an astounding "order" within diverse natural beings, especially but not exclusively living beings; an order that is truly a "wonder" and yet a wonder that creates and supports us. It can be no surprise that all this was regarded as sacred! Finally, in this vision of nature through the hierophany of the moon there is again the clear interweaving of death and life, of dying and rising again. The strange unity of prehistoric fertility rites and the much later hope of resurrection, evident in the late Hellenistic cults, makes new sense in the light of the unity of life and death, of death and new life, experienced in nature itself throughout the history of religious apprehension from the most primordial of religions to the religions of premodern civilization.

Another universal symbol of life is water. Water in its quiescent state resonates with infinity, both endlessness and formlessness; in this state water is the visible primal sign of infinity, felt if not yet conceived by all human life. Water is the formless abyss into which all forms disappear and die; and it is the formless origin from which all forms arise. Yet water is also living, flowing, moving, penetrating, making alive all it touches. As rivulets, streams and rivers, rain, semen, and continually experienced as thirst quencher, water is the creative principle, infinitely potent as the condition of life and as the possibility of new life. Wherever water appears, life appears—or begins again. Whether in or on the earth, whether in the male or in the female, what is moist and wet fosters life, whereas what is dry signals the end of life. Finally, water cleanses and purifies and so is the bearer of rejuvenation, of a new start, of redemption as well as creation.

Each of these aspects represents water as creative alike of life and of the spiritual redemption of life. As the visible medium of the infinite and formless source of formed things, of the principle that makes alive and preserves the life it makes, and of purifying, redeeming grace, water has been central for religious rites and images, archaic and modern alike. And this role in all archaic religions has its dim echoes today in our awe at the infinite sea, our relief at the unexpected appearance of rain or of a spring or of a river, and our experience of renewed cleanliness at the simplest bath. Through water, nature manifests its infinite power to initiate and preserve life, to purify what has been tarnished, even to overcome death with new life—and through a raging water, nature shows its infinite power to destroy. Water is at once the source of all creative finitude, the principle of new life, the redemptive power of rebirth—and hence the window to and mirror of eternity.[16]

As primal a principle of life as water in archaic religion was earth, the Great Mother.[17] For us (ancients and moderns alike), all things rest on the earth as on a stage. It is on the earth that we drive and walk; it is in the earth that we mine; and soil is essential for farmers and gardeners. Nature as earth is our place, our own lot, our sidewalk—the "where" of human activities, until we move to another planet. But the earth was also far different for archaic humans; and, as the ecological crisis shows, their intuition of humanity's real situation appears to have been far more accurate than ours today.

For the earliest humans, all life arose solely from the earth: it was the direct and infinite source and the continuing ground, the Mother, of plants, animals, and humans. All comes from the earth Mother and returns to her when its term is done. Somewhat later rituals depicted earth as mother and sun or rain as father, a cosmic marriage participating in and encouraged by the sacred union of a king and his partner. Still later, earth and plow represented a new form of marital union resulting in a fertile earth. In all of this, earth as source of life represents woman, as in turn woman represents earth. Together they are vehicles, symbols, bearers of the infinite and precious power of life—our power to be—and hence they were supremely sacred. Here again is manifest the clear intuition of the earth as alive, as female, as the infinite and exhaustible source of life, and of matter as naturally teeming with abundant life.

There appears in and through this symbol also the strange unity of life and of death. As the natural life of plants demonstrates, the seed must die in order to give life; and as rites and myths everywhere reiterate, the disappearance of what was once alive into the earth—especially the "death" of sowing and scattering—results in the appearance of life again, the coming of new life after death. Earth is thus the source of life and the fearful abode of death. As the Great Mother gives life out of herself, so with the sacrifice, the dismemberment, and the scattering of her consort—Adonis, Osiris, perhaps the king himself—there occurs a death that results in new life.[18] Death and life are united in earth as they are in water, in moon, and in sun. And all represent the intricate, all-encompassing, creative "system" of nature, an interlocking, interrelated, perfectly coherent and intelligible order of astral, terrestrial, and subterrestrial entities and powers: sun, moon, earth, fields and forests, water, animals, plants, women and men.

This union of life with death and, more relevantly, of death with the appearance of new life, deeply evident in the human encounter with and dependence on the vast forces of nature (sun, moon, water, earth), indicates that confidence in some mode of new life after death is "natural," an evident disclosure through each of the crucial natural processes that the earliest human beings encountered in the nature around them. It is a natural intuition of nature, seemingly disclosed everywhere throughout nature. This intuition was helped by dreams, especially of the dead, and by reverence for and fear of ancestors. But the intuition of a new life after death is hardly the result, as many modern intellectuals think, of a primitive form of "metaphysical speculation" based on unreal and unrealizable wishes. Natural experience would find its denial overwhelmingly counterfactual, against the empirical evidence of almost every important natural force known. Nothing shows more clearly the vast changes in human intuitions of and attitudes toward nature than this difference: the naturalness and so the reality to the earliest humans of continuing life after death, and the unreality, the unnaturalness of this to us. Apparently, only faith in a transcendent power can now intervene to secure this possibility.

The final symbol of the infinite power of life in nature is the plants. Of all the symbols of life, this one seems to many humans today to be the least significant: plants are to us edible, decorative, useful against runoffs; they beautify nature but are not (at least to me) symbolic of the deep powers that create and uphold nature. This was not so to archaic humans: to them, plants, especially trees, represented life power, even the power of the cosmos itself—which is, therefore, life power. The tree is the cosmos in its infinity, strength, and power of fertility and growth; in fact, it represents the *Axis Mundi,* the center post of the world that holds the world together and that mediates between heaven, earth, and the realm under the earth. Again, the tree lives through its death; its leaves go, it dies, and then it is reborn. Hence the tree (like all else in nature) communicates the power to overcome death. All plants are signs of this vast power, the power of life; soma as divine communicates this sacred power by the gift of ecstasy, which lifts us beyond our plodding, daily, dying selves into union with nature's undying power of life.

Agriculture—again, the realm of women—in union with earth, sun, and water, uncovers and frees this sacred power of life. In plowing, sowing, and reaping humans would unite with this power, repeating the primordial sexual acts of divine beings. As with hunting and fishing, then, farming is a "ritual," a cooperation with the sacred powers of nature as life. In archaic religion's view, sacrifice is always necessary for this power to return and for us to participate in it, sacrifice among the gods (Osiris and Adonis) and also among men and women. Thus combined with the apprehension of human participation in the infinite powers of natural life is the sense of human estrangement from them, an anxiety about being separated from the infinite source of life. Religious acts, rituals, incantations, and prayers are hence considered necessary to reconcile and reunite us with these powers on which we depend. We moderns are hardly aware of these needs, but it is quite possibly the case that this is also true for us.

8

Nature, Order, and Value

In this chapter on the order that humans apprehend in nature—just as we apprehend it in other regions of experience—I change the format slightly. The reasons are twofold. First, the philosophical and theological problems raised by order, especially the relations of order, novelty, and value, are so fascinating and complex that they demand a more coherent reflective treatment than merely a careful look at science and then at archaic religion (both of which illustrate these problems, to be sure). Second, the philosophical developments around these themes are so important and illuminating to its discussion that they cannot be omitted. Hence this chapter on order is extended and constructed as a brief chronological account of the human experience and articulation of order, interspersed with reflective comments on the themes swirling around order, nature, and value.

Throughout the discussion thus far, the certainty of and confidence in an order encompassing all experienced things has been revealed as one of the most persistent of human intuitions of objective reality. From the beginning of the human story to the present, order of some sort has been seen to be a fundamental character of natural processes. This intuition has been so persistent that one could well conclude that nature discloses itself as containing an order, which humans are challenged and lured to discover and articulate. This lure to understand the order of things is also universally acknowledged and understood: the uncovering of the order of natural events and our consequent participation in that order represent—so community after community affirms—our only possible entrance into value and especially into secure values. Nature's disclosure of its order is to be met with our acknowledgment of it and obedience to it; in such terms might much of human culture—customary, moral, philosophical, and religious—be summarized. In some cultures, to be sure, moral custom and religious obligation are derived directly from divine decrees, that is, from religious law rather than from "natural law." However, in a great number of other cultures the divine will discloses itself in both the natural order around humans and the traditional order of social life, and the two disclosures are brought to unity in religious myth and symbol and later in religious philosophical reflection.

Two points are at work in these traditions of "natural law." First, the order in nature makes possible our world as world, as cosmos or Tao; without this order there would be no habitable world at all, much less one that offered us fulfillment and secure values (to use John Dewey's phrase). It is through the Tao and the Logos that the world as "world" comes to be. Second, this order provides not only a world for us to inhabit but also, by analogy, the structures, the possibilities, the principles, or the laws by which we may fulfill ourselves, become fully human, and achieve excellence in that world. In other words, the order of the world around us furnishes the basis for "natural law" (cf., for example, the Tao, Dharma, or the Logos), that is, for *our* natural law, the principles according to which authentic human life can be and so should be lived. Here the normative (natural law) is derived from the real (nature), "ought" from "is"—if one understands both "ought" and "is" in this special way. Only when "is" (existence) is understood purely positively or naturalistically—as modern science portrays it—is it vacant of any traces of "ought"; a metaphysical interpretation of reality, of "is," has always been resonant with ethical implications.[1] Hence discussion of fundamental principles of order in nature provides, for most cultures, the basis for any intelligent discussion of values—as, for example, our own Enlightenment tradition of "natural rights" as the foundation of democratic moral and political principles shows. How modern science, especially modern positivism (naturalism), interprets this relation of the order of nature to value is of interest.

Another important theme, especially in relation to modern science and its implications, is the relation of novelty to order. Most archaic and traditional interpretations of order—natural, political, and moral—assumed that the cosmic order was permanent and so timeless: always and everywhere the same. Hence not only the habits of nature but, even more, the customs and moral obligations of men and women remain identical throughout history. In such a static system of coherence, change and what was new represented principles of relative unreality and dissolution. In the modern period, on the contrary, first history and then nature were seen to undergo substantial changes and, most importantly, changes of essential form. As a consequence, in both nature and history forms that are quite novel—that were once mere possibilities—become as real as and slowly even more valuable than those forms that are presently old and traditional. It is now the new, the latest, that is resonant with the possibility of value, not the old or the traditional.[2] In fact—most paradoxical of all—a "value-creating order of change" began to appear, especially in history and biology. This was a "progressive" order, in which what was new replaced the old and represented a greater value—or was thought to do so. Thus the relations of reality to value radically shifted: whereas it had been the *unchanging* character of reality that gave to it what values it possessed, it became a *changing*, not a static, reality that created value.[3]

Several fundamental, metaphysical questions related to science and religion are latent here: How is it possible for novelty and order to coexist in mutual support? How is an orderly novelty possible? Put in other terms, how can order span the gulf between the terms of significant change, between an actuality and a possibility that are really different, between a past and a future that represent fundamentally different epochs? Thus the question of the relation of natural reality to human value—of nature's processes to the human values inherent in those processes—is joined by the puzzle of a progressive sequence of natural forms, thereby constituting for modern reflection two of its most intriguing, fundamental questions.

Generally, in modern reflection, these questions have been answered simplistically and so, it seems to me, unsatisfactorily. Nature's reality is understood as science understands it and thus as in itself void of values, as an orderly, determined system of material (and hence, blind) processes of change. On every level, changes here are determined solely by physical causes, acting according to an order reflected in the objective theorems and formulas of science. Values therefore are internal to each valuer, in this case, to each "species" or phenotype thrown up by this material, vacuous process. Whether this process of change represents a movement toward value, a "progress," is the anthropic question, and it is unanswerable, for science in its inquiries omits considerations of value.

My entire argument has contested this radical sundering of nature and value, of blind objective process and subjective purposing or valuing. First, I have questioned in the previous chapters both the account of science as itself shorn of value and, especially, of a valuing subject and also the account of nature "out there" as representing only the material, determined, blind process that the methods and perforce the limits of scientific method articulate. Naturalism's view of nature in itself "as a realm of valueless matter in motion" represents an unintelligible account of science and an inaccurate (because an abstracted) account of nature. To remedy these nonphilosophical and inaccurate interpretations of science and of the nature science studies, I have suggested the move through philosophy of science to epistemology and thence through epistemology to ontology, in order to unite with scientific inquiry other modes of knowing reality and, especially, other modes of knowing nature.

In this chapter, second, I take up the next part of this argument: namely, the critique of scientific naturalism or positivism with regard to its view of the relation of nature and value. The actual order within nature, especially an order that unites with change and so with the appearance of novelty, is inescapably bound up with values—if nature is to be made intelligible at all. If the order within nature, on which science depends, is taken seriously as also an order of change, then, inescapably, ontological or metaphysical reflection on nature supplements the understanding of nature by science, and with that move, nature as "reality" is understood in terms of meanings and values as well as in terms of its orderly structure. The sharp modern or secular split between objective nature and subjective values makes intelligible neither science nor the humanities, neither nature nor humanism, neither technology nor democracy. Again, some further philosophical or religious mediation of this split in our theory is necessary to effect a more unified understanding of science and the human subject of science, of nature and the human in nature, and, now, of reality as a changing process productive of values. Only thus can we achieve a more moral approach to nature and a more unified "scientific" understanding of ourselves, of democracy and of democracy's moral ideals.

As the previous chapters based on the work of Mircea Eliade and Lawrence Sullivan indicated, the earliest forms of a religious apprehension of nature manifest the disclosure of an order encompassing all aspects of experience. Wherever one enters the world of archaic religion, one finds implicit in each rite, each myth, each magical incantation, and each individual symbol the assumption of a coherent system of entities and powers, a system to be "known," to be participated in, and so to be used by the humans who are parts of that system. Plants, water, moon, earth, snakes, and other animals are all coherently interrelated; structured action in relation to any one of these has an effect throughout the entire system. Each so-called deity—sky, sun, moon, earth—fits into and rules over a discernible order, an intelligible structure of the sacred.

Thus, as Eliade has shown, intuitions of order are already manifest in the earliest examples of religion: in the patterns of aboriginal art; in each religious myth about the complex but consistent relations of a wide variety of sacred powers to one another; in the universal order latent in any sacrificial rite; and in the order assumed as the basis of any example of divination or of magic itself. Each of these presupposes an intricate and all-inclusive coherence, encompassing everything that appears in experience. In each case this coherent system, however bizarre it may seem to us, is in some manner knowable, dependable, and universal. We can, if we understand it and obey its requirements, participate in it and use it. And it is through this participation in objective order that our life becomes possible and receives whatever security, meaning, and value there may be in existence. From the very earliest time, therefore, order and value have been united in objective reality, and participation in order has represented the necessary condition of value; order and the knowledge of that objective order have from the beginning been an ultimate human concern. Not so much is different in this regard in modern scientific culture.

At the very beginning of the human story, the human spirit or mind responds to the universe around it by organizing its world into a system of powers: this represents "disclosure" on the side of nature, organization or ordering on the part of humans. "Spirit" is defined here as self-constitution in relation to a world: spirit arises in dependence on the environment but also in aware separation from it. Hence arise in turn the naming of the environment's aspects or entities and the relating of these into an order, a coherent whole, a "world." From the first moment of its appearance, the human as spirit has organized its world into an order of some sort, clearly in response to what spirit has found already manifest there.

Whenever we look at the order found by another culture, we view this order as a purely human construction. It is to us *their* order; and, queer as it obviously is, it is simply a projection. Our own order, of course, is simply there, "reality as it is," objective and directly apparent.[4] This is the case, for example, with scientific positivism, which views itself as the mirror of objective reality and which understands the order that science implies as simply "found" empirically in the world and not projected onto it. On the contrary, however, in each of these intuitions of order, spirit has distanced itself from its natural environment so as to observe the latter; and by its process of naming and organizing (language) and through relating events and entities one to another into a coherent system of the whole, spirit has created a world, an ordered cosmos, out of its environment. The forms and so the shape of this order, of the world projected by spirit, change as cultures develop and change: from the systematic if, to us, bizarre order illustrated in the earliest religions, through the Tao, Dharma, and the Logos—the visions of the earliest literate cultures—to the modern sense, first, of a mathematical order and, second, of a statistical mathematical order. Clearly, this intuition of order has been a very persistent and deep—and apparently valid—intuition or awareness of the character of reality; or perhaps disclosure is the better term. It takes its place with the awareness of the other as person in community, the awareness of the passage of time, and the awareness of the sacredness manifest in and through all things, as a fundamental intuition of what is real or "really real" in all there is.

In archaic religion, along with the intuition of order there is a continuous and ever-present intuition of disorder, of the waning or disappearance of order—as of the power of life. This intuition is expressed in the numerous myths of the fragmentation of order, of its dissolution, of some primal catastrophe. Many myths of ordering tell two interrelated stories to make reality as we experience it intelligible: first, there is the primordial foundation of order at the beginning by the great god or gods; second, a series of subsequent catastrophes in which this order has been compromised, threatened, made vulnerable—and our present ambiguous experience initiated.[5] Thus most rites and sacrifice are understood as renewing an *original* order of existence, an order currently precarious and elusive; human actions, often difficult and painful acts of real sacrifice, are necessary if the original order is to be present again and human life to be fulfilled. Again, as in human experience throughout its course, order, disorder, sacrifice, and value—structure, antistructure, and meaning—are brought together in a clearer fashion in early myth than in modern experience, where the same elements are dramatically present though not as frankly seen and clearly understood.

As was noted, each culture as it develops reconstructs this intuitive order in its own terms, according to its own vision of reality and of human existence—its own "religious substance." Ancient cultures articulated this disclosure of nature's order in a vastly more complex and extended system of things: Dharma in India, the Tao in China, and the Logos in Greece. For example, in Dharma the systematic coherence of natural and social life, expressed in all primordial and archaic religion, is newly used to provide an analogy for a system that includes but far transcends nature's spatial and temporal life: the endless wheel of birth and rebirth, inclusive of numberless universes of worlds above and below our own; a limitless process governed by a strict and universal moral law, the law of karma, which allocates through an irresistible "moral" judgment how each entity will rise or fall on the wheel. Here all the forms of life are included, animals and humans, gods and demons; here life and death are intertwined as representing steps or stages in a process possibly leading to redemption. Hence a universally valid hierarchy of values is established, governing qualitatively each being at each stage of its life in its ascent and descent (e.g., a good tiger will move up to be a Kshatriya, a good wife to be a Brahman, and so on); and the final purpose and goal, quite different from any such in archaic religion, is freedom or liberation from this entire universe of becoming. Nature, here interpreted religiously and morally, has provided the model of order, which then far transcends the nature with which this interpretation began.[6]

The Confucian Tao provides an analogous extension of nature's "original" order, also deeply moralized and humanized but much more this-worldly and organic. Like Dharma, the Confucian Tao pervades all of experienced reality: nature, society, and individual human existence. Confucian thought characteristically emphasizes the order of social and individual life, a structure disclosed in interrelations and obligations originating in the family and extending its scope thence to all of society. This is, therefore, an *organic* order, one established by the interrelations that are given as life comes to be: parents, children, children's children, and so on throughout the larger extended family. This organic hierarchy of authority, privilege, and obligation, given originally in the family, is further extended to society as a whole, where an analogous system of duties and obligations, of functions, and of privileges is articulated. As the father is to the small family, so the emperor is to the state as a whole; and as the father's (and the emperor's) authority is balanced by his responsibility for his family, for its survival and its order, so the primary obligation of sons (and subjects) is to honor and obey those set above them in this sacred order. Hence the unity of the whole is achieved through the given and unchanging social unity based on the order of natural relations in the family.

Social unity is, therefore, not a rational, chosen, "contractual" unity, and there is no universal set of identical obligations holding for all in relation to all. Yet the Confucian Tao represents a thoroughly moralized order; in fact, this order permeating all existence defines the moral and is held together by obligation. The fundamental duty of a son is to the father, to family, to superior, to emperor, just as each of these has responsibilities downward. Thus moral fulfillment and social renewal come when each acts in this sense "naturally," that is, as his or her function and role (name) imply. The Confucian Tao then represents a "natural law" moral and social theory, echoing in its coherently related obligations the relations of the hierarchy of things in nature.[7]

I turn now to developments in the concept of order in the tradition of the West, beginning with the earliest Greek philosophers.[8] At the very start of Hellenic civilization (seventh to fifth centuries B.C.E.), a remarkable group of figures emerged who wished to understand in a new way the world around them: they were the Ionian philosophers, the so-called pre-Socratics. This process of understanding represented the beginning in the West at once of philosophy and of science. Thus it also represented a departure from a strictly "religious" mode of understanding the world in terms of traditional or mythical stories of origins. Nevertheless, these beginnings of philosophy manifested real continuities with the religions that preceded them: when, for example, Thales (640–546) said that "all is water," he was translating into the discourse of natural experience the myth of Oceanus.[9] But, more to the point, like the myths, these explanations sought to describe the whole and to specify the universal and coherent principles by which "all things" came to be; it was a search for an order available to understanding as the primary principle of what is real. In this sense, early philosophy did not "desacralize" the universe by replacing the gods with concepts of order. Rather, it reidentified the divine as a universal principle available to rational thought; in effect the divine became order. Thus when Thales said, "All is full of gods," he showed that he meant to rename the divine and not to replace or to deny it.[10]

With Anaximander (b. 601) philosophy began: the *arche* (fundamental principle) of existence was now beyond both sensory experience and myth (that is, beyond the phenomenal world) because origins must unite and so transcend "the many" that humans see. This *arche* must be, Anaximander said, the boundless, the unlimited. It is, he argued, apparent to thinking that the ground of all must be infinite, eternal, unlimited. Anything with a limit, either in space or in time, any entity that has a beginning, cannot be itself the origin; and whatever transcends all limits is the "divine." Thought and its requirements begin here to specify the essential limits of reality; order as rational is seen here as determinative of what is real.[11]

Further, a universal principle or law governs all coming out of and all going into this "Infinite." It is the law of Justice (in Greek, *Dike*): "All arise and pass away according to necessity—for they must make atonement and pay the penalty for their injustice according to Time's decree." To be is already "to have too much"; according to the necessity of justice, therefore, time sends us back into nonbeing, into the infinite ground.[12] Here the comings into being and passings out again that characterize all natural and historical existence have been startlingly and originally interpreted through the model of the political community, its laws, and the justice—the order—of those laws: "Justice rules the coming into being and the passing of each out of being." A vision of the universe as "cosmos" (order) has arisen on the inspiration of the polis as a political order, not the family as model. This is order, but not an order of mere natural cause and effect: it is a *normative* order, reflecting (at this point unlike Karma or Tao) a coherent yet also a moral order of things as a whole. Despite the fact that impersonal concepts have replaced the "gods," this vision is not yet very far from myth.

Parmenides appears genuinely strange. He presented his ideas as a religious message revealed to him alone by a goddess and on a special supraterrestrial ride. Here religious ecstasy and philosophical vision unite—and Parmenides's epic is the result. His message is, he says, in the sharpest contrast to the so-called wisdom of men; and Parmenides felt himself charged to proclaim to all "who do not know or understand" and to proclaim a "way" that alone is true and redemptive. Thus the philosopher became the bearer of unique and saving knowledge.[13] This "revealed" knowledge, paradoxically, is in content purely logical, rational in character: "Thinking and being are one and the same." What is, is, and cannot change or cease to be; what is not, is not, and cannot come to be. Hence change and becoming are unreal, apparent only, because illogical: being is, and nonbeing is not. The real is utterly different from the changing, passing world of sense experience, and hence our world is mere appearance; the real is apart, eternal, self-sufficient, mysterious—the object and so the product of thought alone.[14] And yet this vision of order appears in an "ecstatic" insight, otherworldly and mysterious, religious in its form if not in its content. Order as rational here has almost dispensed with the world, with whatever is to be ordered.

Heraclitus (died ca. 478–70) also sounds like a religious prophet: he too had a unique message to bring to a humanity that, for him, utterly failed to understand. The truth he proclaimed was the universal principle of all; but it was, as he recognized, hidden to all. This truth was practical, a way to live. It set us in a common world: "Those who are awake have a cosmos in common, those who sleep live on their own."[15] This truth is the Logos, the rule according to which all things come to be and pass away. Here again, it is the mind, not the senses, that is able to conceive a law that applies to all reality. Reality has become cosmos, order, and the rational mind that can think this order now inhabits in a new way the reality unseen before. This law is again *Dike*, "justice"; it sets bounds and limits: "Even the sun cannot overstep its bounds lest the Erinyes, Dike's messengers, find him out."[16] Reason has, in a way, triumphed over myth, only in the end to find itself expressing myths conceptually.

The law of justice is a unity of opposites, a law of harmony within strife and tension: "You could not step twice into the same river"; "War is the father and king of all." Out of tension comes a harmony that generates and then destroys all that is: "Opposition unites. From what draws apart results the most beautiful harmony."[17] This universal principle of coherence—and of the coherence of what seems chaotic—is "unseen" by the mind and seen only rarely: "Men contradict the Logos though they deal with it everyday." Unity resides in incessant change; in the apparent irrationality of all things lies a deep and abiding justice, as well as rationality or order. This sense of just order, while philosophical, is here again deeply religious: this is the divine principle that rules all and by which humanity can be freed from ignorance, from anxiety, and from self-concern.[18]

Here lay the beginnings of the Greek sense of order: an ecstatic, though thoroughly rational and intellectual, vision of the cosmos's order, a vision that is quite individual and unique (private) yet public in its import. This rule of Logos permeates and governs all. It is not, however, either blind or impersonal; it incarnates values as does the order of community and of self, and knowledge of this Logos is the knowledge that transforms life. In this sense, the order known by reason is the divine. Rationality and the religious have strangely mixed.

As the Hellenic culture flourished, Greek life was permeated with the wonder of order. Order was to them the principle of reality and so of coming to be, of beauty, of fulfillment, of justice, and of healing. This is apparent in the sculpture and the architecture of Greece, in its political and moral theories, in its medicine and in its early science, and above all in its philosophy. I will not even try to summarize the vast philosophies of Plato and Aristotle; for me, order, form, and structure dominate their thought as its final principle, although differently in each one.

For both Plato and Aristotle, order is the principle of reality, of what is and so of all there is; nothing transcends essence, rationality, coherence.[19] The form (essence) is the principle of any entity's existence and its permanence; and its form is the key to its proper functioning and role and so to its fulfillment. The form is known by the mind, not by the senses; and knowing the form is the way the mind relates itself to what really is and what is eternal: an intellectual vision of essence is at once ecstasy and fulfillment. Thus the mind is, in turn, the principal and highest attribute of the human, as form is of reality: rational understanding provides the entrance into reality, the key to ordering the state, and the sole possibility of regulating the self and its body. Hence the philosopher-king, symbolizing the rationality and wisdom of the rulers, and the rationality of the self, symbolizing the control or ordering of the passions and the body, represent the principles of human fulfillment.

The form of a thing, its structural principle, constitutes the principle of the *reality* of a thing; further, it is through reason's control of all the aspects of a given being that the *order* of that being is to be achieved—and so both its reality and its proper functioning achieved. When this order becomes actual, the excellence of that being is realized: it is then what it really is. This fulfillment of its structures is its *arete*, that is, its excellence; the fulfillment is therefore its good, its "virtue," and the principle of its happiness, whether we speak of a state or of an individual person. As health is the proper ordering of the body, so *arete* is the proper ordering of the whole person and of the whole community alike. Thus in each case the "natural law" of an individual or a community determines for each its *arete*. The fulfillment of a person is nothing other than the achievement of the harmony and functioning of the powers latent in its inherent structure. Order transforms and heals the self, cleanses the city, and relates us all to reality. The philosopher who contemplates the idea of the Good comes to resemble the forms he contemplates and is changed into the harmony and universality of those eternal and changeless ideas; for this reason, he can rule the city truly.[20] Order is universal and timeless; it transforms into harmony the disharmony of special interests and relations, special customs and obligations, special perspectives.

As in Dharma and the Tao, order here is qualitative: it is the order inherent in each *kind* of being. Its form or principle of organization is unique to each kind in the hierarchy of being: to community, to humans, to horses, to gods or immortals. Each has its own law of nature, and this "law" is the key to its reality, its worth, its obligations, its fulfillment, its happiness, its *arete*. Existence and norm are here completely united: value and fact, the structure of existence and the possible worthiness of existence, are—as opposed to the modern situation—one and the same in Greek thought.

There is, of course, a principle and reality other than order, namely, that which is formed or ordered: the principle (potentiality) of disharmony, of plurality and disunity, of desires and special interests, ultimately of chaos. This is what must be controlled or shaped: matter; instinct; emotions; and, in community, the many. This dynamic, material principle appears preeminently in Greek religion and tragedy: Dionysus, the earth deities, the Maenads, and the later cults. And in tragedy it comes as Ate, or madness, and as Moira, or fate. The questions for Greek spirituality always are: Is control by reason possible? Will it last? How can the victory over chaos be maintained and the returning victory of chaos prevented, put off—even if never eliminated? The sense of the encroachment of desire, of fatedness, of chaos grows as Hellenic culture moves into the Hellenistic period (200 B.C.E.—400 C.E.)

Further, the image of order here is *Dike* (justice), a harmony of the parts, an image, derived from an ordered polis (community or "city") as a small model cosmos, that then illumined their awareness of reality as a whole, of reality as *Kosmos*. This image represses and so harmonizes the emotional and the organic; all that is partial, special, particular is reshaped by political and moral reason into a cooperative part of the universal whole. This order, therefore, is not organic, "given," family-like, a prerational bond of dependence, affection, and responsibility (as in Confucianism). It is an order established by reason and will, almost by rational contract; an order achieved by personal objectivity, fairness, justice, and the desire for peace. It led much later in the eighteenth century to the ideals of equality, liberty, and personal autonomy that dominated the French and the American revolutions.

The last example of the Greek sense of order presented here is that of the Stoics. This is a genuine continuation of the Greek sense of order; reason remains the supreme principle of order, of control, of freedom, and so of fulfillment, not only in us but in the world process as a whole. Nevertheless, the confidence in the scope of human rational control and so the area in which human rational action is possible are both dramatically reduced. Hence there is here a passivity, a resignation, an aura of defeat (what Gilbert Murray called "the failure of nerve") unknown in the earlier periods. This characterized the Hellenistic world, continuing to the end of the Roman Empire. The two figures examined here are Epictetus, the Greek slave of the late first and early second centuries C.E., and Marcus Aurelius, the Roman emperor of the second century (161–181 C.E.).

Epictetus began with the reasonable assertion that some things are in our power and some are not.[21] Among the first are our impressions, judgments, assessments, "reactions," and above all what we wish to avoid or to possess (our valuings). Among the second are all the things that happen to us, all that lies outside the inner world of the will and the emotions. In this second area humans have no control: that is, over sickness, age, death, political and historical events, and so on. Be attached to the first, said Epictetus, but be indifferent to the second: all that happens to you on the outside is nothing to you. Your will inside is everything to you—control your will, you cannot control anything else. "You can be invincible if you never enter a contest where victory is not in your power."[22] Hence, Epictetus proposed, "Ask not that events happen as you will, but let your will be that they happen as they do."[23]

As was the case for the entire Greek tradition, reason for Epictetus was the principle of order and of that control over "the many" that order necessitates. "Freedom" was precisely the achievement of this sort of control. Hence "nature" or the natural represented precisely this free, rational imposition of order: nature was the victory of intention over what is merely determined or unintended—over what is "blind." One could hardly find a sharper opposition to the modern sense of "nature" as that which is non-rational and must therefore be controlled. To live according to nature would, for Epictetus, be to live a life of strict rational control, bringing order to that portion of the universe allotted to each one of us—again, a sharp reversal of our contemporary use of the phrase "according to nature." The universe as a whole, as we are, is in this view controlled by Reason or Logos, the divine principle in all things, which directs them as our reason ("the divine principle within") directs our inner life. All is guided by a unified purpose that adapts things perfectly to one another—as a look at the purposeful order of nature shows. Thus, all beings and events are directed toward the good of the whole. We can accept them as meaningful even if they seem alien to our own interests. But to term those interests "our own" that go against events, that turn out be failures, represents an ignorant and foolish misinterpretation, for in wanting something other than what we receive, we are "irrational" and "unnatural." Piety, said Epictetus, is thus "to give way to all that happens, follow events with a free will in the belief that they are fulfilled by the Highest Mind."[24]

Marcus Aurelius (emperor, 161–180 C.E.) echoed these sentiments in his *Meditations*: all is determined by divine reason; we can control only our inner reactions and our inner valuings. In the inner world of our own will we have absolute control, and the opportunities for serenity, nobility, courage, and self-direction are unlimited. Marcus added that as rational and communal beings we must also deal justly, fairly, and responsibly with others, performing our social roles in the family and in the community with reasonableness, moderation, and genuine concern: "It is thy duty to order thy life well in every single act; and if every act does its duty . . . be content; and no one shall be able to hinder thee so that each act shall not do its duty . . . nothing will stand in the way of thy acting justly and soberly and considerately."[25]

Outside, in the stream of events that make up history, all seemed pointless to Marcus: "Soon, very soon thou will be dust and ashes, or a skeleton, and either a name or not even a name." But "things themselves touch not the soul . . . nor have they admission to the soul, nor can they turn and move the soul; but the soul turns and moves itself alone, and whatever judgements it may think proper to make, such it makes for itself the things which present themselves to it."[26] And Marcus (fortunately) showed amazing confidence in the possibility of achieving virtue, if nothing else: "Now it is in my power to let no badness be in this soul, nor desire nor any perturbation at all";[27] "No man will hinder thee from living according to the reason of thy nature; nothing will happen to thee contrary to the reason of universal nature."[28]

It is evident that this Greek sense of the cosmos as Logos and of the soul as also Logos is a legacy of the earliest Hellenic vision eight centuries before. And, as then, for the Stoics following "nature" by exerting rational control over matter and destiny was the path to *arete*, a path open to all who had the courage and the strength to set forth on it. However, here the area over which reason can effectively operate has diminished to the mere island of the inner self; all else on the sea of events is beyond human power to shape or even to direct. Despite this serene confidence in Logos, it seems as if that which is irrational has expanded to take in almost everything except the inner self.[29]

Next I turn to the question of order in medieval Christian thought, and again, I present only a summary of this quite complex matter. If medieval civilization can be conceived as a union of Greek and "biblical" (Hebrew and early Christian) influences, what happens to the concept of order I have here been tracing? A brief answer is that order as a fundamental principle and reason along with it were very significant elements in medieval Catholic culture; in fact, one may say that these constituted the elements that were Greek in this culture. Order and reason were, however, included within a larger framework established on a different set of principles, Hebrew and Christian principles—and thus order is bounded by quite different themes, and order is *transcended by* as well as *included in* the divine. It is helpful to begin with a short statement of how order was included in the medieval synthesis.

God in Hebrew and Christian faith may transcend our reason ("His ways are not our ways"), but God is not irrational, against reason itself. In medieval culture this principle meant that the Greek concepts of reason and logos become important aspects of God, just as Sophia was an aspect or attribute of Yahweh in late Hebrew thought and as the Logos was the principle of self-manifestation or revelation in the Johannine tradition. Thus for orthodox Christianity—beginning with the first theologians in the early second century—the Logos (the rational principle of the divine being) was the "second God" (Justin Martyr); the Son of God begotten of God (Origen); and the creating, ordering, revealing aspect of God (Augustine). It is through the Logos that God creates ("God spoke," and it came to be) an ordered world; and it is through His Word (Logos) that God reveals God's self; and it is God's Word that becomes incarnate. The coherence, that is, the goodness, of creation as a rational order—an idea presupposed by the Greek Christians of the early centuries—thus was conceived as the result of the work of God's Logos;[30] and the natural order of human being, an order that represented the goodness and so the *arete* of each creature, was the result of the divine Logos. All this is thoroughly Greek.

Order as the Greeks understood it, however, was not in this Christian view the primary attribute of the divine, as it was no longer the primary characteristic of human being—or of cosmos and history. There is the mystery of the Father as well as the coherence of the Son and the enlivening presence of the Spirit. But order clearly was included among the most fundamental of Christian notions; how to include it became an issue of great debate in the so-called Trinitarian Controversy of the fourth century between the Arians on the one hand (who said order was a strictly subordinate power) and the Athanasian "orthodox" on the other hand (who maintained that the Logos represented an equal and eternal aspect of the divine).

The importance of this notion of the divine as rational order—or truth—and of human existence as structurally and essentially "good" through such an order is shown by many themes in medieval theology; I mention two here. First, it is because of the *rationality* of God and the corresponding presence of rationality in us—a Greek correlation—that we can "know" God and speak of God. Augustine, following Plotinus, discovered (i.e., "proved") God as the divine Light or Truth present in the mind when it knows anything that is true at all. And then he found traces, images, or analogies of God in both nature's order and the self's rationality or capacity for the truth.[31] Centuries later, Thomas Aquinas found or "proved" God by reason because of the coherence and the rationality of the cosmos: a dependent universe rationally requires a first cause; a contingent universe rationally requires a necessary being; and a universe full of obvious purpose (cf. the Stoics) requires a divine purpose or source. Although these rational arguments were changed to fit the contemporary Christian situation, still they harked back to Greek rationalism; only in a rational universe would these arguments, embodying as they do a logical sequence, be held to describe reality. Thus they depended, as they did for the Patristic thinkers, on the Greek context, namely, on a sense of a divine order permeating the entire universe and thus leading the mind through the structure of that dependent cosmos to its divine intelligent and beneficent Creator.

The second important inheritance in the medieval period from the Greek was the conception of "Natural Law," fundamental for medieval ethics as it is for modern Roman Catholic ethics. The natural law—whether for the state, for family, or for individual persons—is here thoroughly Greek: it is the law required by the structure of a kind of being, the order that makes the existence and the fulfillment of that particular sort of being possible. As the *arete* of that sort of being, it represents the moral duty or obligation (two words introduced by the new Hebrew-Christian environment) of a person or a community. Moreover, the content, as well as the form, of the natural law was Greek: for humans these requirements were courage, prudence, temperance, and justice—the moral requirements for the "nature" of a rational and social creature. Again, however, this Greek inheritance is embedded in a larger framework: beyond the requirements of the natural virtues for lay people were the "supernatural virtues"—faith, hope, and love—the requirements for all "religious"; and insofar as laity were as Christians directed to "their supernatural end" and not simply to their worldly relations and obligations, they too were called to exhibit faith, hope, and love.[32] But as in the Greek world, natural law set the moral obligations of ordinary "secular" and so "natural" life. Traditional Catholic ethics continues this Greek tradition of natural law, especially with regard to marital and sexual moral issues.

The Greek sense of order was in the medieval world surrounded and transcended by other elements. To start with, God transcended as well as included the principle of order: God's being is richer than order, and God's rationality is much more than our own rationality. God remained, therefore, a mystery even to the best of human thought; negative concepts were necessary in order to describe the divine (cf. Augustine: "Whoever thinks he has understood God, does not yet speak of God"; "We know what he is not and not what he *is*"),[33] and positive concepts were at best analogical. This transcendence by God of order had two important concrete results: (1) God is the source and ground of *matter* as well as of form; and (2) God goes "beyond the law" (order) in *love*, which becomes God's central attribute. As God's being transcends order and God's truth transcends our truths (even our rational truths), so God's will transcends, in the grace of God's forgiveness, the requirements of even God's own law. Thus in principle—if not, sadly, in fact—the material world and with it the organic, on the one hand, and, by implication, the impulsive, "prerational" level of human existence and the emotional, uniting power of love, on the other, are made equal to order and rationality as first principles of the divine and so of what is of worth for humans. I said "in principle" because it has taken centuries for these "earthy" implications of the transcendence as well as the inclusion of order to be seen and appropriated by Western Christianity.

Perhaps, however, the sharpest break with the preeminence of order and rationality came in the analysis of human existence. There is one area, Epictetus and Marcus had said, echoing their whole tradition, where I as the representative of reason do have control, namely, my own control over my own will; here I am quite free to become what I will to become. Although Augustine (354–428) agreed with much of Epictetus ("Retire within to know the truth"; "The care of the soul is the sole primary care"; "I wish to know only two things: God and the soul"), on this point he totally broke with his Greek inheritance and followed Paul. The one thing I cannot control, said Augustine, is my own will:

> I can move my arm, but I cannot, try as I will, change my love. I want to become continent, but my will doesn't want what I want. Nothing else outside me determines me here [here he agrees with Epictetus]; . . . But my will, free of all else, is *itself* bound to *its own* false loves, its love of itself and its love of the world. It cannot rescue itself, and thus does it depend on precisely what is not itself, on what is outside itself, namely on God's grace which transforms the will into a loving will.[34]

Arete as human fulfillment thus proceeds from "Other Power" and not from "self power," to borrow two traditional Buddhist categories. Here is an entirely new principle. Not only is the will responsible to become a *loving* will (which is not Greek); it can become this only through the presence of the Divine Spirit. Matter, love, and Spirit, therefore, are words that here came to appear alongside order and rationality. This all changed again in the birth of the modern world.

With regard to the concept and role of order, the modern world began, I believe, with the rise of modern science in the sixteenth and seventeenth centuries, not with either the Renaissance (a return to Greek humanism) or the Reformation. This new world is, therefore, expressed in the thinking of Galileo Galilei, Isaac Newton, and René Descartes, and it received full expression in the Enlightenment of the later seventeenth and eighteenth centuries. This "modern" conception of order still dominates the intellectual mind of the West, although (as with the Stoics) its scope and with it the scope of reason have tended in recent decades to diminish rather dramatically.

The main point in this history is the development of a quite new understanding of order and with it a dramatically different concept of natural law. With Galileo and then with Newton, "nature" was seen to manifest an astoundingly universal, even necessary, rational coherence or "rule of law"; this was a conception of order in nature that was, in relation to the tradition I have just rehearsed, radically new.[35] These "laws" governed all material events alike; they were expressible in mathematical formulas and theorems; they excluded all qualitative and purposive elements whatsoever; and each of these features was dramatically opposed to their Greek counterparts. Not only, therefore, were the material events that were determined by law "colorless" and "soundless," without what may be called qualities;[36] even more, to use Aristotle's language, this change meant that the formal and final causes (rational principles and guiding purposes) that structured the Greeks' Logos were eliminated from all material events, and that the material forces that determine those events were perceived as necessary and so "blind," oblivious to values and ends alike. Material and efficient causality—matter and agency—became the sole dynamic factors in events and thus their sole principles of explanation. Moreover, this reign of law was indifferent to "kinds"; explanations according to scientific principles of this sort applied equally to stars, rocks, cells, horses, humans. And they applied everywhere, to the furthest reaches of space and (later) of time. Suddenly (at least, in principle) the "real" had become a solely material realm, dominated by necessary law and shorn of "spirit": of rationality, intentions, norms, and goals, and certainly vacant of deity.

In the early Enlightenment this mechanical realm of matter was represented by what Descartes called "extension," and it was balanced by the equally real realm of "thought," the "substance" participated in by the scientific subject, the thinker and knower. And for Benedict de Spinoza these two, extension and thought, are equal attributes of the one divine substance. For Immanuel Kant, this realm of extension becomes the world of experience, the world in part constructed by our own senses and by our mind, the *phenomenal* world organized by science; but it is balanced by the *noumenal* world of the "thing in itself"—on the one hand, external to our perception, and on the other, the inward realm of the intellectual and moral subject. Gradually, however, as the authority of science has increased, the noumenal worlds of the knowing and valuing subject have receded into the merely "subjective"; and, as was demonstrated in Part 1, Kant's realm of phenomena, the world as known by science, has slowly become the one real, objective world. As a consequence, for most of the intellectual public, objective reality is constituted solely by "extension"; reality in itself remains as natural science describes it, a realm of order but one characterized by a merely material, determined, and blind order. For most members of the scientific community, if one referred to "thought" as a mode of reality, they would not know what was meant—although, with Descartes, they are scientists "living off" thought!

In the Enlightenment, as a result of classical Newtonian physics, the world was pictured as a vast, intricate machine. Such a model of order has two apparently opposed implications. On the one hand, this machine image or model of nature systematically excludes mind, intentions, norms, ends, and values from the objective world; on the other, this image or analogy seems, as do all machines, to imply a divine engineer—a purposive and all-knowing Designer and Maker—if this harmonious system is to be intelligibly explained. No machine produces either itself or its order; only a purposive mind can create a machine—for a machine is a complex instrument *for* something and so it represents an order imposed *by* someone. It points beyond itself (although few who now speak of the "mechanical" interpretation of the world see this point). Thus arose, as the religious response to the Enlightenment, the deistic conception of the divine as the creator of order while yet a creator outside the natural order—as the intelligent mind and benevolent will of the "scientist" remain outside the determined order pictured by precisely that scientist.

Moreover, because reality was for the Enlightenment thoroughly rational, exhibiting elegantly mathematical harmony and order, Nature and Reason fit together so as almost to be synonymous: what is natural is rational, and the reverse. Thus there were also universal "natural laws" for society, corresponding to the universal physical "natural laws" of material existence: these are the laws of human rights, justice, liberty, equality, and fraternity, so important to Enlightenment revolutionary theory; and the laws of the free market, dear to capitalist economics. Despite the vast changes in the conceptions of order and of law, therefore, elements of the Greek inheritance reappeared in new forms in the new setting: the conception of the divine origin of natural order; and the conception of the social, economic, and political relevance of that order.

There is one further large change to mention: the appearance of *develop-*

ment as qualifying the form of order in Western self-understanding. Slowly appearing in the eighteenth century as the clue to the order exhibited by history (cf. the concept of progress, e.g., in G.W.F. Hegel and later in Karl Marx),[37] the concept of development in history expanded into a cosmological concept with the sciences of geology, biology, and later astrophysics in the nineteenth century. Here the universe itself, and with it all its celestial, terrestrial, and especially botanical and biological forms, is viewed as in a process of developing change, a "historical" process. Thus the adaptation of forms of life, first within the unity of the organism itself and then between the organism and its environment, no longer was seen to require an external "designer" but was explained by the process of coming to be (out of one another). Mind, purposes, ends, values—the whole world of "spirit"—thus arise out of the blind order of nature rather than represent the prior, explanatory principle of that order. This origin of mind out of the "natural" (and so "mindless") process is assumed in the sciences of genetics, physical and cultural anthropology, psychology, sociobiology, and sociology and again marks a sharp reverse of Greek presuppositions.

The origin of mind out of mindless process—nature as natural science portrays it—seems to many, however, less of an answer to the problem of order than the cause of new puzzles. To begin with, order is disclosed—and has been—universally in human experience and is presupposed by science and by all its operations. This order encompasses all events and processes in our experience; and this universal presence is as strange to us in the scientific age as it was in the entire history portrayed in this chapter. It is an aspect of nature as fundamental as power and the possibility of life. Even more strangely, it has since the beginning been "correlated" with mind: with the practical needs that the mind sees, with the obligations that organic life entails, and with the rational and logical sequences of abstract thinking—and in the modern world, with the mathematical powers of the inquiring mind. Nature thus represents an objective as well as a subjective logos—an "anthropic" principle resident in the order characterizing each event in far-off space and time. If the processes of natural development have produced mind, these processes in doing so have illustrated and obeyed an analogous order of changes, objectively present in nature from the beginning. Just as the early Greeks intuited, modern science itself, in and through all that it establishes, witnesses to the presence of Logos in the flux of things that determines the order of coming to be and passing away.

Further, this order is a *temporal* order of changing forms. Forms come and go, and novel forms not present before have arisen through orderly processes as older forms have receded. Thus order spans not only space, as Greek and Newtonian rationalism saw, but time, the movement from the actual into the merely possible, uniting the conditions from the past with the new actualities of the present in a discoverable order. Here is even more of a puzzle for reflection. If all is genuinely in flux, so that no continuing and determining substance remains from moment to moment to bear this continuing order, how is it possible that the sequence of events exhibits the same order that makes possible a world, a cosmos—continuing entities as much as continuing galaxies? The past cannot guarantee the order of present and future, for the past has already vanished; nor can the future determine our relations, lest there be no spontaneity or freedom in the present. Actuality vanishes and thus cannot determine the present as the present appears in being; possibility is only possible and cannot therefore determine its own arising "causally," its coming to be into the present as actuality. A puzzle is thus left by the overlapping of novelty and order, by the interweaving of radical change with continuity, with, that is, the appearance of new forms different from yet continuous with the old. As order is one "trace" of the divine that has long been disclosed to the minds of human beings, so the order within radical change is also a "trace" to modern minds of some deeper principle. These puzzles are addressed more fully later.

To many in the early years of evolutionary theory, the fact of developing order in the processes of change therefore raised an old question in a new form: Whence came that order? Could it be "chance" that explained the appearance of novelty, a novelty representing an *increment* of value during the duration of process (to use Alfred North Whitehead's terms)? As Anaximander and Heraclitus had seen, a world of orderly change required a principle of order within it, not just blind process. And even more, a world of progressing change, where novelty unites with order to create value, needed a principle of progressive order. Such a principle of order ("the wider teleology") was what the modern observer could call "God" or the developing "evolutionary" principle, as such diverse thinkers as Henry Drummond, Lyman Abbott, Samuel Alexander, Henri-Louis Bergson, F. R. Tennant, A. N. Whitehead, and Pierre Teilhard de Chardin have argued.[38] Again order, value, and reality have been realized as associated intricately with one another, each defining the new meaning of the other; and again the principle of the unity of these three is and must be "the divine"—albeit an order and a divinity of quite different forms from those of the early Greeks. It must be recognized, however, that those "metaphysical" inferences from order leading to a "natural theology," persuasive though they may be, are not regarded as either "scientific" or valid by most of the scientific community. The positivist temper of the West is sovereign; what cannot be empirically "proved" is not cognitive, even if it represents the metaphysical basis of all empirical proof!

As I have tried to show, most of the scientific and intellectual community, at least in the twentieth century, has not drawn a theistic or religious conclusion from the new concepts of development. To them, the natural process is just as science describes it, quite without mind or purpose, and it does not manifest or imply any "values." Such values are viewed as at best subjective, late, and local products of the blind mechanical processes of this immense universe science discerns—and not as the universal and very real generative principles of the orderly cosmos that the early Greeks saw. So-called facts and values therefore remain sundered, as do reality and mind. No wonder a religious interpretation of the modern sense of order has had a difficult time!

In conclusion, I briefly mention the points where the modern conception of a determined and mindless order seems to call for more than itself and thus for supplement from philosophy and religion. This conception is, as the word implies, "reductionist"; taken as the exhaustive description of what is real, this view excludes from reality as so described mind, subjectivity or inwardness, purposes, freedom, norms, and mystery. Although this seems satisfactory to some, it is by no means persuasive to all reflective people in the West. There are at least two reasons for this.

First, as already mentioned, such a conception of deterministically ordered reality finds no place for the scientific mind that has conceived it, for the intentional will that has, in persistent scientific inquiry, uncovered it, or for the purposes that obviously prepare and then use this knowledge in technology, industry, medicine, communication, and defense—in fact, in all the rest of modern culture. Although these applications of human enterprise seem clearly to reveal freedom, initiative, intentions, and so norms and ends—that is, "spirit"—it is only the theoretical results or conclusions of science, not its human conditions (as in Greek thought), that impress the modern academy.

Second, the social results of science—its uses in weapons, industrial expansion, and so on—show the vast ambiguity of knowledge or, more precisely, of the knower and user of knowledge. The modern use of science in war and potential war, in an expanding industrial empire, and in the devastation of nature and the modern co-option of science by irrational and fanatical ideologies show that the determined, "valueless" order known there can be accompanied by the *demonic*—and prove destructive not only of value but of science itself. Order, if "end-free," has shown itself to be oppressive as well as destructive. The call to liberation, against modern forms of order in both the East and the West, represents a significant demand that cannot be denied. Is this also "subjective"? Or is order itself, here as in the industrial and military use of order, partial, biased, and to be criticized and supplemented by such elements of reality as are more than order?

Order is an aspect of nature and the condition for major aspects of human value. But the potential of order for deep ambiguity, for the demonic and oppressive uses of order, in hierarchical and traditional societies and in capitalist and Marxist societies is especially evident today. No more than in the Greek or medieval periods can reality be interpreted as solely characterized by order—especially by a determined and blind order. The West, as much as if not more than India and China, needs to reconceive its vision of order, scientifically, politically, and morally, and to reconceive that vision in sufficient religious and philosophical depth as to unite the diverse elements of life rather than to exclude them.

9

Nature as a Realm of Meaning

In light of the discussion of nature as power, life, and order, I now approach a much more nebulous, perhaps even ambiguous, set of themes. Power, life, and order can all be directly "seen" in the human encounter with nature, that is, in contemporary daily experience and in scientific inquiry alike, and especially in archaic religious experience. Each of these characteristics of nature seems to initiate questions or puzzles about itself ("limit questions," I have called them) that scientific inquiry can neither usefully discuss nor answer, although it was precisely scientific inquiry that raised these questions. Now the discussion turns to glimmerings of meanings, which are much less direct and clear but nevertheless of sufficient definiteness to warrant serious reflection.

One of the most important points developed in this discussion of nature has been the great effect that the evolutionary hypothesis, both in actuality and in potential, has had on our understanding of the human. By that effect I mean to indicate our total understanding of the human, the human in all its aspects: the human as the inheritor of the genetic legacy, as a physical organism with needs, as a social creature with significant relations, as the constructor of its world, as communicating and self-communicating through symbols, and finally as projecting its actions into the future and outward onto the environment. Hence it is "out of nature" that the human realm of meanings has arisen: the realm of symbols, of projects, of purposes, of memories of past defeats and victories, of anxiety about future catastrophes, of dreams of future fulfillment—the entire imagined and projected realm of possibilities, of the "not yet" in juxtaposition to the hard reality of actual fact, of the given. Meanings reflect an organism in temporal process, moving from given conditions into an open future; an organism on a precarious passage through time and within its environment from incipient to possible fulfillment or disaster; an organism that can in itself make the "bridge" between given fact and impending possibility and hence envision what might be, what might not be, what threatens, and what beckons—and tell the difference. Here, beginning at the simplest biological level, are the initial signs, the seeds, of needs, desires, goals (in short, of "values"); of threats, dangers, and perils (in short, of proximate and ultimate negativity); and, finally, of preservation, fulfillment, reproduction (in short, well-being).

Meaning, as the word is used in humanist studies (literature, arts, drama, philosophy, and perhaps especially religious reflection), connotes this question of the varied relations of life to value, to questions of fulfillment or destruction, of serenity or loss. Such usage is neither subjective nor arbitrary: life can lose its meanings, and it can regain them, and it can begin again. This is the world where faith and hope have their purchase, the world of religion as well as of existential and moral meanings. This world recedes back far into the mysterious life of nature. Such meanings, as they develop in the various levels of life, signal the birth of what I have called "spirit," which, as the modern world sees it, is itself a child of nature, as with all else we know on earth.

But the principle that human existence is to be understood in terms of its natural sources, in terms of what we know of "nature" through physics, chemistry, genetics, biology, and physiology, is, as Alfred North Whitehead remarked, a double-edged sword.[1] It means that nature, in turn, is to be understood by all that we experience on the human dimension in terms of spirit: that is, we must understand nature precisely in terms of *spirit's conditions in life*—for example, long before humans appeared, in the genetic code itself; in the simplest animal's psyche; in apprehended needs and unconscious purposes; in all the urgency, the drives, the fears, the meanings of animal existence. All these traits of "latent spirit" are also nature, if we are nature and developed out of nature—unless we posit precisely the supernatural jump that natural science repudiates. The only other path is an irrational reductionism that insists that the human be understood univocally in the terms of inorganic life or, at best, in terms of the life exhibited on the simplest cellular level—a position I have sought throughout this book to dislodge as self-contradictory if it is adopted by "science." Hence one can legitimately seek to discern in nature what I have called the "seeds of spirit": latent signs of the political, the moral, the inquiring, the intellectual, the reflective, and even the religious in the life of nature and, even behind this, in the mysterious "fertility" of matter—out of which all this arose.

Here, then, is a two-sided principle of great interest: we are of nature, and hence we are also an example, a paradigm, of nature's richness. This is by no means a new thought: the theme of "microcosmos" and "macrocosmos," of the parallelism of the human and the cosmos, has appeared and reappeared in religious, philosophical, and literary thought up to the modern period—in India; in China; in the Renaissance; in the "deviant science" of the early modern period, which spoke of microcosm and macrocosm; and most recently (in the incognito of the white coat) in the anthropic principle. This would be a rich lode to explore in the reinterpretation of nature in the light of the human as seen as the fruit of nature's changes—but that is for another volume.

Meanwhile, this chapter explores further the relation of nature to meanings. Meanings are correlated with values, and values with the realization or actualization of being: with preservation, with fulfillment of potential, and with propagation (in all its senses). In our naturalistic culture, meanings are all regarded as exclusively "human," at the most subjective to each species with its own peculiar needs and so its own bizarre fulfillments. In a sense this is valid enough: the form of the good for us is a human good and must be so for it to be "good."

My point, however, is to call attention to our double-edged principle and to maintain that meanings, on all levels, are intrinsic to natural life and so to nature. Nature as life exhibits a *telos* toward fulfillment as realization, actualization of its potentials, and continuation of those potentials—a "superject" into the future through propagation. These meanings and the symbolic powers to express and to receive them are intrinsic to nature. Nature as life is saturated with needs and so with values; with interests and so with striving; with fulfillment and loss; with life, new life, and death—it too is a realm of meanings.[2] Thus nature is the preparation for the human life of culture and of history—the human dimension—when a "world" is established by symbols and lived in with intentionalities, established by means of expression and fueled by passion, eros, and commitment. With this onset of "spirit," these meanings—of life, of family, of work, and of the community and its existence in the future—stretch by way of consciousness and self-consciousness infinitely into meanings encompassing the whole of things in space, in time, and beyond both space and time. At this point, where myth, obligation, inquiry, and reflection as spirit have arrived, the human dimension is fully present, and we are in the midst of culture and history. But all of this is prepared long before within nature. Just as the principle of indeterminacy on the inorganic level prepares the way for the mobility, self-preservation, and self-direction of life in the freedom of a risky future, so the needs, purposes, and values—the meanings—of animal existence prepare the way for history, that is, for the contingencies, the given destiny, and the freedom into the future of historical existence. The developments of cosmos and of life in the cosmos manifest the deep sources in material being of these possibilities of life and later of spirit; the development of life in all its variety shows in turn that living matter, the organism, is capable of, in effect the harbinger of, other dimensions leading up to spirit.

All of this scientific inquiry "shows" in silence: these reflections are left as limit questions. But they are undeniably there as science looks at nature. Thus, as a whole, nature is yet a mystery; a mystery with many layers, obviously filled with immense possibilities, open at every level to meaning and the hope of fulfillment. A redefinition of nature is made necessary by scientific knowledge itself.

Nature as life is, therefore, a realm of meanings; the cosmos, as providing the conditions for life, is indirectly such a realm; its order over eons of radical change, a puzzle; and its itinerary toward our world of explicit meanings over almost endless improbabilities, an astonishment. One can hardly prove the presence of meaning or purpose here, for one can discern them only as if disguised in the behavior of all life; but the puzzles remain materials for endless myths and rituals, for philosophical reflection, and for responding religious gratitude and worship. Our human existence, however, is not merely one of unfolding meanings; of movement through growth, through relations, and through actions toward fulfillment and the actualizing of possibility into completion. At every level of life such unfolding is frequently, often fatally, thwarted or negated. Disasters too varied and too numerous to list appear at each turn; existence is laced with the tragic as well as the fulfilling. And this occurs on every level of nature's life, in each epoch of human history, and to each small family—if not each person—in our human story.

Being—expressing the fullness or actuality of developed existence—is thus balanced by nonbeing in all of existence, fulfillment by negativity, salvation by "condemnation," lostness, and annihilation. These symbols of the negation of life and its meaning are as prevalent in the human response to destiny as are the positive symbols. Together they make up the symbolic content of the religious; and the intertwining of good and evil, of meaning and the loss of meaning, is the thread that runs through most of the religions and at the deepest level has animated the myths that give expression to culture, as the liberal and the Marxist myths of progress show. This ultimate issue of the encounter of meaning and its loss spills over from its expression in religious myth (cf. the "religious substance" of a culture in Paul Tillich's usage) into the other areas essential to culture—morals, law, politics, art, and literature—and it dominates practical daily life devoted to survival and to material well-being. The clarification of values—of what is the good, of right and wrong, of justice and peace, of virtue, of integrity, and of beauty—may seem an esoteric quest; but the economic, political, legal, and practical, workaday worlds are as much structured by these issues and their values (which provide, after all, the necessary "ends" of activity) as they are by the practical exigencies of getting something (anything?) done.

Insofar as values or meanings animate the existence of all forms of life, and in explicit form the human, the threat to these values—the negative—represents a dominating presence throughout existence. Therefore in the above description of nature I spoke only of traces of the sacred: power, life, and order. These were only traces of meaning or value and hence of the latter's presence in the silence of the cosmos and the mutations of life. Throughout experience, natural and historical, these traces of value seem to become continually submerged by some antithetical force; for power wanes; life is wounded and dies, vanishes; and order becomes threatening disorder. In nature and in history, negation accompanies fullness of being at each step.

In 1989–1990, almost all of history seemed to be unfolding toward value and fulfillment. Tyrannies suddenly collapsed, and the promise of freedom and fulfillment seemed present everywhere in the end of the Cold War, as in the appearance of spring. Then equally suddenly in 1990–1991, dark threats suddenly reappeared—in bitter new and yet old conflicts throughout most of the now rescued world, in the new imposition of conflict and tyranny in, for example, the Balkans and Somalia, and in the sudden and unexpected war with Iraq, in which still uncounted civilians perished—and the happy (to Americans and their allies) end of that war has only ushered new dilemmas and new suffering on every hand. What are we to make of this dialectic, this continuing polarity of being and of nonbeing, of meaning and its negation, of suffering goodness and regnant evil?

These are the deepest questions of religion in almost all of its infinite varieties. Contrary to much opinion, religion is not primarily the response to the presence of goodness and promise in nature, history, and personal life. Most religions do not ignore the evil seemingly swirling around them and devote themselves exclusively to the good also present in life. On the contrary, as its myths, its doctrines, its rituals and its sacraments, its modes of worship, and its obligations show, religion appears precisely out of the midst of this conflict of good and evil, of value and disvalue; it recognizes, in fact builds on, the presence of evil and centers itself on the celebration of the experience or apprehension of rescue from that apparently one-sided conflict. Its most fundamental symbols are renewal, reconciliation, redemption, the unexpected return of meaning after its evaporation has left us desolate. Meaning (like good politics!) must surmount the tragic, the negative, in our existence if it is to be real; it cannot long escape or ignore evil and be relevant to real life.

If this is a fundamental characteristic—if not *the* fundamental characteristic—of human existence, expressed in myths, art, literature, and common wisdom alike, what are we then to make of nature? Are there in nature seeds of the spirit in this sense, signs of the nonbeing that is later to erupt in the

agonies of the human spirit in the face of suffering, meaninglessness, alienation, death? Here perhaps appear the profoundest of the theological—if not
also the literary—questions about nature.

As has been my wont, I first turn to nature as seen by empirical science, in
this case especially biology. When one looks for the role of the negative and
the tragic in the coming to be of natural existence, one finds that role to be
essential. Surprisingly, negation is fundamental to the appearance of things
out of one another, to their preservation over time and space, and to their
propagation into the new generation. The process of coming to be—whether
it be organic or inorganic—repeats a strange dialectic between an achieved
determination as the entity in question has been formed out of the past and
an openness to new possibility in its coming to be in the future. Achieved
actuality moves through the present into relevant possibility, to use Whitehead's words; or destiny appears from the past into the present and then
becomes freedom, openness to possibilities, to paraphrase Tillich. Intrinsic
to becoming, therefore, is an aspect of indeterminism, of open and varied
possibilities, of "randomness," in the movement into the new: the new of
the next moment of life or the new of a mutation, a change in the form
of life, possibly to a more complex form (but possibly not). This randomness or
experimental openness on the organic level leads to all sorts of possibilities,
because process is, apparently, really open. On a still different level, in the
experience of humans of their own being, "openness" leads to the experience of choice, decision, planning, and enaction—necessary aspects of the
enterprise of scientific inquiry, as they are of political and moral processes.
Correspondingly, some of these new possibilities (on each level) do not
work; in fact, many fail and lose their actuality. Many are overwhelmed by
contingencies beyond their power. The temporal becoming of things out of
what is past, out of the given, makes possible the becoming of possibility
into actuality; by the same token, temporal becoming makes possible novelty,
new modes of actuality that arrive as new ventures in space and time—and
thus may also expire. Possibility and the new (contingency and new ventures
in history) have an underside, a darker face—the chance of failure and,
beyond that, of extinction.

Even more, new possibilities as such signify, even necessitate, the vanishing of what is now actual. Young, brilliant, new professors require the
retirement of old "fuddy-duddies"; a new generation with all its varied
possibilities requires the recession of the older generation out to the periph-
ery and, ultimately, its disappearance into memory. Temporality and process
mean the possibility and appearance of the new but also the vanishing, the
loss, of the old. Hope in the morning brings with it the mourning for what

is now gone. Just as openness and randomness entail the chance of not fitting in, of extinction, so on an even more fundamental level does any new generation, any new form—temporal change itself—bear as its shadow the death of what has already been. On both counts—the temporally new and the qualitatively new—in nature's passage, life arises out of death; each example of life replaces another example in time and space; and new forms of life arise out of the extinction of the old. More complex forms are made possible by forms that have failed, as also they depend on the perpetuation and the continuing presence in their environment of so-called lower levels, for them to use and to consume. Life lives off life: in time, replacing the old with the new; in preservation, by feeding itself on life; and in space, by removing the other so as to move, to breathe, and to act in new ways. The loss by one entity of its being, by one self for the sake of the other (what might be termed involuntary agape or sacrifice), is thus intrinsic to nature— as early *homo religiosus* apparently saw clearly. Negation is the ground, along with being, of both actuality and value: "The great Dying yields the great Renewal."[3] The role of death is intrinsic to the appearance and the preservation of life in all of nature as modern science views nature. Interestingly, the relatively nonscientific Greeks saw this dialectic of living with dying, of all growth with decay, with utter clarity; we know much more about nature than did they—and we too all die—and yet we ignore this whole side of what is evidently real.

In archaic religion, this juxtaposition of negation and affirmation in natural existence made a deep imprint on the human intuition of reality. It was deepened immensely by the awareness that values recede, that nature's power as life and as order recedes, and thus that our existence in nature is doubly precarious. Hence in appropriate response, dependent humans acknowledged the need for sacrifice, for the appropriation of negativity on and in themselves, if they were to share in the powers of the life of nature. To modern humans, this side of early piety is superstitious if not masochistic and sadistic, based on unreal guilt or neurotic fear of the angry father: "How neurotic to have to give something up in order to get something from nature. Let us appropriate these values directly, 'naturally.' "

Actually, however, not so much has changed. It is now all too evident that as much as they, we can deal with ourselves in relation to nature only in terms of genuine sacrifice, that is, a regime of genuine self-control and self-discipline so that we may become prudent. Unless industrial production in its use of natural resources and its development of nature's spaces is disciplined—and that means sacrifice—resources will be used up, rain forests will be cleared, wetlands will be dried up. Unless nuclear power is controlled, life may well cease. Unless pollution and toxic waste are eliminated and then prevented, nature will be fatally despoiled. All this means sacrifice, the giving up of something intensely valued. All these requirements or demands could also be ignored; and then our lack of discipline in these activities may well pave our way to destruction. If there is strong awareness of guilt here, so much the better; such guilt is surely valid when responsibility for the destruction of something so important is undeniable. As Eastern Europe's devastation clearly shows—not to mention our own—here we are not dealing with merely a runaway Oedipus complex!

The unity of life with death and of death with new life—and of both of these with rebirth and ultimately with immortality—has been clearer even to the religious consciousness than it is to the modern biological observer. This theme is, in different modes but nevertheless with striking similarity, intrinsic to archaic religion, to the religions of the great early civilizations, and to the universal religions of redemption and salvation—Hinduism, Buddhism, Christianity, Islam, and Judaism. In all of these religions, life and its values are experienced as deeply threatened; in all, negation is felt to be in part alien and yet also in part not unwarranted, and strangely essential to fulfillment; in all, acceptance of the negative, participation in it, and passage through it are seen as necessary for renewal.

This unity of death with life, of nonbeing with being, is perhaps most clearly articulated in archaic religion. Everywhere the unity of life and death seems to be obvious to anxious *homo religiosus:* new life, fertility itself, arises out of the dying, the sacrifice of the old life. The rebirth of nature becomes possible only if some sort of death precedes. The earliest religious intuitions of nature and current biological overviews are in total accord here. As a result, almost universally the sacred powers of life—sun, moon, water, seeds and plants, earth, serpents, and so on—represent also the sacred powers of death, the lords of death. For the religious consciousness, each power enacts or suffers the entrance into death and shares in our communion with negativity or nothingness—the sun sets, the moon wanes, seeds die, water inundates, earth receives its dead—and as a result, each power effects and bears witness to the wonder of new life, as that wonder also arises from the opaque waters, from the dark earth, from the womb. In all its varied aspects, nature seems to make this paradoxical conjunction and to teach this lesson: life arises out of death; death is the narrow passage to new life and to continuing life.

The intimation that just as natural life arises out of prior dying, so may another immortal life arise beyond earthly death appeared therefore quite naturally, as the consciousness of the value of life rose and so the question of the ultimate end of life became more prominent. Hence in the Hellenistic (late Roman) period many ancient, pre-Roman fertility cults became the sectarian vehicles of immortality, "mystery" cults.[4] This conjunction of "natural" fertility with the hope for immortality astonished young modern students of religion when they discovered that it was precisely the fertility religions, with their symbols of life in the here and now—that is, symbols of agriculture and of sexual fertility—that became later transmuted into redemptive religions, vessels of the promise of immortality beyond the end of earthly life. What had been neither seen nor guessed was this biological preparation for the unity of life with death: that even at the level of "natural" or "worldly" life, of the life nature's power has offered to us, life and death are already entwined together; and hence that for the archaic religious consciousness, the fertility of crops, of animals, and of humans arises out of an initial passage of some sort through death into life.

The clearest example of this quite intelligible transmutation of early fertility religion into later redemptive religion is found in the dying and rising savior figures of the Hellenistic cults of immortality. In the prehistorical Mediterranean world, prior to Hellenic culture, these "heroes"—for example, Adonis, Osiris, and Mithra—represented powers or instruments of agricultural, animal, and human fertility. In the myths about them, these young consorts of the great Mother Goddess die (were once sacrificed?); their bodies were then spread abroad in the fields and, as a result, new life appeared in the spring. Much later, these same figures functioned analogously in the mystery cults of the Roman Empire, to guide and to bear the souls of the dead through the dangers of the passage into death and thence beyond death into a new level of immortal life. They represented the powers of life sacrificed, opened thereby to others. Hence they were "mediators," enabling devotees to participate in that life—power even over their own death.

This is scarcely an objective comment, but as the church long viewed the history of the covenant with the Hebrews as a "preparation" for the new covenant in Jesus, so one might view this strange dialectic of fertility and immortality as a preparation for the dying and rising of the Christ. There was, first, the level of natural processes themselves, where all natural new life seems to emerge from prior death in one form or another; and then there appeared the fertility myths and rituals responsive to those processes known in nature and eager to encourage nature's fertility; and then, at a still further level, there were the myths of immortal life of the later cults; and finally there was the historical "event" of the death of Jesus and his proclaimed resurrection on the third day. In this strange sequence, there is the most unexpected of all transmutations: from visible natural sequences through religious responses by way of myths on two distinct levels—myths of natural life and then myths of eternal life—and then back again to "history," at least in the sense of an affirmed event concerning a definite person in a definite place and time.[5] Yet it was an event that promised a life even beyond the life and death of nature itself.

This universal intertwining of death and life, deeply appropriated by the earliest myths as a fundamental principle of nature's order, called for an active response on the part of humans if they would participate, as they surely wished to do, in the natural processes of life. What was seen, therefore, to be a principle in nature became quite naturally the model for an appropriate responsive set of actions for the human colleagues of nature and, in the end, a number of assumed and binding customs. This response is manifest in the universal role of sacrifice in all relations to the forces and the bounties of nature, inspired, I presume, by a sharp sense of the appropriateness for humans thus to share in nature's travail and in nature's burdens if we are to participate in nature's creative and recreative life. Embedded here is also probably a sense of alienation from nature and of the consequent possibility of the recession from us of nature's limitless powers. Sacrifice thus has dual role: our participation in the life-giving powers of nature, on the one hand, and our efforts to aid in the renewal of these same powers, on the other. Illustrated everywhere in religious life is the principle that something must be given in response to a gift from beyond us. We cannot just receive passively; as autonomous, self-constituting beings, as responsible beings (felt long before these aspects of the human were articulated), we must respond by sharing, by obedience, by commitment, by appropriate action. Much has changed as religion has changed. But even in those religions of grace most wary of magic, of materialistic superstition, and of meritorious rules, these requirements of our spiritual and our active participation in response to grace remain. Self-discipline, obedience, active loyalty, and above all self-sacrifice are the ways the power of grace is appropriated, received, and embodied by faith and by service.[6]

In this sense again, there is a continuity as well a discontinuity in the changes in religion (I hesitate to say a progression). What begins, most appropriately, as the serious act of the sacrifice of the first fruits of our labors culminates or at least reappears in modern experience as moral obligation, self-discipline, and finally agape—a love that gives itself for others. And if these are practiced in relation to others, why not in relation to nature too? These "heights" of human *arete* in the face of the negative represent the inward and spiritual extensions, first, of the processes of nature's life and, second, of the respectful and very appropriate response of human religion to the threats to those processes that appear and reappear.

As I have said frequently, this whole side of the archaic religious relation to nature is by no means as irrelevant to us as we seem to assume. When early men and women in respect and fear propitiated the powers of nature; when they "gave" of their own to those powers or to the gods, in order to share in the gods' benefits; when they disciplined even themselves, purged themselves, lacerated themselves in order more and more to participate, we look at them with mingled pity and scorn as deluded, superstitious, and neurotic, and above all as incapable of affecting and controlling nature as we moderns can. Yet our "effects" on nature have been so disastrous that now we are faced with our own set of humbling spiritual requirements if we would live on in nature. We may not have to put offerings everywhere or sacrifice a first Buick or even fast; but we do need radically to discipline our greed, to limit our use and misuse of resources, to reduce our waste, to control our pride for power and gain, and to moderate our demands—if we are to continue to live in nature. If we do not, nature's powers will surely wane, and then all our capacities will be reduced to vanity. We live on nature's powers and bounties, or we do not live at all.

One of the earliest myths tells us that the true life (the tree of immortal life) can be found only when the tree of wisdom has been located. Mistaking wisdom for scientific knowledge and technical capability, we have sought thence directly to gain life, abundant life ("you can have it all"). But, as the myth itself states, that way in the end is the way to death. Nothing in our present situation in relation to nature challenges the validity of that myth—but as yet we do not believe it, and so self-discipline vis-à-vis our consumption is the last thing on our minds.

10

Nature and the Human Care of Nature

Nature is our parent, our mother. Yet we ignore, use, and use up nature. There should be a Mother's Day for nature to remind us of our ultimate dependence on her. Nature has for some time represented—or seemed to— little threat to us as a species. Perhaps this is one reason, among others, that we appreciate nature less and less. In the last century, human creative intelligence and ingenuity have come easily to dominate and hence to employ for our own purposes most of nature's forces. As has been the case so often in history, it is the gift of our creativity that poses for humans our greatest dangers. Only at rare intervals does the independent power of nature over against our use reveal itself. Thus storms, floods, earthquakes, and volcanoes all represent occasional signs of our radical dependence on that ordered power. But we heed the sign in order to avoid its consequences to our lives and interests, not to read in it the lesson of the deep reality of our dependence.

Our modern relations to nature are indirect, utilitarian, and contrived. The direct relations of continuous mutual dependence, of uneasy cooperation balanced by uneasy threat, are relations evident in the hunter, the herder, the farmer, the householder, the sailor, and the traveler, relations characteristic of most of human history. These mutualities are now largely gone. Through technology they have been replaced in almost all these callings by more dominating and so more secure relations, complemented and reshaped by urban concerns (which seem so natural to us) with production, commerce, and leisure. For our practical existence, our day-to-day life, nature is primarily the storehouse or warehouse of raw materials for the goods and services necessary to comfortable modern living. Our dominant relations to nature—logging and pulp production, mining, fishing, and herding, which used to be crafts characterized by mutual dependence and respect—are now business enterprises intent on salable products. Even farming has tried to see itself (until notices of eviction arrived) as merely one business enterprise among others and not as a special profession, a unique vocation.

Only our need for leisure (our finitude often saves us from our creativity) promotes a different relation to nature: that symbolized by the weekend, perhaps by the summer vacation. Here mutuality is sought, but not, I think, necessarily achieved. What is sought is the somewhat artificial, certainly "smoothed over" mutuality of viewing, climbing, skiing, camping, rafting, sailing.[1] Only for those who supervise these vacation enterprises is this *work* or is it really mutual—though typically, boat trips are also a business, the beauty of nature its raw materials and the sail around the harbor its salable product. Nevertheless, if it were not for the political weight of this role of nature for our leisure, crying out that nature, its wilderness parks, its waters, and its woods be unspoiled and its forms of life extant, the other practical relation to nature of production would log, strip-mine, and develop the whole thing clean.

Science has provided our main and now our sole *cognitive* relation to nature. It is through science—physics, chemistry, geology, and biology—that we assume that we know what nature is, that is, what its reality is. Books on nature are books written by scientists, culminating in an evolutionary cosmology inclusive of the development of galaxies, solar systems, earth, life, animals, and even of society and of the human in society. Some want to continue this scientific account of reality through neurology, behaviorist psychology, and scientific sociology and thus tell us all there is to know about the reality of *us.* Of course, there are other books on nature—one thinks of Rachel Carson, Loren Eiseley, Gregory Bateson, Aldo Leopold, Gary Snyder, and Bill McKibben[2]—but to most of the scientific community what these persons add to science is "poetry," creative but purely subjective reactions to nature that have little cognitive value. It is a dogma of our time that our only way to know is through science, and so nature is as the relevant sciences define nature.

The heavy consequence for the topic of this chapter, ecology, comes from the fact that scientific method objectifies whatever it seeks to know. Nature known by science is therefore a system of objects, entities with external relations, with no inwardness—no "for-itselfness," as German philosophy would say—a system to be understood only insofar as we understand the invariable and the determined character of these external relations. Thus regarded, nature, as John Dewey proudly intoned, is now rendered by science into a system made up of homogeneous, quantitative, and purposeless parts; and because it is not "for itself" and so has no value or purposes of its own, it is not a reality in itself. Hence it is a fit realm to be used by our techniques for our purposes, that is, to be "humanized." Nature, said Dewey, has in itself neither purposes nor intrinsic value; we insert our values into nature and thus, he believed, we beautify and ennoble "natural" nature. Thus he spoke in the year 1921–1922, with its incredible optimism about technology and about the "intelligent" humans who develop and use technology.[3]

Present scientific knowledge of nature, of course, continually—if mostly without being noticed—overleaps these grim objectivist limits. Unpredictable spontaneity appears in this account of nature in every event, however apparently determined. Life arises, and with life self-awareness, self-organization, and self-direction appear out of this homogeneous, quantitative mass. Changes of form take place randomly. Finally, out of this process of change comes (however our objective rationality may deny it) "development," an amazing story of emergent values. Nevertheless, science officially knows only quantity, homogeneity, and "causedness": an inert, "vacuous" (to use Alfred North Whitehead's scornful term), purposeless, valueless, material nature. The correspondence—the congeniality, even—of this theoretical picture of inert nature with the requirements of technical industry, namely, nature as raw material, is too obvious to miss. No wonder Herbert Marcuse said the picture of the world science provides is the ideological justification for the economic exploitation of the world through industry.[4] The scientific understanding of nature as a system of objects and the scientific development and underpinning of industrial technology have prepared first our minds and then our instruments for our present exploitation of nature.

Another factor, however, has also been at work: our religious traditions. I do not intend to place the entire blame for our disaster relative to nature on so-called biblical religion, on our joint Jewish and Christian traditions.[5] I have already indicated other sources of our deteriorated relation to nature. But that does not excuse these religious traditions. This is not a matter simply of the word *dominion* or even of the command to dominate the earth. To countless generations that command meant hunting, herding, clearing, and farming, precisely the cooperative relations of mutuality that preceded modern life. It did not, because it could not, imply the absolute control that makes exploitation and desecration possible. Whatever they did to their own towns, medieval men and women hardly polluted Europe's rivers, made toxic its soil, or killed its forests with acid rain. Dominance became destructive only when the theoretical know-how and the right instruments were there to enable an absolute control—and that has been only in the last three centuries. Nevertheless, our religious traditions are sorely lacking in relation to nature. I think it is fair to say that as a consequence they unquestionably share the blame for our disastrous Western understanding of and relationship to the nature around us.

What is it that has been amiss? There are, I think, two elements here, which, not surprisingly, are aspects of the very creativity of the so-called biblical view—for, as in all things human (including science), the creative side of a religion can become a source, under the wrong conditions, of disastrous consequences. The first element is the *desacralizing* of nature. Because God is one and is in some important regard transcendent to nature, the divine in this common tradition is not identical with any of nature's wondrous and terrifying forces. Hence nature ceases directly to participate in and to manifest the divine; it is in this important sense desacralized, stripped of divine and demonic powers. This represents a gain in understanding God, and that gain is illustrated in every major aspect of both Judaism and Christianity. But it contains a more ambiguous set of consequences for our understanding and appreciation of nature; for unquestionably, this desacralization prepared the way for the strictly reductionist, mechanical, and objectivist understanding of nature that appeared with the development of modern science and modern technology just after the Renaissance. In theological terms, the desacralization of nature stripped nature of its sacred power and so of its inherent value, its power and value in and for itself. More importantly, our traditions failed to replace that sacred status with the apprehension of nature as a sign and instrument of the divine glory, as they might well have done.

Second, for our common Jewish and Christian traditions, insofar as there is a common element, it is not nature's powers and values that hold center stage (either for God or for humans) but people, and with them community and, further, history. God is concerned above all with the establishment and nurture of a truly moral and religious human community, the People of God, the Kingdom; thus the moral and religious law, the true worship of God, and true love for the neighbor stand in the center. The religious relations of God to men and women; the moral relations of men and women to one another; and the commands, promises, and expectations relevant to these relations represent almost the sum of true biblical religion, however otherwise that true religion has been interpreted in Judaism and in Christianity. In none of this does nature figure in any significant way; it is, in effect, the backdrop (as Karl Barth accurately put it),[6] the stage on which the drama of the relations of God to human beings and of human beings to one another is played out in history and beyond history. God is *our* God, the God of a covenant with us, the God with concern for human redemption. Thus nature has been religiously ignored and demoted in our faiths, representing in effect a religious vacuum, a house swept clean, into which other interests and other interpretations therefore could and did rush.

I do not for a moment condemn this emphasis on the human, on community, and on history. It represents the creative heart of our religious traditions. And the positive values of this emphasis—for our religion and for our moral and social traditions—are evident for all to see in the development of higher moral standards, of legal and political rights and obligations, of more humane social theories and practices. But these creative moral commands to honor, love, and serve humans did not apply to nature. Nature was not "made in the image of God"; nature had no soul. Hence it was there only as an object among objects, for our use. Nature was at best a means to be wisely used; it was never an end to which we were unconditionally obligated, as we were to other humans.

I note in this discussion how our scientific knowledge, our technological and industrial power, our religion, and our present sociological locus (most of us live in a human world, a world of human constructs—towns, cities, highways, colleges, factories, and office buildings—not in nature) have worked together to lure us into forgetting nature. Nevertheless, that forgetting is by no means complete; for with the other hand we pillage, rob, and exploit nature, and for these purposes we do anything but forget her. In fact, these are the purposes for which we "know" nature! Neglect, indifference, even ignorance as spiritual attitudes are in no way innocent when they cooperate with—in fact, make possible—a "knowing" exploitation. All of us condemn those conservative forms of religion that have studiously ignored social issues and yet which have profited from social injustice. The same is true in this case: the churches and synagogues—and certainly their members—that have ignored nature have also participated indirectly in the exploitation of nature; and when they have not, they have happily helped to consume the products of that exploitation. The creative side of our two faiths has betrayed us into acts we had not intended; or have we betrayed that creative side?

Nature does represent a problem, a problem of the very deepest concern; an ultimate problem. Now, through our creative power, nature is in danger—and that puts us all in the same danger. As dominant over nature, we threaten nature; as dependent on nature, we are thereby ourselves threatened. Because we are more than nature, we can and do threaten nature, through all that makes us "more": our intelligence, our practical ingenuity, our infinity of will—in fact, the "image of God" in us. But we are also part of nature, its child, a natural creature among other creatures; and so we are at the same time threatened. In the ecological crises are revealed at once our ontological ambiguity as transcendent to, yet dependent on, nature; our moral ambiguity as dominators and exploiters through our skills; and even the vaster ambiguity of our destiny, the fate of our earth. Through the very wonder of our science and technology, the terrible vulnerability of our contingency and finitude as well as our greed have become strikingly mani-

fest to us. Even if the universe is infinite—and we know anew its vastness—
the nature that supports us is very finite indeed, itself vulnerable and mortal;
and that humans did not know before. Thus, like any creature, nature can be
killed, and we can do it whenever we will to do so.

If we were rational, we would at once control ourselves. But we are not
rational; such self-control is at the moment hopelessly ideal, utopian.[7] Yet
ironically it is our rationality, as modern culture defines rationality—scientific
inquiry, technical innovation, industrial practicality, and organizing genius—
that threatens nature and with nature our rationality! (It is precisely the
pragmatic managerial class, capitalist or communist, that spurns action for
the environment, in the name always of practical reason.) The paradoxes of
human being—at once infinite and finite, self-transcendent and creaturely,
willing the ideal and yet enacting what is destructive, image of God and yet
fallen—are evident here. To our surprise, we now appear as the prime
example of this paradox of creativity and the demonic long articulated in
archaic myths. An ultimacy of power has been placed in our hands, in the
hands of a particular consciousness and a particular will which are themselves ruled by pride and greed. The resultant mortal ambiguity of human
nature is as vividly portrayed in our modern scientific and industrial
encounter with nature as it was in the most primitive of fertility myths and
ritual sacrifices. History now, for the first time, can threaten the nature on
which it depends for its being—and so nature has returned to center stage in
our two historical religions. And dominant now over the fate of both
history and nature is our oldest enemy, our own waywardness. Here our two
Western traditions uncover an unexpected similarity to Buddhism: for to the
Buddhists, there is a force ruling over our science, over our technology, over
our industry, and so over our common history, and that is "desire," *tanha*;[8]
or, in the terms of our tradition, "concupiscence," an infinite greed driving
our rationality and our wills to capture, possess, and devour the entire
world, the very nature on which we depend.[9] This grim assessment by both
Buddhism and the Western traditions of the current prospects of an industrial culture—prospects made possible by modern science and its child,
technology—seems to be an uncomfortably accurate judgment on the politics of ecology.

The rescue of nature is first of all an issue for science. It has been morally
concerned scientists who have understood and warned us about these imminent dangers and who know, if anyone does, how we might profitably deal
with them.[10] It is, second, an issue for public policy and for politics: a
matter of forming and enacting concrete and practical policies that control
our exploitation and help to heal nature's wounds, her loss of blood.

Fundamentally, however, these are spiritual matters, matters of attitude, on the one hand, and of moral choice, on the other. By "attitude" I mean our fundamental spiritual relations to nature: our sense of kinship with nature; correspondingly, our sense of respect and of moral obligation to nature; and as a consequence the desire—it is to be hoped, the drive—to act in creative harmony in relation to nature. Even more, it means a fundamentally new relation to ourselves: Who are we and what are we about? Do we see ourselves as so far above the nature that bore us that we can destroy her? And if we reject this superior self-understanding, do we have the moral self-discipline to be as prudent as we like to believe we are? Unfortunately, as in the most ancient religions, sacrifice, even self-sacrifice, seems necessary on our part if we are to restore our relationship to nature. And it is precisely the recognition of this requirement of sacrifice if we will save the environment that makes the public, almost as much as the managers, wary of any legislation that controls or limits our industrial use of nature. Such legislation costs money, threatens industry and thus jobs—and hence requires sacrifice, however modest that sacrifice may be. Who would have thought that these primitive themes would return as relevant for modern scientific, technological, and industrial civilization?

This emphasis on spiritual attitudes and moral obligations sounds woolly-headed, out of touch with the real world of bottom lines, job security, and survival. But the ecological crisis is very real, as is the possibility of the death of nature. In the event of the onset of the latter crisis, of the diminution of the power of life in nature, there are no more bottom lines, no jobs, no survival. Furthermore, spiritual matters lie behind fundamental political movements and changes. It has been because of changes in spiritual attitudes in our country—in matters of respect for the other, commitment to justice, and the discipline necessary for self-control—that our tragic racial situation has somewhat eased, that new roles for women have appeared, and that new political possibilities in both areas have opened up to us. When spiritual attitudes change, laws change—not before. The issue of ecology is thus, in its resolution as in its origins, in important part a religious issue. At the base of politics lie spiritual attitudes: toward self, toward others, toward nature, toward God. And nothing can be done without commitment, decision, and surely in this case the willingness to sacrifice some important level of economic well-being.

How we use our science, how we control or do not control our industrial machinery—these political decisions that we make for or against nature depend on our most important spiritual attitudes, namely, our moral obligations and our moral decisions. And these issues of the spirit are, unfortunately, the responsibility of those of us who assume leadership in our dominant religious traditions. How, then, do attitudes, moral judgments, and ethical decisions change (for they can and do change, as is evident in issues of race, of gender, of other religions)? How can those in the biblical traditions begin to rethink nature, to refashion their understanding of nature? That is the point in these suggestions: a rethinking of nature, not in the first instance a rethinking of God—though to rethink nature we probably do have to rethink both God and human beings. And such inward changes in us, the dominators, are in this case especially important. Here there are no exploited voices to cry aloud, no oppressed persons to march, protest, and act in political rebellion. We, the dominators, recently having become "the ruling class," are the only ones who can be active, who can change the situation—unless, as Robert Heilbroner warns, the impersonal forces of war and starvation and their ultimate consequence, depopulation, reduce our predatory powers.[11]

First of all, attitudes toward an entity, a person, or a community depend directly on how we assess or judge the reality of that "object." If, in the realm of human affairs, certain persons have been (as frequently has been the case in history) judged to be of little worth, an "inferior breed"—inferior in being and so in status—then our attitudes toward them will be despicable. If, however, they become for us of intrinsic value, "created equal"—replete with dignity, integrity, and so worth—then our attitudes toward them will or may perceptively (if gradually) change. In the same way, to "know" nature's reality as an inert, mechanical, "vacuous" object, of little value in itself or for itself, is to encourage an attitude of deep disrespect and so a behavior of use; it is to make nature into merely a means for our own goals and needs, into "raw material." New spiritual attitudes give rise to the possibility of new policies; but behind spiritual attitudes lies a new sense of how we know the reality of an entity or a person and so what their reality is. It is thus that the issue in theology of the "essence" or "nature" of nature—how we view nature's reality, how symbolically we name nature—arises as an important condition of healthier and more creative attitudes toward nature.

I begin with a suggestion that both is obvious to us now and would have been heretical in the past. I propose that we not only admit but proclaim and teach that nature is an "image of God," *imago dei;* a creature of God, to be sure, but with that also a sign of God, a symbol of God, just as are we. Hence, as made in the image of God, nature has, as we do, a value in and for itself, an inherent integrity, order, and worth, which we must respect as we do in the case of another person.

As Martin Buber reminded us, nature is a Thou,[12] an image of its creator and thus an "other" to us. Historically, our traditions have emphasized humanity as alone the image and likeness of God; and this has helped to foster human dignity, value, and rights. But it also led to the ignoring of nature. We forgot—though the Psalms and Job might have reminded us— that God is also the creator and orderer of all the vast and wondrous variety of nature. And because God is the creator (and again, we are reminded of many psalms),[13] nature inescapably shows forth or mirrors as an image the glory, the power, and the wisdom of its creator and preserver. In fact, the God of the Hebrew and Christian Scriptures is a God imaged continuously through and so conceived by means of the signs and traces provided by the grandeur, power, order, and beauty of nature; it is through analogies from nature—as well from human persons, community, and history—that God becomes God.

Where do we experience and know transcendence and immensity, infinity and endlessness—the first signs of the divine? Surely it is only through the sky and the heavens, words crucial to the biblical vision of God: "For as the heaven stands high above the earth, so His strong love stands high over all who fear Him" (Ps. 103:2). Where is overwhelming, vast, creative, and threatening power known? Through nature's power (e.g., in Job 9, 12). Here the deepest nature of the divine as the creative power that establishes all things is imaged or symbolized, that is, made available to our worship and reflection through the awesome grandeur of nature. Further, experience of *life* in nature, of life in ourselves as parts of nature—that is, of our existence in nature—puts us in touch with the awesome and infinitely valuable reality of life, the wonder, power, and terror of life: fertility and birth, blood, breath, vitality, ecstasy (cf. Matt. 22:32; Josh. 3:10; 1 Tim. 4:10; Heb. 10:31). These signs of life are vivid in both our outer and our inner experience of nature; they are also signs throughout the Scriptures of the living God, of the God of life and the power of life.

Finally, the order and beauty of nature—the regularity of its changes, its coherent system despite its variety—also are signs of God's wisdom and of God's power, sung over and over in both Psalms and Job (e.g., Psalm 104; Job 28, 38–39). It is on this astoundingly intricate and yet orderly structure, this welcome coherence (adaptability, as we now call it), that we depend for our being; it is because of this order amid the immensity and the power that we feel at home in nature. And unquestionably, it has been this pervasive experience that has led humans to conceive of God as order, wisdom, and logos, as well as power and mercy. These signs of God in nature—transcendence and infinity, power, life, order—are not, I believe, materials for a proof of God; nor do they (as again the Psalms show) make up even the major or culminating nature of God as the God of the covenant, as law, as justice, as love, as compassion and mercy, as "unfailing love" (e.g., Psalms 36,

40, 41, 42). In regard to these major "attributes" of God, history and persons must provide the signs or symbols of the revelation of God's character. Still, without the former attributes drawn from nature, God would not be God. Nature is and has been a genuine image of God; it is high time we admitted this, concentrated on it, and learned from it.

Now, if in these important ways—and there are many more—nature is a sign or image of the divine power, life, and order, then nature has in itself its own integrity and value. It incarnates and embodies—as we do—powers and values that we associate with God and therefore respect, revere, and cherish: infinity, power, life, order, uniqueness or individuality, and self-affirmation. This integrity, this value in and for itself, must be respected; nature, like humans, must become an *end* as well as a *means*. This value for itself must balance its value for us and temper and control the latter, lest our legitimate concern for ourselves becomes, as it so quickly does, our greed. Greed, nurtured by the pride that we represent the sole end of creation, has together with that pride brought forth the infinity of our exploitation of nature.

Corresponding to these changes in the "status" of nature with regard to God and our sense of nature's reality in itself must come changes in our apprehension of our relation to nature, that is, our apprehension of nature's value to us and so its status in our own eyes. Nature is not only something for itself, of value to God and to itself; it is also something of ultimate value for us. And this is what we have forgotten, in our science, technology, and industry on the one hand and in our religion and moral values on the other.

Nature is the source of all life, of the power and continuity of life, and so of the future of life. Nature thus is, as nothing else is, our mother and creator. We now know (thanks to science) that it is directly through nature and nature's developing processes that God has brought us into being; it is through nature that God has created us. Nature is thus not only a sign, an image of God, but also the most direct and encompassing instrument of God's creativity. Our dependence on the divine for our existence in life is directly expressed in our dependence on nature: in nature we live and move and have our being.

I here elaborate on this point. Our changed scientific understanding of our origins has transformed—or should soon do so—our sense of our dependence on nature. Heretofore, most Western men and women recognized their immediate dependence on nature for air, food, rain, and so on. But traditionally, the creation of men and women by God was seen as a separate event from the preceding creation of nature by God. Now believing Jews and Christians, insofar as they also accept the evolutionary account of our origins in nature, understand God's creative work in a quite different way. God has created us as humans *through* the long slow processes of development in nature, the long cosmic, geological, and finally biological processes that produced first our cosmos, then our earth, then the other forms of life, and finally ourselves. In this sense, as for the earliest religions, nature is our mother, the instrument or, better, servant God has used to produce us—much as God creates each one of us as individuals through our mothers and fathers. Our dependence on the divine for our existence in life is directly expressed through our dependence on nature. Modern science has explicated what archaic religion knew well: our utter dependence on nature for our being and for all the attributes of that being.

Primordial and archaic religion knew this. Nature contained for them the sacred powers of life: fertility, community, health, and security—all that on which life depends. Clearly, such a religious intuition of the sacred in nature saw something in nature we are now not able to see: its power, its life, its order—its sacred and demonic dimensions. Both our religious traditions and our scientific inheritance have blinded us to these aspects of nature. Perhaps it will be by seeing nature partly through the eyes of these archaic religious traditions that we can begin to apprehend nature's reality and real value, instead of the abstracted versions of nature given by either our religious or our scientific traditions.

I referred to nature's *reality* because—as humanity is beginning to realize again—our dependence on nature is absolute, and that is also part of the reality of nature. Nature is thus not merely an objective system of physical processes or even the inert stage for the human drama. Nature is the encompassing source and ground for us of the sacred power, life, and order on which we depend. Nature's reality is therefore much more than either scientific inquiry has found or even our religious traditions have celebrated. That "much more" has been sensed and celebrated in myths, rites, and art throughout human experience. It is perhaps possible for humanity—even for us moderns—to recover it. We have been dazzled by our scientific brilliance and technical ingenuity, by our moral and religious rectitude, and by our independence, knowledge, and power. We have forgotten whence we come and the ground on which we must continue to stand. Fyodor Dostoyevski said that when God is forgotten, humanity also quickly vanishes.[14] One can perhaps now add: when the sacred presence in the natural world vanishes, nature is not only forgotten but in the end misused, used up, and destroyed.

Finally, one may ask how it is that we have been so absent-minded in relation to nature—in fact, ignored those elements of our traditions that might have redeemed our relation to nature. Why is it that our cognitive and technical powers have so consistently externalized nature into an object for our exploitation? In answering this question, one uncovers perhaps a point where our religious traditions, for all their other failures, manifest their strength, depth, and profundity. As I suggested, the contemporary Buddhist has here a surprising but helpful contribution: modern men and women, says Nishitani Keiji, have through science and technology succeeded in understanding, ruling, and using for their own purposes the heretofore uncontrollable powers of the nature, of the world, around them. They consider, therefore, that their minds and their wills freely and reasonably dominate and so control all that is outside them. Actually, however, unknown to them, their own minds and wills are ruled by an even deeper force, *desire,* which drives their use of nature outside them into misuse and ultimately into destruction. Hence this same force, which has driven all other civilizations, will propel modern scientific, technical, and industrial civilization toward annihilation and death.[15]

For me, the answers given by our own traditions to this same question—why we have exploited nature—are even more subtle and profound, impressive though this Buddhist view undoubtedly is. An essential element of the biblical understanding is that what is most creative in our life—and in the life of all creatures—can become the demonic, the destructive; and this truth applies even to the image of God, namely, the intelligence, the ingenuity, and the strength of will, on the one hand, and the spiritual depths, the religious devotion of human beings, on the other. Thus (according to the old story) could the original pair, although created good, nevertheless fall; and their Fall was not because of instincts, desires, or sloth but precisely through their highest capacities and goals: their thirst for knowledge, their longing for moral insight, their urge for autonomy—for being "God-like." Thus also could the leaders of even the chosen people do wrong in the sight of the Lord, bow down before idols, and persecute the prophets. Thus could the select followers of Jesus abandon and so betray him. Thus can a religion of love and self-sacrifice turn into a domineering and persecuting force over other religions, especially over its nearest kin, Judaism. Only if each community sees this "demonic" possibility and repents for the continuing actuality in itself of that possibility—if its members see that it is their very creativity that can become a point of pride, of arrogance, of heedless self-concern, and so of infinite greed—is there any hope of a new beginning through grace, through "the unfailing love of God," as the Psalms say.

This theme of creative being, betrayal, judgment, and the promise of rescue runs throughout our common Scriptures. And it illumines, I suggest, our present situation vis-à-vis nature. The most creative elements of our common culture—the intelligent inquiry into truth, begun in Greece and creatively renewed in a new form (influenced by the Hebrew tradition) in the early Renaissance—flowered into empirical science, into scientifically established technology, and into an expanding industrial order (the justifiable pride of Western culture, the foundation of its modern imperial glory, and the envy of other cultures). Surrounding this scientific and technological center of modern Western life had long been the precious inheritance of biblical religion: its emphasis on history and community, on the sanctity of the person, and on the ultimacy of the moral law capped by the power, wisdom, and infinite mercy of God—a tradition that nurtured most that is humane in our common culture as the scientific and technological inheritance fed its effectiveness and power. No wonder this combination of creative elements, intellectual and spiritual, gave birth to the confidence or belief in cultural and historical progress! This progress, in turn, focused on (1) the final dominance and control of nature for human well-being: in medicine, in the production of material necessities, in the satisfaction of fundamental human needs, in a creative leisure; (2) the achievement of a democratic, free society; and (3) the realization of moral persons in a human society.

Much of this has been achieved. But creative achievements (as both Greek tragedy and biblical realism knew) have their destructive side. Precisely in and through what is here most creative—through science, through technology, and even through such a religion—the demonic has also manifested itself: in the continuation in the modern era of old inequalities and injustices, in the continuing threat of ultimate war, and above all in the new and infinitely dangerous exploitation and potential destruction of nature. Continuing reliance solely on the celebrated and hence untransformed creative achievements of human being will only hasten the ultimate destruction. In this ambiguity of what is creative—and hence, in the need for repentance— lies the mystery of a fallen as well as a creative history, which optimistic secularism has never understood. Yet despite this ambiguity, the creative is creative, new life is possible, and even this demonic history may be redeemed. The point is that *if* the presence of the demonic within the creative is recognized and admitted—if, through humility about even the best in our scientific and religious traditions, we can reassess and reform what has been given to us in both those areas—we may see ourselves, nature, and God in a new light; and a new world may become again possible.

It is apparent that the reality of nature manifests itself to us as richer; deeper; more of a mystery, an ultimate value, and an ultimate concern than modern scientific, industrial, and religious culture has articulated. Granted this, why move on to a *religious* perspective? Why in our age begin again to speak of God? Why not speak only of the sacredness, the value, of nature and leave it at that?

First of all, the contemporary ecological problem has revealed at last that nature is incurably finite or, in theological language, in its being a creature among creatures. It too is vulnerable and mortal, limited in power, in life, and in order—despite its awesome participation in all of these. It points, as Augustine had said, beyond itself to a further ground, a further source, of the power, life, and order it so splendidly displays. In our age this has become obvious. We have come to dominate and exploit nature too much ever to worship nature again. If we do, it will be because nature has been used for some other end, transformed into the instrument of a political, and so very human, ideology for antihumanistic purposes. Such an ideology, appealing to "nature" as its legitimating principle and myth, must be more than balanced by our traditional emphasis on humanistic values.

Second, in contrast, the ecological crisis has at the same time uncovered the insufficiency of humanism. Our modern concentrations on the human in our religious traditions (as sole image of God) and in modern pragmatic culture (as the sole source, criterion, and arbiter of values) have teamed together to represent a disaster for nature. Human creativity has been much greater than we ever dreamed; but it is also much more ambiguous and dangerous. "Value for us" has inexorably led to exploitation, to "value only for us." Our ultimate concern, our sense of the source of reality and of value, must reach beyond the human, even transcend the human, if we are to control and dampen the modern anthropocentric binge that now threatens the life of nature. Yet this deepest of concerns must also include nature as it includes the human. We must find a religious transcendence that relates creatively both to nature and to the human, nature's child.

As Ludwig Feuerbach pointed out, when the divine was totally resident within nature, when nature was the locus of all divine and demonic powers, then the human was hardly able to distinguish itself from nature.[16] As a result, the creativity and value of the human, while surely already present in latency, were subordinated to nature's vaster order. With the slow development of culture, largely under the inspiration of religion, the human has distinguished itself ever more clearly from the rest of nature. And with that distinction, humanity's almost infinite capacities for creativity have appeared. But with the establishment of human creativity, the domination of nature has slowly followed, and history is now frighteningly sovereign over nature, apparently holding the power to determine nature's life and death—and so its own. Experience has shown that human well-being, "value for us," is too ambiguous for one so dependent on nature beyond us and especially for one so irrational and imprudent as mortally to endanger its own being in the name of its enhanced well-being!

To mitigate and limit that human dominion over nature, therefore, some supreme and yet inclusive object of ultimate concern is necessary. This is not an argument for the truth of theism or its other religious equivalents; it is an argument for their potential value for us today. In any case, whereas the political tyrannies of the entire twentieth century have shown us the value of humanism, the human tyranny over nature at the end of the century has questioned the ultimacy and the wisdom of the humanistic concern exclusively with the human.

Part 3

Nature and the Sacred

11

Human Viability in a Nature That Is Mortal

I begin this chapter on viability with two concepts, both of which are fundamental to our entire theological tradition and crucial to understanding our question of viability: contingency and temporality. Both are essential aspects of the theological definition of the creature, a finite, created being—in our case, human being. When I say we are contingent, I mean we may or may not exist. We are not necessary; on the contrary, our existence is precarious. We are now, but tomorrow we may be gone;[1] we are "being bounded by non-being," as Paul Tillich put it,[2] or "made out of nothing, ex nihilo,"[3] as the earliest tradition insisted—all of these symbols being made concrete by the rude ending of each life in death. Temporality rounds this out: we are in passage, temporary and not permanent; an "event" more than a substance. As the Greeks saw and Alfred North Whitehead repeated, nothing here really *is*; all is becoming.[4] It is, and then—poof!—it is not. Contingency and temporality help to define each other.

As was noted, the Greeks saw this union of contingency and passage—as did the Hebrews ("All flesh is as grass")—with great clarity. All that grows, decays; all men are mortal; all is flux, coming to be and passing away—and only the gods are immortal. Similar insights into the contingency and temporality of all things under the sky characterize ancient Indian, Chinese, and Japanese cultures. Only modern Western culture seems to have ignored this clear implication of ordinary experience—an interesting case of ideology overcoming evident data, however clamorous. Temporality has for us been *progress*, not decline. In the case of the human race and its history, there is, said John Dewey, growth and not decay; process is everlasting, and it unfolds in an increment, an accumulation, of value.[5] God does not, in order to be God, transcend contingency and process, as in the classical theological tradition; on the contrary, God is process or is in process, and process is everlasting and cumulative.[6] Throughout our century, however, this nineteenth-century confidence in "contingent temporality" has repeatedly been challenged. As one example, the question of the *viability* of our species, and of the nature on which we depend, has been raised for us as never before. Are we viable as a species? Far from being a necessity, is our survival even a possibility? Can we, contingent as we surely are, have hope for our common temporal future, and if so, under what conditions? Can a contingent, temporal being survive? I explore these questions of viability by looking at humans and our survival, first, as beings generated out of *nature* and its strange processes and then, second, as beings also immersed in *history*, a medium also produced by nature but posing in a significantly different way the issue of survival or viability.

We come to be from nature. We now understand this in a quite different light than we used to: all that we are as human beings, all our cultural powers and our historical character, develop out of nature's developments. History and we as, in part, creators of history are children of nature. Thus everything else I say in this chapter—and all that humans may say about history—is itself a product of nature, the way, I believe, God has created us as humans. This does not mean, however, that all this, including history and our viability, is to be understood exhaustively as we understand nature, in the terms through which we understand nature scientifically. Nature understood by our inquiries is an abstraction from, a limitation on, nature as our source and ground; or, as Whitehead remarked, to understand human being as a part of nature also requires that nature be understood in the terms in which we understand human beings.[7]

Nature is laced with contingency and temporality. All in the natural order—even galaxies, even dinosaurs, even humans—comes and then goes; none is necessary, and then all die. This apparently is as true of species as it is of individuals, of phenotypes. Many of both may still be around; but we know that their time will also ultimately come. Ancient cultures have always known this. The modern display of fossil remains and the evolutionary theory resulting from the discovery of those fossils make it even plainer, though for decades we have failed to see its implications for us as a species. In fact, natural selection as a theoretical explanation for evolutionary change presupposes and so underlines the contingency and the temporality of all life and of all forms of life. Only through the processes of death and of dying— through selection—does life, especially new life, arise.

This relation of being—of being there—with contingency; of life with death; of death with new life; and of both with temporality suffuses all of nature and all of our experience of nature: the barrenness of winter is the possibility of spring, the apparent death of seeds makes possible new plants, one generation's passing is the condition for the appearance and flowering of a new generation. In all its ordinary processes, nature moves into significant change, change of individual and of form alike, by means of loss and death—that is, by means of contingency and temporality. The question of viability, of survival, is originally a question within natural process: How in this wheel of natural coming to be and passing away can we contingent and temporal beings survive? How can we be viable for our allotted time?

The classic human answer to this fundamental (and very existential) question has been technology: tools, organization, planning, and more and more knowledge—the entire equipment we now term "intelligence." Nature strangely developed our immense brain, set us upright, and gave us thumbs—all of this providing some of the conditions for language and for technology. But the cumulative development of technology has depended on more than this original and necessary but standard equipment. It requires also knowledge, and specifically the accumulation and almost infinite proliferation of knowledge that culture, especially modern culture, has fostered. As Francis Bacon saw, knowledge is power: power, through understanding causes, to work our will on things—on the environment—and so power to adapt the environment to our needs. It was, I think, this faith in knowledge as power or, to use Dewey's words, faith in "organized intelligence to reshape the environment in line with our needs," "to *secure* our values,"[8] that has allowed us to overlook our contingency, our mortality, and so not heretofore to raise so sharply the question of viability.

Two new factors (or new recognition of two old factors!) have qualified this modern confidence in technology—and behind it, science—as the sufficient answer to viability. One of them is the fact that, no matter how much technology advances, human technology cannot exhaustively control its environment; cannot, in other words, adapt us successfully under all circumstances. The environment can, in one way or another, become uncontrollably hostile to our existence—in fact, to all life—and it may well do so. Nils Eldridge has shown that this has happened with some regularity in the past; on four occasions, radical changes in the wider environment have eliminated most of the then extant life—and only bits and pieces sneaked through![9] In these extreme cases the ability to adapt was irrelevant. Even with the most advanced technology, we are subject to the wider contingencies of nature in process. Our viability may in the end be determined by forces quite beyond our control.

The other factor that is raising with a new urgency the question of viability is our recent recognition of the deep ambiguity of knowledge and so of technology itself. Until only four or five decades ago, scientific technology was regarded as the sufficient key to human adaptation: it seemed to be an unequivocal success in guaranteeing an always increasing human security. "Whereas the savage leaves nature as it was, leaves the desert a desert," said Dewey in 1921, "the modern scientific man, 'organized intelligence,' turns that desert into a rose garden."[10] Applied intelligence permeates "objective nature with more and more secure human values." When I read this to classes at the University of Chicago, they shook their heads in disbelief. "You've got this thing turned around; it is technology," they insisted, "that turns the garden of nature into a desert!" At least as we use it in agricultural and industrial development, technology is too ambiguous to count on; as we have come to know, technological expansion may destroy our habitable environment, becoming an instrument in our *inability* to survive instead of the dependable means that humans possess for their own survival. What nature developed by way of the large brain may not be enough—or may even prove to be our fatal flaw.

To make further sense of this discussion, however, it is necessary to move to that other environment produced by nature and surviving in and on nature: history.

I here speak of history rather than of culture. The category "history" continues with new sharpness and emphasis the themes of contingency and temporality, raising each to a new level of intensity and so of turbulence. "Culture," in contrast, connotes an enduring, even a monolithic, tradition, one slowly evolving; society seen as a substantive entity perduring through time and at best evolving slowly and consistently according to law. History is society seen as a realm of events; culture is society seen as an enduring and developing subject. History is laced with—in fact, constituted by—intentions and so meanings; with memory and foresight; with decision and so with open alternatives; in history, therefore, unexpected and devastatingly lethal failures appear, sudden turns toward good or toward evil, toward renewed life or toward renewed carnage. If, in nature, life and death, viability and extinction, are intermixed, this is even more true of what G.W.F. Hegel, optimist though he was, called "the chopping block of history."

Many discussions of nature and of nature's processes move easily into the arena of culture and comfortably carry with them their field equipment from genetics, biology, and physical anthropology; therefore they speak naturally and serenely of "cultural evolution."[11] They can hardly do this (though they may try!) with the category of history, however, where not only language, tools, technology, and cumulative knowledge appear but also communal and so political uses of these, uses determined now by intense structures of meaning, by deepened anxieties, by invigorating hopes, and by deadly fears. Technology in history reveals itself not just as the human principle by which nature's hostile forces may be controlled and turned to our uses but also now as a threat to our very viability. How are we to understand this new role for intelligence and its child, scientific technology?

What is crucial for the theme here is that it is in this turbulent realm or context of history, where contingency and temporality have become intensified, that the question of our viability has recently been raised. To be sure, it is still technology that raises the issue, and it is the threat to nature that poses it; the same triangle operates here, that made up of nature, our knowledge of nature, and our use of nature. But it is technology as a *historical* force, as a power utilized by historical communities, that here enters the scene and thus has become the threat to nature. Technology has in the last century "entered" history as one of history's major driving forces. And with this development, history has regained the power not only to reshape but even to destroy nature.

Still, this difference having been specified, it is important to remember that history in all its variety, diversity, depth, and contingency (that is, its utter unpredictability) is itself the child of nature's mysterious processes—or, to put it theologically, both are created by God, with the one, history, having been created by the instrumentality of nature's processes. Hence is all of history latent in nature; its "seeds" are there, "incognito," in earlier forms of life, ready and waiting to flower under the conditions of human life.

Natural process forms a unity (so I believe) under the infinite God. Nevertheless, there are in this unity diverse levels or dimensions, which it is important to distinguish and to recognize. If we do not distinguish these levels in nature, we either reduce all to the lowest level or unconsciously think in terms of an incoherent dualism—for example, of reality as a system of merely material causes plus the scientific observer who perceives, tests, and thinks that material cosmos! Among nature's dimensions, there appears first the important level or dimension of life, then later the significant level or dimension of history. In moving from dimension to dimension, all our fundamental categories shift: space, time, causality, and substance. They do not lose their meaning, but nevertheless their meanings shift and become analogous and not literal: causes are causes among organisms, but in organisms causes are subtly different from those in inorganic societies. So, further, in history causes are still more complex, including now explicit intentions and decisions mysteriously united with physical causes and unconscious tendencies—as we all experience in ourselves and in others. The same applies to temporality, as Augustine discovered: in humans temporality is experienced both inside and outside; it includes memory and anticipation—

a before, or a past, and an after, a future. It is temporality still within passage but nonetheless one that transcends and so can span time's passage. It is a temporality generated by and so in touch with eternity (and with anxiety!).

This analogical shift is particularly apparent with our central category: contingency. If all in nature is subject to change and ultimate dissolution, coming gradually to be and then passing away, this is so much more the case in history. In history all is much more in flux: not only is each individual life contingent, a precarious passage through our brief time; even more, communities and societies are contingent, coming to be and passing away, even vanishing, with bewildering and disturbing alacrity. Who among us has not been stunned by the virtual disappearance of the seemingly permanent Communist bloc and, most recently, the Soviet state itself,[12] following so quickly on the destruction of Adolf Hitler's "Thousand-Year Reich"—not to mention the earlier dissolution of the Austro-Hungarian Empire and the Ottoman Empire, each dominant for centuries as apparent historical "substances"? The West has recognized this contingency of past societies ever since it knew of the disappearance of Macedon and the fall of Rome and, later, when it succeeded in uncovering behind them the remains of imperial Egypt, Babylonia, and Sumeria. But it was able to view the contingency of these imperial substances with serene indifference (as with the disappearance of dinosaurs) because it believed that Western civilization, thanks to its wondrous science and technology, was both permanent and progressive; that in this one case temporality contained an essential core that was not contingent.

Now we are not so sure. There are no permanent substances in history, not even our own; there are trends and communities that last, but none is everlasting. All substances in history are *events*, precarious, temporary, viable, and yet also threatened. If finitude is "being bounded by non-being," so much the more is this the case with historical finitude, human being. And one of its deepest problems is that it knows this from the inside: it knows its insecurity in the ever-shifting and unstable environment of history. It is aware of its own uncertain future, and therefore it is anxious, in desperate need of courage to face this heavy compound of contingency, temporality, and uncertainty. Sharpest of all, it is now evident that in history, technology, which was counted upon to increase our viability vis-à-vis the natural environment, has now apparently reversed itself and increased our vulnerability. Technology now poses a threat to our survival in nature, as well as offering a promise for our adaptation. In history, creativity becomes a threat as well as a promise—a sure sign to the theologian of the relevance of the symbol of the Fall!

It is important to recognize in this context the role and significance of politics, of the political—messy, corrupt, ignorant, and self-seeking though politics undoubtedly is. It is through its politics that, for better or worse, each community seeks to deal with the essential and unavoidable contingency and temporality of its historical life, to "steer" the community through the passage of time, out of present dilemmas and into more security in the future. Politics is thus the way that communities hope to preserve, secure, and enhance their own being and well-being in an unstable history. Through the political—whatever its form—communal decisions are made and programs enacted for the impinging, uncertain, and dangerous future. Politics, temporality, and contingency go together, and all are inescapable.

It is now perhaps clearer how it is that history is constituted by both "nature" and "spirit"; by natural pressures and needs; by external social threats; by dangerous internal divisions; by our very precarious assessments, judgments, intentions, goals; by genetics and physiology; by physical needs and desires; and by the use of our fallible intellects and wills. History is immensely complex. It cannot be understood or dealt with if it is reduced.

The point of this discussion of the dimension of history is that just as fundamental ontological categories shift and take on *analogous* rather than *literal* meanings, so the rules and principles relative to viability shift as one moves from the inorganic through the organic to the historical dimension. Of course, the physical and material requirements for survival remain: a community must have food; relative warmth and protection; and defense of its members, its property, and its essential activities in order to be and to continue to be. Security in this minimal physical sense is essential and remains. One could add that a community needs air, a stable range of temperature, water, and fertile earth in order to live—in fact, all the riches that nature now lavishes on us. Thus is history—and all the communities of history—utterly dependent on nature for its viability. However much history may be "more" than nature, its dependence on nature remains inviolate. Hence the issue of survival appears in this ultimate form of dependence on nature in history. A threat to nature's viability becomes a threat to history. Without nature, history cannot last until morning.

However, as firsthand experience of any community shows, attainment of a level of material security is not enough for humans; nor is victory, even continuing victory, over a community's external enemies enough. The survival of the fittest in this simple adaptive sense represents no sufficient rule for historical communities (as Socrates and Augustine saw so clearly). As Reinhold Niebuhr said in one of his earliest books, the will of the organic realm to survive turns in the human realm into the will to power—another example of the ontological shift that history introduces. Thus communities conquer, rule, and in so doing subjugate others as well as defend themselves;

and thus ruling classes not only lead the community politically but also dominate, enslave, and oppress those they lead. The lust for power and for goods—pride and greed—springs "naturally" from our insecurity and the anxiety that knows that insecurity; and both have their roots in spirit's awareness of our contingency and our temporality.

But the human problem of survival is compounded by the fact that communities cannot and do not survive, either as oppressors externally or as tyrants internally; sooner or later, such injustice (note the appearance of that word) destroys itself through internal revolt, through external conflict, and a new political structure arises. Augustine saw this clearly as he contemplated the dismemberment of the apparently permanent historical "substance" that Virgil had called "eternal Rome." Each community, Augustine said, longs for internal peace and for outer harmony; but the peace it establishes favors its own partial interests, and the harmony it achieves is for others an unjust order—and so in the end it falls.[13] One can see precisely this lesson in the astounding fall of communism—not to mention in the prior demise of the West's own colonial empires!

Therefore, in history, *justice* is one necessary ingredient for political viability: historical contingency requires, as well as material security and self-determination, some measure of justice inside and out if a community is to survive over time. This complicates enormously the question of viability. Justice is strange indeed, not least in its queer relations to actual communities, to their politics, and so to their history. Is any community just? No. Is any community then quite void of justice? Not for long. Whence does it come and where is it—eternity, as Plato thought? Or is it a projected ideal, a requirement of divine law, merely a hope, or an ultimate promise for the final End? These are strange, unavoidable questions; all that can be said is that justice is a requirement, an "impossible possibility," an "ought" that must also in some sense be an "is" if the community is to survive. Speaking personally, I experienced this requirement vividly in an internment camp, where the increasing injustice of our common life in the end threatened our survival as directly as did any of the shortages of material supplies from which we also suffered.[14]

Justice is, moreover, not only puzzling but also a complex compound constituted by several very different ingredients, especially in communal affairs. It requires *discernment*, of the situation and its needs; it requires *prudence*, a rational practicality that will see the real self-interest represented by justice—mere self-interest will seek only to secure the self and its community, and thus it will fall. And for both discernment and prudence a lot of *courage* is necessary and also more than a little *detachment*, that is, an ultimate lack of or some control over nagging self-concern. A self or community too anxious for its own life is unable either to be prudent or rightly to discern the real situation—as those who for economic reasons balk at necessary ecological controls show so well! Justice thus moves closer and closer to love: to self-affirmation and self-love, to mutuality in respect for the other, to agape in the willingness to undergo some measure of sacrifice. Without these "highest" levels of spirit lodged securely somewhere in the community, the community can know no justice—and it will fall. She who would save her life must in the end be willing to lose it; reconciliation must enter each conflict if either party is to survive. Thus does love shore up justice, just as in history justice in turn shores up viability or physical survival.

In the complex realm of history, a realm on the one hand compounded of natural needs, physical security, social unity, and communal self-direction and on the other hand shaped and driven by meanings, survival itself becomes immensely complex. It is no longer merely a matter of fitness and the struggle with the rival—of the gene's successful drive to perpetuate itself. In history an unconditional victory, if not tempered by reconciliation and so by justice and love, breeds tyranny, enslavement, and so in the end renewed conflict. And in history the uncontrolled urge to survive, fueled by an infinite greed, can dispose not only of rivals but also of the storehouse of nature around us and the gift of life within us. Survival on the human level is, therefore, a moral and a religious issue as well as a utilitarian and a technical issue. The wisdom of every tradition has seen this; but few communities, then or now, really believe it to be true. A prudential self-interest, always necessary in historical life, turns out to be barely possible in worldly politics!

What has been argued so far has been characteristic of history since its beginning, since a consciousness of historical passage and so records have appeared. Something new in our day has, however, entered and shifted radically this complex interrelation of natural needs and historical requirements, of the material and physical well-being of communities with the social, political, and moral interests of communities. Nature and history have in our day arrived at a new interrelation—a new state of intimacy, one might say—and it is this new shift that begets in a new and sharper form the unsettling presence of contingency and temporality and so raises our present question of viability. Therefore, to assist in understanding the present dilemma before us, my next task must be to articulate this new interrelation of nature and history.

An interrelation in historical communities between natural, material needs—issues of physical security—and moral requirements—justice and self-control—has always existed. No community can survive without food, shelter, and security of its properties; and, as is well known, the onset of storms and diseases has changed the course of historical events. Thus every community, the species itself, and so history utterly depend on nature for their life. Correspondingly, no community can long survive without some measure of justice, of an order inside and out that discourages rather than promotes conflict. Too much concentration on survival can lead to defeat, even to extinction, in history—and that is the dilemma. So how has the contingency of communities in relation to nature combined in a new way with the contingency of communities in their historical relations to one another to raise the intensity of the question of viability (for that, I am arguing, is our present situation)?

What is new here is the cumulative ascent, within the cultural life of historical communities, of the particular developments of natural science and its consequence, scientific technology. In the modern period this ascent has been at the heart of the dynamic character and of the incredible power of the Western community, which only now is receding from its long-term dominance (because of this very technology) over other historical groups. Spreading slowly over the globe, modern scientific technology has transformed our common relation to nature and has vastly increased our ability to resolve our natural needs, the better to secure, as Dewey put it, our natural values. We can control nature as never before; we can extract from nature materials and services to answer all our needs, real or imagined. We have, in other words, reduced dramatically—in many places in actuality and everywhere in principle—the contingency of human life in relation to its natural environment. Knowledge is power, the power to control our natural environment and to secure life. If this were the only sort of contingency in our human condition, present life would, in truth as well as in hope, be infinitely more secure and fulfilled. That this contingency was in fact our only "enemy" was the dream of much of the nineteenth century; it remains the explicit faith of many within the scientific and engineering communities. Hence the people of the last century and their present-day descendents have believed happily in the promise of progress toward security and fulfillment through science and technology.

The control over nature to secure human needs, "to secure our values," is, however, not just an aspect of our relation to nature. It is, unfortunately, also an aspect—a very large one—of our current history; for the control over nature represents, in the strange dialectic of historical life, also the power to dominate, to exploit, to desecrate, and ultimately to destroy nature—at least, to destroy the conditions of life here. This we once did not believe. "Organized intelligence" creates science and surely directs any application of technology; would not, therefore, our use of technology also be intelligent (that is, prudent), directed at our real self-interest? So an optimistic culture once thought. But even intelligent humans are not necessarily prudent. On the contrary, technical rationality—in military advances, in industrial expansion, in agriculture, in all sorts of property developments, and in the proliferation of chemical compounds—has been, we now know, wildly *imprudent*, heedless, almost willingly ignorant of its own baleful consequences. As a result, this rationally produced but imprudently directed "binge" by now threatens nature's order and so the possibility of continuing life.

This expansion must be slowed if not stopped—a political requirement, unfortunately, rather than a cognitive (scientific) or a technical one. And not surprisingly, political control over industrial and agricultural technology proves itself to be almost infinitely difficult. As Robert Heilbroner has asked, Will any community voluntarily reduce its gross national product? Can the question of viability be resolved politically? But the causes of the problem—the rise and the uses of technology—and the political dilemma—the control of technology—are historical. As historical, these causes are subject to the terrible and unnerving contingencies of history: ignorance, human bumbling and error, but especially greed, lust for power, the rivalry of classes and of groups—and the "stuff" of politics. Our relation to nature has, so to speak, left the pasture and entered the sophisticated but ungodly realm of urban politics; this is our difficulty. To put it in larger terms, nature, on which history depends for its being, is here at the mercy of history's decisions and so history's vagaries. Put theologically, the fate of nature—as the Genesis myth intimated—is now subject to the baleful consequences of the historical Fall, and so it shares in the tragedy of an estranged history.

Evident here is a validation not only of the relevance of the symbol of a fallen history but also of the religious insight that the most creative of human powers, if estranged from itself and from its own good uses, can become destructive, the most mortal of threats. Nothing the human spirit has created has been more an apparent blessing than the ability to know, to uncover and assent to truth, and the capacity to apply that knowledge instrumentally in resolving real and threatening problems—in short, science and technology. Yet this creative power, so full of promise, represents at present our greatest long-term threat. As a consequence, it is the use of this creative power—a historical question—that will determine its status from moment to moment, year to year, as promise or as threat. Technology has become historical in a new way, subject to the moral and the immoral decisions of fallible, greedy, and self-interested groups. Lest it destroy us, technology has thus by its very brilliance inexorably placed itself under the norms of the political: of justice, of self-control, even of some sacrifice. The besetting sin of its use is not at all ignorance but greed; not too little science but too little self-control. Its salvation will not be through new advances in scientific knowledge or technological expertise, new discoveries or new inventions; on the contrary, its salvation will depend on prudence, a reasonable dose of communal self-control, and even some openness to self-sacrifice. A scientific culture, by the inexorable development of its power over nature and over society, now depends on the *humanistic* excellence of its institutions and of its moral sensitivities—a strange reversal indeed. Nature and nature's contingencies have unfortunately become subject to the deeper contingencies and ambiguities of historical life—and hence, as always, our only hope is greater humanistic self-understanding, more moral strength, and so practical wisdom.

Are we viable? If my analysis is valid, the answer given to that question will depend especially on one's assessment of the rationality or irrationality, the self-control or the greed, the prudence or the selfishness of human beings, particularly of human beings in political, communal, and historical affairs. Increases in scientific knowledge of nature and of technological possibilities contain, and will increasingly do so, both threat and promise. They do not in themselves possess any antidote to the new threats of technological advance. If, therefore, scientists and engineers are optimistic about our viability, it is because they believe that scientists and the intellectual people who rule a scientific culture are rational, that is, prudent—not because of what the scientific community "knows" scientifically. An understanding of history and its ambiguities, including an understanding of the uses and misuses of science and technology, is more sobering. Our track record for political wisdom, for self-control, and for the possibility of a modicum of self-sacrifice has not been great—but we have squeaked through!

Theologically, there is much to say both ways. We know religiously—whether we be Buddhist or Judeo-Christian—that we are governed by *desire* (the Buddhist word) or are prone to *sin* (our word) and so quite capable of self-destruction, while under the illusion that we are being very wise and very good. But, also religiously, we know that in every situation courage is possible, and on that basis (and on it alone) genuine rationality is possible. We can, if we have enough courage and so serenity, control ourselves enough to be prudent—it *has* been done. Anxiety is here the greatest menace, anxiety for the self and for its community; for anxiety tempts us to dominate what unsettles us, and greed tempts us to confiscate everything we think we need—and these two can quickly combine, not just to threaten other communities but now, even worse, to destroy nature. In this case, the relevance of religion is obvious: faith and detachment are essential if we are at all to be intelligent in the world. Religion in existence is an essential condition, not the enemy, of worldly, practical reason. And not least, we need the confidence that only the knowledge of providence can gain. Such confidence is the securest and most dependable ground for courage, that is, for the faith and the detachment necessary if we are now to be viable.

12

Nature as the Image of God

In Chapter 10, the deviant but nonetheless important suggestion was made that nature represents an *imago dei*, an image and likeness of its divine creator. This is important because if nature is in truth an image or mirror of the divine, then nature, like humanity, has an integrity in itself, a value for itself. It is not just an object for us, a means for our use, but an end in and for itself, in and for God. In this context image is taken to mean—as John Calvin interpreted it[1]—a sign or symbol of the divine, a mirror, in that sense, of the divine glory; or, as I have discussed nature, an image replete with the power, life, order, and redemptive unity bestowed on it by God. It is in this important sense that humanity has been considered to be an *imago dei*, namely, insofar as humans manifest in and through their humanity the intelligence, will, freedom, and love that are—or can be—characteristic of human existence.[2] In neither case is this imaging obvious to any random viewer, to just anyone reflecting on nature or on human beings. Many persons look at nature or at humans and do not find there traces of the divine. In neither case, therefore, is this an issue of proof, an uncontestable argument that the characteristics of power, life, order, and redemptive unity in nature and of intelligence, will, freedom, and love in human being are in fact images or mirrors of God. However, in both cases the characteristics— or the traces, as I prefer to call them—are there, present in nature and in human existence, for anyone to observe and to ponder. They are there, but to see them as traces of God is an act of "faith"; it presupposes that through these media the divine discloses itself to us and that we respond to that disclosure with acknowledgment and assent—and obedience.

The task here, then, is to draw out, articulate, and so bring into a clearer view those traces of the divine, of the activity and presence of God, that have been discerned dimly and in passing in this entire discussion. Whether these are in fact traces of God and who that God may be are for the moment left open. In viewing them, it becomes apparent why they can be so apprehended, but there is little necessity to do so here—other interpretations are possible. However, with this caveat it must also be said that other interpretations would encounter formidable intellectual obstacles: either they deny the presence of these traces by way of a reductionist process that ends in self-contradiction (monistic naturalism), or they save the facts at the expense of coherence (dualism). There is present here, therefore, an argument that a theistic interpretation makes coherent sense of the width and the depth of our experience of nature as no other interpretation does. But behind and with that argument (and theologically more important), there is also present the theological affirmation, grounded in faith and its witness, that nature so viewed discloses significantly if not exhaustively the glory of God, that it represents an essential if not yet a sufficient mirroring of the divine. Even more important, however, than urging through this discussion a richer interpretation of our religious tradition by the inclusion of nature, it is hoped that this interpretation of nature and its theological implications may serve as a "lure" to all who read it, a lure toward a richer experience of nature and of its mystery, and so a lure toward a more creative relation of modern men and women to the nature on which they depend.

To introduce this discussion of traces, it is helpful to remind readers of two major themes in what has preceded. The first is what might be called the multilevel or multidimensional knowledge of nature. I have argued that nature is known through a number of different avenues or means. These work together to make any specific sort of "knowledge" of nature possible, that of empirical science as well as that of practical common sense, art, philosophy, or even religious understanding. These modalities of knowing are correlated, intertwined, in any sort of knowing. They represent, therefore, an "extra-scientific" mode of knowing, yet one necessary and essential for science.

First, there is the *self-awareness* of the subject doing the knowing, an awareness of itself as perceiving, naming, organizing; as defining, deliberating, formulating, and supposing; and finally as judging in relation to the new evidence. Here we know ourselves as intelligent inquirers, as minds or subjects in operation. To put this in other language, finite being here is, to use Martin Heidegger's language, "inwardly illumined"; it knows itself "from the inside."[3] Because our minds as well as our wills—our entire "person"—are products of nature, nature is in part but also in truth known from the inside; or better, here nature knows itself from inside.

Second, there is the awareness of the *other* as a subject, as "Thou." This is, if anything, probably in origin prior even to self-awareness: we become subjects in a community of subjects.[4] This awareness is also necessary for science. From it arises all our training, understanding and sense of community: of the goals and standards of the community, of our responsibilities to the community—and of our dependence in turn upon its traditions, its expectations, its judgments. This awareness of the other—what I term a "personal" relation and so a consciousness of a "person," a Thou—is also the product of natural processes. It thus reveals, as does self-consciousness, the richness of nature, the capacity of its mystery to produce the personal and awareness of the personal.

Third, there are certain general apprehensions of nature—of the reality around us and in us—that become, as formed by our culture and so "inherited" as well as intuited by us, the *presuppositions* of all our knowing: apprehension (1) of the reality that discloses itself through experience; (2) of the temporality of that reality and its extension in space; (3) of its order despite passing, variety, and change, and despite its projection into the future; (4) that this order spanning temporality and spatiality is, even more strangely, in some way congruent with the processes of our language and our thinking—that logic is relevant to reality and that inquiry is therefore relevant to our being and the being that surrounds us; and, following from that, (5) that reality and the knowledge of reality are of concern to us, of value for us, and thus that reality has "meaning"—or, in Platonic language, that truth is "good." These are the foundations of an ordered experience, of "world," of cosmos. They provide the presupposed structure within which the empirical cognition of external reality, which we now term knowledge, becomes possible; they make possible a systematic world of experience, the discrimination of "facts" and of "theories" necessary for knowledge. They are the conditions of inquiry and so of science. By means of these persistent intuitions of reality, the infinite variety and confusions of experience are given the formal structures for knowing and acting, for receiving disclosures, and for reshaping what is given—because it is through experience and the organization of experience by the subject that we are enabled to chart, to know, and to deal with the reality outside us and in us.

These various modalities of apprehending or knowing interpenetrate among themselves and with our sensory contact with the world to establish knowledge. The self experiences and knows itself in a world through and in its communion with others; cognition is an inward and a social process as well as a sensory and an intellectual process. Cognition is, therefore, also a participating, involved operation: objectivity and noninvolvement, or "rationality," with regard to data, theories about data, and projects in the world, depend directly on self-discipline, the eschewing of temptation, and so commitment to the truth, as well as articulated certainty that reality can be known by means of experience and reflection on experience. These interpenetrating modalities of knowing—of other and community, of self and of world—are more than the basis of empirical science; they also usher in, establish, and shape the other aspects of cultural life. As Alfred North Whitehead said, it is the metaphysical presuppositions of knowing and acting in experience that ground "civilization" in all its aspects.[5]

Our modes of interacting in any given culture—in our vocations, crafts, courts, markets, and legislature; in the home, the factory, and the offices of government—are based on these assumed intuitions about worldly reality, about others, and about self. The arts of culture are fed primarily by these modalities: the visual arts, music, literature, "science," philosophy, and moral debate. Finally, these intuitions are explicitly shaped, expressed, and articulated in the myths, rites, and laws of religion and reflected on in speculative thought.[6] And on each of these levels, from crafts and daily customs to the arts, philosophy, and theology, the imprint of the particular cultural gestalt is present: each level is "Greek," "Chinese," "modern," and hence differentiated. Nevertheless, this "religious substance" of each culture (as Paul Tillich described the ideals of particular cultures)[7] expresses also, in all their variety, the same fundamental intuitions basic to knowledge and to action. Thus it is the entire culture, not just the official cognitive wing of that culture, that gives expression to our apprehension of what is real and of how all that is real is structured. If nature is the source of us, inclusive of all our cultural aspects, then ultimately the distinction of objective and subjective in "naming" nature recedes in importance. The richness of all our powers and of our subjectivity itself is a richness of nature itself. In any case, it is only within the context of the multidimensional character of human knowing that the question of "traces" arises, when nature is experienced and known through all of these modalities and through all of them in some mode of unity.

Alongside the theme of the multidimensional character of knowing, that of the ambiguity or duality of "nature" has appeared and reappeared throughout this discussion. For science, for reflection, and for religious apprehension, especially in myth, "nature" as a word and concept has filled two quite distinct roles and thus has implied two quite discernibly different, though interrelated, referents. These two meanings and their implied referents have tended to slide back and forth into one another. First, on the one hand, nature is represented in both archaic religion and modern science as the all-encompassing source or ground of all there is in concrete experience: the entities, inorganic and organic; the system of nature; ourselves; and even historical communities are products of nature. As long as nature is not reduced to the second sense (which follows), it is appropriate and accurate to say that in this sense history is a child of nature and is thus "natural"—a treasonable suggestion from a twentieth-century theologian if ever there was one![8] Nature in this sense represents our widest and most direct environment, and in so doing—as evolutionary science has taught—our immediate and direct source.

This was clearly recognized by early religion; it became increasingly forgotten in the urban technical, philosophical, and religious milieu that the developments of culture represented, especially in modern biblical and humanistic culture. It has reappeared in theoretical form in modern cosmology, evolutionary biology, and social biology and in existential–ethical form in our common consciousness through the crises of the environment. Ironically on this point, modern naturalism represents as knowledge (as theory) much, but not all, of the ethos of archaic religion, namely, that nature represents the all-encompassing source of every aspect of human being, of human community, and so even of history. In any case, as source of both objects and subjects, what we experience and ourselves as experiencers, what we know and ourselves as knowers, nature represents an essential "mystery," partly known, comprehended, and articulated but escaping always complete formulation—not only because of its dynamic character and its depth but also because it includes and thus transcends knower and known alike.

Second, nature as a word, a concept, a symbol, signals on the other hand our distinction from, even our distance from, this environment. Nature here is contrasted with culture and art; in modern terms, therefore, it represents the object of scientific inquiry, an inquiry that itself is a part of culture and not of the nature it studies; for as is evident in the conceiving and in the writing of every scientific theory, nature as studied, organized, and formulated by scientific inquiry and as manipulated by technology represents a system of objects over against ourselves as inquiring subjects and as acting technologists and producers. Nature as cosmos, as the organized, intelligible system of things comprehended by the sciences, is in part the construction of mind, the object of an active, intelligent, and purposeful subject. In being made thus intelligible, nature is here distinguished from the mind that knows it; its description is made precise and validated according to the rules of scientific method, and hence it is reshaped into a homogeneous, quantitative system. In becoming known, nature loses that all-encompassing character of its first meaning and loses as well its mystery; it is, so to speak, "finitized" into a coherent object, an object of knowledge and of manipulation.

If the concept of nature as source is an extrapolation of imagination and reflection from ordinary experience to encompass the ground of that experience, so accordingly nature as cosmos, as classified, organized, and known system, represents an abstraction from the richness of our wider experience, which is inclusive of objects, inner subjects, and communities of subjects. It is, first, an abstraction from the subject, from the subject's participation in nature, in others, in communities, and in one's own self-direction as a subject; and it is, second, an abstraction into the special disciplines that make up science—physics, chemistry, biology, and so on—none of which encompasses (except through a reductionist process) the whole of the system of nature, the whole of the cosmos. Formal empirical knowing is in this sense an "objectification" as well as an abstraction: (1) in the more formal homogenizing, quantification, classification, and control that both manipulating and theoretical comprehension exert on what is known, and (2) in the deliberate abstraction from all "self-knowing" of the subject doing the inquiry.

Further, although nature as a system of objects may neither now nor ever be completely comprehended (there may never be a theory of everything), understanding may well transcend its own relativity enough always to point beyond itself. Thus nature as "system" always carries beyond its known parameters a penumbra of mystery. Nevertheless, this sense of the "mystery" of the cosmos, of cosmology as "not yet fully known," represents a different sense of the mystery of nature from that of nature as the all-encompassing source and whole inclusive of us, of community, of history, and so of science itself. The most fundamental questions for the special sciences may concern the relation of the special sciences to each other and of them all to the system of nature understood in a unity of the sciences—the question of cosmology.[9] However, beyond even that question is a more fundamental question about nature, namely, that of the relation of nature as all-encompassing source, as the whole beyond objects and subjects, to nature as known by subjects, as made into a cosmos by the unified knowing of the scientific community. Both questions represent "philosophical" as well as scientific questions—but they are significantly different. In any case, it is only when one sees nature in these two dimensions and asks these more inclusive questions that one can speak reflectively of "traces." A new sense of the richness, the depth, and the mystery of natural being—of finite creation—clarified immeasurably but by no means exhaustively by modern cosmology and biology, is necessary for the sense of the sacred to appear in our experience of nature.

For most of the human story, nature was teeming with power, with life, and with an infinitely valuable order. These aspects of the experience of nature seemed to archaic men and women without question to represent disclosures of the presence of the sacred, to represent infinite powers of reality and of value resonant in and working through the entities and forces of nature that both surrounded and appeared within men and women. As I have tried to show, much of what was thus apprehended as "sacred" and hence dealt with by the means of archaic religious rites, sacrifices, myths, and obligations still appears in a modern, "scientific" account of nature. Power, life, and order are definitely there when we study nature or theorize about nature; but their sacrality has been quite lost for us. Nature now appears as one-dimensional, and hence nature is for us reduced from source and ground of our being to a level below us; to a means; to a system of objects to be examined, manipulated, and used; to a warehouse for goods needed by us. Because these signs of the sacred are there but disguised, incognito for us, one suspects that we as well as nature have been "desacralized"—that the desacralization of nature in traditional Christian faith, in order to make room for the growth of the religious vitality and value of the human, has in the end helped to desacralize both human being and nature. Perhaps when nature becomes secular, so do we—and these signs are ignored in the rush to appreciate and enjoy the benefits of nature.

These signs are both there and visible to inquiry, and yet they are ignored. At best they are signs of the variety of modes of knowing nature and of the glimpses or hints of the sacred throughout the rest of ordinary experience, disclosing themselves to those who are looking, to those who are conscious of the mystery of nature—or in classical theological language, to those who have "faith."[10] Faith in this broad sense does not create these signs; their presence in and around the scientific account of nature indicates that. But faith looks at them directly rather than away from them, ponders their import, and accepts them as also disclosures of what is real and significant.

Is faith necessary for seeing these signs as *signs*, as signs of the sacred, of the divine in creation (or in history)? Yes. Does "faith"—our subjective receptivity—therefore create these signs so that they can be said not to be there objectively but to be illusions, so that there is no discourse about them as they appear in ordinary experience? No. Why, if these signs are present in nature to be looked at, can we not describe them and speak of them as "pointers" to the presence of God (a kind of natural theology), as well as signs of God for the faithful? I think we can. Is this a tenable, coherent position? I don't know! But let us see how it works.

First of all, nature discloses itself as power, a power in process, converting itself into energy and into matter; appearing and then vanishing; the basis of all being in experience, continuing as definite and defined into the present and apparently projecting itself into an open future. Because power in this sense is equivalent to existing, to coming into being, remaining there, and projecting into the future, power is for us of ultimate value, a unity of being and value that we experience not only in things around us but within ourselves in the power to be and to be active, which we share with all that is. The origin and continuity, the dependable presence, of this power is thus an "ultimate" question for us, a question for our own existence and its meanings (a religious question) and a question for reflection (a philosophical question). Science also raises this question about power but can answer it only by reductionism on the one hand or by ignoring its implications on the other. It is a "limit" question that, because of its existential as well as its reflective aspects, will not go away.

Power, like life and order, manifests itself on different levels, in a kind of hierarchy of modes which modulate and suddenly change as they appear in different ranges of finite being. Power on the inorganic level seems nonpurposive, almost determined or caused in its career, amazingly predictable and comprehensible in terms of quantitative, mathematical, and homogeneous categories of analysis. Power on the level of life discloses a modulation: life becomes here vitality, a vital "force" not purely comprehensible in the categories of physics and chemistry; a force that can vanish in death; a force directed at the preservation and propagation of life. This is a force dependent on the unity of the organism; it is partially self-maintaining and self-directing. Power in humans combines physical power and organic power but adds another dimension: vitality here includes "meaning," purpose, the fulfillment of a goal. Human vitality recedes as meaning evaporates, when the will finds itself empty of purpose and goes limp: as Casey Stengel said, "You've got to have heart."[11] Finally, in historical communities, power becomes political and infinitely complex, inclusive of meanings and assent, of the uneasy balance of unity and diversity; and yet such power cannot be without physical power, in all its facets.

This hierarchy of power, made up of these analogous levels, is undeniable and yet ignored. Each discipline plies its own trade on one or another of these levels.[12] Again, the limit questions of the origin, the description, and the unity of power arise: Must there not be some permanent, necessary, and unconditioned source of all this, in which the same levels appear? Can it be sensibly said that all levels of power arise out of the lowest level, for if one says that, then the mystery of nature as a source is made almost impenetrable?

Second, in all religious awareness disclosure is accompanied by demand, a presence signaled by law or obligation, which is acknowledged and witnessed by obedience and service. The ultimacy of what is real, of power, is thus balanced by an ultimacy of obligation, an undeniable and unavoidable sense of "ought" that has accompanied each religious tradition from its beginning. One may try to translate that "ought" out of its uncomfortable apodictic status (and along with it, religion) into the more comfortable region of prudent self-interest or even of the prodding of the genes; but those who so translate the "oughts" of others reveal in the last chapter of their sociobiologies, a chapter devoted to the ethical implications of their inquiry, that even they are "called" by moral obligations (mostly of the liberal sort) that they cannot refuse and which they do not consider to be self-serving.[13] No one escapes this demand and its accompaniment in what we call conscience. The forms of the demand, the laws or ideals seemingly required, change as cultures change—and so, accordingly, does the content of conscience. But both appear universally, whether in what we call religion, the traditional religion of the culture, or in the ideals of culture generally, what Tillich called the "religious substance" of the culture.

Humans have always been able in part to comprehend and hence to use for their ends the power coursing through themselves and through the things around them. With the advent of science and its offspring, modern scientific technology, however, this knowledge and this use of power increased immeasurably. Knowledge is power, said Francis Bacon, and he meant precisely this: the power to use nature as we will to use it.[14] Through recent science, the power within things, the power of finite being to be, has been in part understood and in that understanding has become our power, power in human hands, and thus, as Bacon predicted, power directed by our intentions, our intelligence, our purposes—our "freedom." This has turned out to be a much more ambiguous and scary eventuality than Bacon had foreseen; for then modern scientific culture realized to its surprise the *ultimacy* of this power (the power to be or not to be), its transcendent awesomeness, its terrible finality. And with that disclosure of the "sacred" power of things has appeared the corresponding demand, the unavoidable voice of conscience, of the "ought," which has shaken the scientific community and motivated many—though by no means all—within it radically to control our use of this power.

As in the archaic experience of nature, the awesome power around us and in us brings with it a demand and hence requires, if we are creatively to share in its benefits, self-discipline and sacrifice. As we are discovering, power is hedged about by innumerable taboos, constraints on our free use of the power our knowledge gives us. This lesson is plain before us today, both with regard to nuclear power and with regard to our power over the environment; but most of us have proved too "modern" to have heeded this lesson. Here, then, in the experience of an ultimate demand, an ultimate obligation concerning our use of nature's power and so our use of our own power, we apprehend the moral responsibility that accompanies every disclosure of the sacred. Power, as an ultimate threat and an ultimate demand, is one "trace" of the sacred in our experience of nature.

Third, nature exhibits an order, one apprehended universally by the humans participating in it and witnessing to it but one sensed differently by various cultures and so articulated in widely diverse symbols in that human response to order. That the order is somehow there is as indubitable as the power that illustrates it; it is presupposed in all social life, in all the arts, in all reflection, and perhaps most significantly in empirical science and in the technology that flows from that science. Nevertheless, its presence and character raise or imply ("drive towards," in Tillich's phrase)[15] recurrent questions that no special discipline can intelligently handle, "limit" questions that point our discourse—the mind—beyond the experienced order within observable things (and so within the special disciplines) to order's mysterious source or ground.

This order combines paradoxically with radical spontaneity and openness; thus it is an order without rigid necessity and with a continuing possibility of novelty—an intriguing union that begs for fuller understanding. It is, moreover, a self-maintaining order. Because the order exhibited in nature is often referred to in terms of "laws," one is reminded of this intuition's ancient roots in political experience. And in speaking easily of these laws of nature, we continually appeal to this analogy—and then quickly forget that it is an analogy. But here there are no police, army, or courts; if "obedience" to these laws is continuously observed, such obedience must be conceived as totally self-imposed, self-maintained by the nature of entities themselves, and hence illustrated in all that they do. The union of such a self-maintained order with spontaneity and ever-present novelty represents an almost eerie puzzle, a question calling for reflection.

Above all, order, like power, appears in analogous forms as one moves from one level or dimension of nature to another: the order illustrated by an inorganic event is similar to but also, in significant ways, different from the order illustrated by an organism and its relations to the environment—as all biological discussion of functions and roles shows.[16] Further on, the order of organic life becomes much more complex; on the human level, conscious purposes and meanings mix with physical and organic process—and form an order with them. Finally, the order of the community, of a state, of history itself is even more complex, as is the disorder. Again, puzzles have appeared out of both ordinary daily social experience and scientific experience that point beyond the realms of our special discourse to a further level of metaphysical discourse, of metaphysical symbols, and even to a transcendent unity of power, order, and value implied in each special realm of discourse.

Amid perpetual change and passing away, amid confusion and radical novelty, amid the continuing impingement of disorder, order has nevertheless appeared and been sustained. Moreover, the ordered characteristic of things has a strange if fortunate correlation with the order of our systematic naming, our norms of thinking, and our logic and mathematics. What this means is hardly known; but it gives to order the welcome role of mediator, of representative, between ourselves and the otherwise infinite strangeness and mystery of things.[17] This texture of order has therefore always been deeply enmeshed with value. The close relation of order and value is reflected throughout the being of nature, up and down the modes or levels: on the cosmic level, with the "compossibility" of our world, that is, the order within it that makes it possible as a "world"; on the biological level, with order as presupposed in survival, security, greater well-being; on the psychic and social level, with propagation, community, and intimacy; and on the cultural level, with the creative enhancement of community life and the fulfillment of common meaning. On every level of this hierarchy, there is no value or maintenance of value without some participation in order, just as there is no increase in value without contrast and novelty[18]—which in extreme cases provides threats to value. Hence as a foundational but fragile characteristic of reality, one of the pervasive and ultimate traits of things, and so one of the deep grounds of value, order has always been apprehended as sacred, as a god or goddess (Apollo, Athena, Indra), as the divine itself (Tao, Dharma, Logos)—or, in our secular age, as a strange presupposition of discourse and inquiry, an unexplained character both of reality and of our thinking.

The intuition of order and its relation to value—of form as both sacred and "good"—has been almost universal. Modern scientific knowledge about the process, its randomness, and the radicality of its changes has seemed to drain our interpretation of nature of this sacredness, of its moral and religious implications; do we not, as physicist Steven Weinberg asks, now know that it is all pointless?[19] But there is more to the modern picture than its emphasis on material and official causality. What has become the "wonder" of modern cosmology (foreshadowed in the eighteenth century in the modern intuition of history as progress) is the fact that in natural process, order combines with novelty and yet remains order. Change and order were thought by the Greeks to be in radical tension, and novelty was certainly considered to be antithetical to order—almost the principle of disorder. The modern vision of a changing process continually exhibiting new forms and yet illustrating precisely in these changes a universal order is new in history, and it represents the most compelling "limit" question of modern reflection. Quite aside from the question of the "progressive" character of these changes (the "story" or "purpose" in them), there remains the question of how novelty can combine with order, how order can tolerate novelty and yet remain order. What power or order mediates between the past, which illustrates one set of forms, and the future, which illustrates another set of forms? Any explanation presupposes an order spanning these two modalities: achieved actuality and not yet possibility. How is such a mediation possible? How or what thus spans past and future, making possible a self-sustaining order among new actualities? There has appeared almost universally a religious intuition of some ground of permanence and abiding value amid change and passing.[20] This intuition responds to a trace of the sacred, a sign of the divine in ordinary experience; and it raises a most intriguing "limit" question for reflection.

Fourth, with each disclosure of order, there again comes a corresponding demand. The identification of order with value is nearly universal; however, the identification of the pervasive patterns of things with the "ought," with what is morally and religiously required, is not. Many forms of religion, as forms of culture, derive their obligations not from the order within natural, human, and social processes but from special disclosures "outside" of these ordinary patterns. Nevertheless, for many human communities what we are required to do to be human is fixed by the transcendent and ultimate order of things, perceived analogously in the laws of earth, of its animals and birds, and of the heavens and "known" especially in the order of relations in individual being, in family, and in society. In this case, order is not only what we do and what we do to achieve or participate in value but, even more, what we "ought" to do; and if we do not do what we ought, we know we are not merely to be fined but that we are wrong and that retribution must be made. Thus in the hierarchy of order, above unity and harmony, there is justice, the order that incarnates value and goodness (to each his due); and above justice there is righteousness, the divine power that upholds the order of all things and the morality that fulfills all things. Here the hierarchy of power and the hierarchy of order unite in "nature's law," in the rationality of natural law, and finally in the divine status of natural law as God's law.

Set within archaic religious or mythical symbols, this hierarchy of reality and value now seems bizarre and unreal to most of us. Translated into our own symbolic universe, however, the identity of nature's power and order, on the one hand, with the highest values and norms (ideals), on the other, is disclosed every time we speak of the equality of all men and women, of the inalienable rights of all men and women, and of the sanctity of each individual—and so of the ultimate obligations thrust upon each of us thereby. Again, disclosure of ultimacy and categorical demand go hand in hand.

Fifth, not only does the process of nature exist and embody an order, which is strange—and fortunate—enough, but it seems that this orderly process exists in an improbable way and embodies an improbable order. For one thing, it has, as far as we can tell, a beginning—and thus its existence and its order are not self-explanatory. To one who believes deeply, as much religious apprehension has, in the radical contingency of all things, the characteristic of nature as non-self-explanatory, as throughout and in itself contingent, has seemed evident; hence nature, merely in being there, seems to point beyond itself to a further noncontingent ground.[21] This intuition, expressed reflectively as a proof, has surely been buttressed (not founded) by the "fact" of a beginning, which even more persistently seems to call for a ground beyond nature. Thus the scientific hypothesis of a beginning of our process—that big bang or singularity with which all that we experience started—has raised its own "limit" question and calls at the least for more careful reflection than just to state, as if it raised no issues (as most cosmologists do), that "in that event something came to be out of nothing."[22] In coming to be at all—and, reflectively stated, coming to be "out of nothing"—the natural process seems faintly but persistently to disclose an ultimacy of being in the ever dimmer background of that far-off event. Such reflections are intriguing as representing the intellectual articulation of a deep religious intuition of the divine being, in its power and its self-sufficiency; but they are not, it seems to me, in themselves useful as proofs.

This process of radical changes over immense time and space embodies a very strange form. To many this form, having produced us, is full of meaning: it illustrates an ultimate, divine "purpose," much the way our own acts, which lead to much less meaning, embody purposes. Even some scientific observers have been existentially moved by the "wonder" of this immense and blind process, producing the scientific observer, and have recognized that a genuine if elusive question is here posed. What gives this question a special force as a genuine puzzle or wonder is the immense, almost infinite improbability of this process taking the fortunate path it did. Were the cosmic changes that took place immediately after the singularity, the improbable changes that made possible our stellar universe and so ultimately our earth, really random, purely chance? Were the mutations and recombinations explanatory of developments of life forms genuinely random, or is there in this process, unseen or unseeable by the inquiries and so the perspectives of empirical science, something at work, some direction of some sort? The "story" of creation and of life, in its modern scientific even more than in its literal biblical form, provides a genuine trace or sign of the sacred, of the deep and unexpected unity of power, order, and value—of the very sort of hierarchy of power and order revealed elsewhere in nature, namely, one where causes on one level unite in a variety of ways with unconscious and even conscious intentions and purposes on another level.

Sixth, nature has apparently prepared for the various unexpected levels that are a part of it. This is, to be sure, an aspect of the "story" just referred to; however, I would highlight another facet of this strange and beneficent character of process, one incidentally now disclosed by evolutionary science. We now know as never before that inorganic matter contained the possibility—perhaps the ingredients—of life, however that emergence came about; that the earliest life contained the possibility of more complex mutations (where did they come from?—as Whitehead remarked, "Possibility cannot float in from nowhere");[23] that these expanding complexities in life contained the "seeds" of psyche and then of spirit: of purposes, intentions, values, expressions and symbolism, goals, fears, and hopes—projects on the one hand and despair on the other. Thus all of culture—art, myth, morals, politics, practical crafts, and even science, all of the facets of spirit and of reason—stretches back into the dimness and mystery of matter, of nature as our source and ground. Here nature as matter—and as known by physical science—shows its deeper, more mysterious union with nature as the source of psyche and of spirit. Nature as source of all objects is united with nature as the ground of subjects; nature as power and order discloses itself as inclusive of nature as source and fulfillment of meaning. These too are traces of the sacred, evidence of the presence of the divine in and through the mystery of the system of things.

Seventh, the final trace of the sacred is the strangest of all. Perhaps it should not even be called a trace because it is, if anything, too paradoxical and enigmatic, too much an "incognito" in itself, to mediate a disclosure of any sort. I refer to the strange unity of life with death throughout nature, especially as modern evolutionary science understands nature; and of the fascinating, but to modern religion "primitive," unity of death and life expressed throughout early religion: in the powers of life that are also the lords of death; in the gods and goddesses that preside over both life and death; in the recurrent myths of consorts dying that crops might arise. Later in the Hellenistic age, the same strange union of death with life had another goal, namely, that souls might ascend to another realm. The same unity appears in the gods of other cultures, for example, Shiva, the lord of creation and of destruction, of life and of death. Clearly ancient men and women apprehended this dialectical movement of life to death and, out of death, new life as, on the one hand, a sacred process and, on the other, a process that in uniting death with life did not so much extinguish value—as modernity would surely conclude—as secure and increase value. How is this union of life, death, and value in the divine possible? How could the dialectic of death and life in nature become a sign of the divine? And how might it become a "trace" for us?

The discourse above on life and death in nature and on the religious response to that natural dialectic in the myths and rites of most ancient religions has landed us squarely in the midst of the problem of evil. If God is all powerful and all good, how can there be an experience of evil? If God created and rules the world, how is the tragedy of death possible? Is God the ground of death as well as of life, of that which threatens value as well as that which creates and increases it? If so, then what could we mean by identifying God with value: how could God be the God of mercy, love, and grace if God is the God of tragedy and death as well? These are the questions that press in on us when we view nature as science describes it, when we view early religion, and not least when we seek to relate God to our own personal lives and to contemporary history, where deaths occur to those we love and where tragedy stalks almost every corner of every continent.

In all of these, death threatens and yet intertwines itself with life and with value. How can we understand God, not to mention human values, if both are separated radically from all traces of death and so from both history and nature, the realms of life within death? Can there be value anywhere without the negative, being without nonbeing? Can there be meaningful life without death—but can there be meaningful life with death? These represent the ultimate questions of religious reflection and of theology; although I cannot settle them here, I must briefly take them up.

The apparent contradiction between life as value and death as the negation of value—the problem of evil—has been as sharply raised in this chapter on "traces" as it was in the descriptions of life in nature and of myth, ritual, and sacrifice in archaic religions (see especially Chapters 7 through 9). In both nature as seen by science and nature as seen by archaic religion, death and life were paradoxically joined as the twin sources of value and of hope. In this chapter, in contrast, every other "trace" of the sacred (especially the third, fourth, and fifth given herein) was identified with the mystery of the appearance, the continuation, and the increase of life and of the values of life. If in our analysis "God" is identified and defined as the source of creative value, as in most modern liberal religion,[24] then how can one jauntily go on to this final point—the identification of God with the dialectic of death and of life? How are the third, fourth, and fifth traces related to this seventh trace (not to mention the second and the sixth, on "demand"—the demands to support the values of life against the threats of death)?

The most baffling and most pressing problem for reflection is the opposition and yet the unity of life and death, of value and the threats to value, of the positive and its negation, of being and of nonbeing. No one escapes this painful and disturbing problem. How can there be meaning to life when it is dominated, as it is throughout and especially at its end, by death: the death of others, of ourselves, and of all who follow? No form of religion or important philosophy can avoid this question. How is the structure of life, closed as it is by the parentheses of death—a structure that governs our finite and mortal existence throughout its course—related to the meaning of our common life, when the latter is a meaning dependent on the values within life and thus on values subject to the definitive negation of death, the epitome of disvalue?[25]

If, however, the dialectic of life and of death represents a direct trace of the divine, is that not a signal from the nature around us and in us that this dialectic itself is a clue to the relation of life to meaning and of death to meaning? Then the profoundest themes raised in the end by nature's child, humanity, in myth, in the arts, in literature, in philosophical understanding, and in religious reflection are themselves echoes of nature's most mysterious pattern; for human existence, existence in and through spirit, has to unite meaning with the impingement of death, life with death. If there are the seeds of religion, as of morals, in the long developments of organic and animal life in nature, there are as well in nature's patterns the seeds of the explicit dilemmas and puzzles of the spirit: anxiety and fear, pain of wound and dying, despair at the collapse of meaning and at the evacuation of hope. Nature's being is not as opposite to human existence as had been supposed: our deepest questions and nature's most mysterious patterns are in some strange way correlated. Both are grounded in power and life, buoyed by the prospects of value, and now burdened with pain, suffering, death, and despair. In nature the patterns of life, death, and new life issued in the appearance of life and its meanings; in the "story" of nature, the dialectic of life and death issued in the appearance and increase of values evident in animal and human existence.

In answer to the questions posed, I must begin with the disclosure in nature itself, witnessed and repeated in archaic religion, that although death conquers life and its immediate values, life precisely arises again out of death. The most pervasive patterns of nature in the realm of organisms, in plants and in animals, manifest this: a generation dies that another may rise. Vegetable and animal life alike is used up for the sake of other life; even species vanish that new forms may arise out of them—and so on and on, even to the solar systems and galaxies! Apparently one cannot create, receive, or accept values without creating, receiving, and accepting death.

One way to deal with this is to try radically to separate these two: some powers are of life and are good, others are of death and are evil; in short, some gods are good and others evil. But such is the dialectical mixture of power, life, and order, of dying and living, that the separation bogs down soon enough. Another way is simply to identify the leading powers of earth and of life with both—as in the gods of life and death in archaic religion, in the figure of Shiva, and in social Darwinism—and to leave the question of the unity of value aside.

A third way is to recognize the dialectic as inescapable and to seek to transcend the dialectic to a higher plane: a transvaluation of the values that separate the questions of ultimate meaning from the natural and historical cycles of life and of death. Thus the religions of karma and transmigration, especially Hinduism and Buddhism, seek a level of meaning and of life beyond the wheel of life and of death. Much of the tradition of Christianity made the same sort of move: the dialectic of life and death and the inevitable loss of meaning in this life are overcome by the promise of another level of life beyond death, where the dialectic will be no more. These have been perhaps the profoundest of all resolutions; their problem is their tendency to drain this earthly life of its values, to resolve the threat of death by relocating meaning so thoroughly beyond life that the latter's values are themselves shorn of meaning.

Needless to say, modernity, in both its secular and its religious areas, has been so enthralled with the possibilities of the values and meanings within life that it resolved the dialectic by ignoring it, by in effect forgetting death and despair and so seeking here and now life without death and value without negation. This solution has not worked either:[26] it not only tends to ignore the inevitability of the negative and so to encourage despair rather than consent when the negative appears, but, even more, it overlooks the need, even the requirement, of sacrifice, self-sacrifice, and self-discipline if value is to be created and preserved. The unity of life and death, in nature and in personal existence alike, must be accepted in consent; and yet the value of life must also be affirmed and embodied. This is the trick, and a difficult one it is.

The strange fact is that the dialectic of life and death spreads out from its natural origin into the very midst of human, personal, ethical existence; nature in this sense leads into the very deepest levels of spirit. We cannot live truly and with integrity unless we are willing to die. No value can be defended in history, much less embodied, without the willingness of life to sacrifice itself for that value. And life withers and shrinks as it proceeds unless it can accept and acknowledge the possibility of its own death and even the coming of that death. Life must have dignity if it is to have and create value; but a life has no dignity if it cannot accept its death with courage.

The embodiment in existence of this paradox—the enjoyment of life and of its values within the courageous acceptance of death—represents a spiritual achievement of impressive magnitude. It is possible, I believe, only as a gift, as grace, insofar as courage, self-giving obedience, and trust, as well as love of life and moral dedication, qualify our life. This courage appears universally in human existence; its appearance is not dependent on a creative religious faith or a particular cultural life. But its source lies beyond our finitude, because it is precisely our finitude that is here threatened and overwhelmed. It is itself a sign of grace, a trace of the presence of the transcendent.[27] The presence of this courage, then, points to a resource beyond ourselves who are at once called to life but threatened by death. If left on our own, that call to life could survive only if it ignored the threat; and thus, if left on our own, the threat of death could easily submerge in despair this call to life.

If this is so, what must we say of God, the source of life and death and also the source of the grace to live in the face of death? As personal existence, our common fate as mortals, and the strange dialectic of nature reveal together, God creates and rules both the realm of life and the realm of death: for it is out of death that life and new life arise. Life is the supreme value for life; all of nature discloses this. But the condition of life is dying, and with consciousness this condition becomes the ultimate willingness to die. Death and life can unite with value if in existence the courage to die is joined with the commitment to life and to its values; the transcendence of the cycle of life and death is not necessary for the values of life to be affirmed and embodied. This dialectical relation of value to the sacrifice of value, of life to death—a dialectic disclosed in nature's processes—is first clearly seen on the human plane in high religion: in Socrates's requirement of the sacrifice of world if the soul will live in integrity, in the new way beyond desire of the Buddha, in the willingness to die for the Kingdom on the part of Jesus, and in the call to give one's life if one would find it in the New Testament. The God who creates life and death and wills a world structured in terms of both is also the God who calls us to life and also to face death for God's sake—and who promises an existence beyond life.

The God of nature and so of life and death—and so also the God of history—is hence the *Deus absconditus* whose mystery within this dialectic is impenetrable. But this God has disclosed an even deeper dialectic: that of the call to life and its values; that of life, death, and beyond death, new life; and that of mercy, forgiveness, and eternal grace. God is not only power and life and so life and death; God is grace, life, and eternity. And most relevant of all, in disclosing the importance of value amid negation, of love amid death, God has in many symbols and modes, but above all in the covenant with Israel and the life and death of Jesus, disclosed the divine participation in our suffering in death and thus provided in the divine power and grace the means to unite and overcome the dialectic of life and death.

13

Nature and Nature's God

This book has examined with some care the picture of nature, as science and archaic religion have painted that picture, to see if within it are any signs of the sacred, traces of the divine presence and activity. An outline of the traces that were glimpsed and the questions integral to and surrounding them appeared in Chapter 12. But the investigation of these signs and puzzles presents more of a description of nature—of its richness, its depth, and above all its mystery—than it does a portrait of the sacred or the divine in itself. Of the latter at this point we have very little notion indeed—unless we surreptitiously import into these hints or traces elements of what may be "known" of God elsewhere.

Hence I ask a different question here, one not so much about the mystery of nature as about the mystery of God: What do these traces in nature and the structure of nature's processes as they have been described say about the sacred in itself, about "God"? First, it must be asked whether nature's processes imply a god at all and second, if they do, what sort of god they might imply. These types of questions are a part of an old tradition, that of natural theology, in which an overview of nature, of history, or of human existence itself is taken to be able to lead us to a rationally secure, if religiously incomplete, "knowledge" of God.

Although what follows here can fairly be called a modest and somewhat hesitant member of the family of natural theologies—perhaps a distant cousin—I emphasize two points about it that diminish, if they do not extinguish entirely, the confident claims of most natural theology.[1] The first is that natural theology represents philosophical reflection or, better, logical reflection of a philosophical sort. It is generated by the urge to understand, with as much coherence, clarity, and accuracy as possible, the entire welter of experience, to articulate the structure and the meaning of the whole as we experience that whole in all its variety and ambiguity. Religious existence is usually generated in a different way: it arises out of sharp awareness of the dilemmas of life; when life is experienced as estranged, at sea—and some disclosure of rescue, of reconciliation, of illumination is received. Such experiences have arisen for humans continually in relation to nature; when they did—as throughout archaic life—nature was experienced as laced with the sacred.

This early kind of religious relation to nature is vastly different from the relation implied in a scientific inquiry into nature or in an engineering use of nature. With nature turned over to science, to technology, and to leisure, our modern religious disclosures—our myths, rites, and religious confidence—have mostly concerned the human self, its community, and its history (as the great modern "myths" of progress, the material dialectic, and humanism illustrate). Religions arise out of disclosures to selves in community, in relation to the crucial realities in which they exist; if that reality is nature, then religion centers on nature in relation to community. With us, however, our crucial environment is social and historical, and hence it is there that fundamental religious disclosures arise. The common thread, often remarked, between modern historical and humanistic ideologies on the one hand and the religious traditions of Judaism and Christianity on the other is that in all of these, persons in communities and communities in history represent the loci of disclosure (these are the so-called historical religions), whatever other differences may be exhibited between the ideologies and the religious traditions.

The effort of natural theology to understand and to articulate the whole of experience, it seems to me, never represents the initiating source of "religious knowledge"; hence this effort cannot function as the final criterion of this knowledge. The center of religious apprehension lies elsewhere: first, it does not appear out of inquiry itself, scientific or philosophical; and second, it does not arise for us in relation to nature but rather in relation to the existential dilemmas of existence, of self, of community, and of history. In our tradition it is among the people of God that disclosure takes place, not in scientific or philosophical reflection—though much in the latter may open one's eyes and ears to the disclosures within the religious community. Correspondingly, Buddhists' "knowledge" appears in the higher levels of consciousness in meditation and in participation in the tradition, not in the sort of philosophical reflection that Buddhist philosophy represents. The reflections of the religious consciousness on the structures of nature or of history—natural theology in this modest sense—do not, therefore, either initiate or exhaust the knowledge of God. The important knowledge of God is not philosophical; it is "religious," that is, it is on the one hand existential and on the other communicated through symbols to the community that acknowledges the most fundamental disclosure and witnesses to that knowledge.

In fact, the philosophical sort of reflective knowledge of God does not tell us much. Like the "traces" that point our minds beyond the processes of nature, such knowledge raises questions about that process, and it begins to suggest an apprehension of the divine presence there, the dim outlines of the mystery of our origins. What it does significantly is to represent the first step in the articulated relation between what we know religiously or existentially of God in relation to our community, ourselves, and our history and what we know elsewhere by other sorts of inquiry, of community, self, history, and nature. Thus a "doctrine" is a correlation of what is known of God in revelation with what we know by other means of self, of community, of history, and of nature. Here I am interested in what nature can tell us of God—and this is only the smallest enlightenment of the divine mystery, but it adds an important illumination to all the rest.

Second, and as an implication of the above, what is known of God in nature by no means represents the center of the knowledge of God for the Christian. The mystery of being and of our being is at best only partially unveiled or clarified here; far more important for our tradition, as for its biblical roots, is the presence and activity of God within history and especially within the communities of the covenant, the Hebrew community and the community established around the person and work of Jesus the Christ. If in nature the divine power, life, and order or law are disclosed through dim traces, and if the divine redemptive love is revealed only in ambiguous hints in and through the tragedy of suffering and death, it is in the life of Israel, in the life and death of Jesus, and in the historical pilgrimage of the peoples of God that all of this is disclosed in much greater certainty, clarity, and power. Moreover, once God is known in this historical disclosure to the community, these traces in nature relinquish much of their dimness and become genuine signs of the power, of the order, and of the will of God. As John Calvin put it, when one puts on the spectacles of Scripture, the signs of God in creation are seen truly for what they are.[2]

The consequence of these points is that what I am doing here is important, but it is not the vital center of Christian theology. It is important because the deeper understanding of nature's mystery and value in and for itself is very important and because the relation of God to natural processes is an essential part of our understanding, not only of nature but of God and of ourselves. How else are the immensity, transcendence, wonder, order, and glory of God to be experienced, known, and articulated? How else are we to know ourselves as truly children of nature, yet as ones called by our common Creator to responsibility for nature's integrity, nature's value for itself, and nature's preservation? And finally, it is, I suggest, only through a knowledge of nature that is inclusive of these signs in nature of transcendence, ultimate power, order, and value that the mystery, the depth, and the richness of nature can be experienced, articulated, and valued by us. An important part of our knowledge of nature's reality is a religious apprehension of nature as well as a scientific, a technological, an aesthetic, and a responsible (moral) knowing of nature—and basic for all of these is treasuring and encouraging a bodily as well as a spiritual joy in nature, in nature's beauty, variety, and richness, experiences that we have almost lost. What I am now doing, therefore, has its point as a theological–philosophical articulation of the presence and activity of the divine in nature as I have herein sought to portray nature.

To start, it is helpful to examine the picture of nature drawn through reflection on the contemporary sciences and their apprehension of nature. Scientific knowledge of nature represents an extraordinarily reliable (valid) picture of the way nature's forces work; it is also, I have urged, a limited picture, an abstraction from the richness and depth of nature, one that not only omits much of the mystery within nature's processes but even more omits the subject—also part of nature—who conducts the scientific inquiry and paints the present picture. What sort of world, then, appears from that perspective—from that valid yet partial understanding?

First, nature is a dynamic process, a stream of energy coalescing into events, into matter, and into the larger societies of events that we call entities. Second, it is strangely determinate and defined as it reaches actuality; here lie the unavoidable, even necessary conditions in its past for the character of each present actuality. Yet each such present also faces indeterminate possibilities in its future; it is open to alternatives, to unpredictable jumps, "changes," "mutations." What consistency it represents at this point seems hardly necessary or determined but only persistently predictable.

Third, this passage from actuality to possibility is itself characterized by order, an order spanning the ongoing stream of events. Thus it is an order reaching into the defined past and yet pervading the movement into the open future—a movement characterized by indeterminate microcosmic events, by indeterminate mutations of organisms, and by the more radical indeterminateness in continuity of historical process. It is, moreover, an order running through each dimension of the hierarchy of nature, as does the stream of power. Causality and order pervade natural existence as its constituent parts, but they appear "analogously," in different dimensions, on different levels in nature.

Fourth, there is continuing novelty in nature, a novelty that represents a break with the conditioned past but also a process in continuity with that past. The genuinely new appears in process: not only change *within* given forms but change *of* forms. Thus new possibilities, still not in existence in the immediate past, become actuality; open alternatives become definite choices; openness is transformed into what appears to be necessity. Time and its passage effect a modal change from possibility to actuality, from the openness of infinity of options to the definiteness, even the necessity, of finitude.[3]

Fifth, this sequence of novelties, of new possibilities becoming actual, seems itself to embody an ascending order, an order of increasing value. Value is, as Alfred North Whitehead suggested, intensity of experiencing, of feeling, of self-reality combined with creative interrelations beyond itself; value is at once value for itself and for others, richness of experience united with richness of relatedness, of relations in the present and for the future— in combination and in contrast.[4] There seems little question that if this is a useful description of value (and another set of standards of value would also serve) then there has been an increase in value in the whole process as there has been a fundamental morphology of forms. As this discussion of hierarchy indicates, there are now beings who in their self-awareness and in their interrelating with others experience value for themselves, value in others, and value for others to an extent almost infinitely richer than was the case in the early organic world and certainly in the inorganic one.[5] The biologists seem inescapably to recognize this ascent of forms, and so of value, whenever they write about organisms—and yet, as soon as they do this, they deny it officially. Of course, whether that increase of value, even if admitted, is the result of chance (i.e., of random mutations) or of some kind of inner teleology or even of some form of divine providence remains at issue. If it is admitted, however, it creates a reflective problem for a purely naturalistic view of things.

These five principles (what Whitehead called "the metaphysical situation") seem to be aspects of nature and nature's processes entailed directly by what science knows of nature, though they represent inferences not always drawn by scientific accounts. Many scientific accounts are intent on an analysis that reduces their explanatory principles to the more universal and abstract terms of physics and chemistry. The "quest for certainty" can lead reflection in science, as in religion, to ignoring many facts and their implications.[6] Actually, these aspects of nature are on the way to becoming principles of ontology or of metaphysics. Because they are drawn from the inquiries of the physical sciences, they represent abstraction from the whole of experience and so, by implication, from the whole of experienced actuality. For, as we noted, they omit the subject of inquiry and of reflection on inquiry—and thus the entire "inside" of being as we experience our own being as knowers and doers. They omit the experiences of the other and so the ontological character of organic and human relations, of community, and of history. They omit the order and the possible teleology of process both outside and inside. Thus there is left the fascinating problem of how a self-maintaining system of things can be understood to embody both an order (there are no police) and an order moving into genuine novelty, much less an order moving into levels or dimensions of increasing value.

When all these omitted but crucial factors (ranges of data, one might say) are taken into account, the resulting reflection about the structure of actuality—now both nature and history, both scientific objects and scientific subjects (scientists), both scientific theory and science—becomes ontology or metaphysics, the effort to understand the structure of being qua being, of what it means for any entity at all to be. Insofar as any theologian asks what the major symbols of his or her tradition mean or imply with regard to the structure of reality and seeks to explicate as fully as he or she can that meaning (of creation, of providence, of human being—and so of nature), that theology must borrow an ontology or forge one for itself. Thus arises from theology's side the interesting problem of the relation of theology to ontology or metaphysics—as in our discussion in Part 1 the *epistemological* issues of the knowledge of science, of philosophy and of religion, and their interrelations, had already to be gone over thoroughly.

Reflection must reach this philosophical level for two reasons relevant to the present enterprise of natural theology. First, if the implications for science of this understanding of nature are to be articulated and not left to wither in a reductionist side street, science necessitates a wider metaphysical base or framework (which it already implies), if it is to be rationally and not irrationally grounded. Second, if the corresponding implications for theological construction—for our understanding of our traditional symbols in the light of our contemporary world—are to be articulated, theological reflection must include an ontological explication of its symbols, if those symbols are not to be conceived literally and "ontically" on the one hand or as empty of content on the other.

There is, however, a further reason in religious reflection for this philosophical level of discourse. If any attempt at all is to be made to show the reasonableness, the credibility, and the persuasiveness of a religious symbol in relation to ordinary experience and its data, then such a reflective structuring of all of experience—a metaphysics or ontology—is essential. Proofs of God of all sorts—strict, "hard" proofs and loose, "soft" ones; those that demonstrate,[7] those that suggest,[8] and those in between[9]—are "if–then" propositions, whatever else they may claim to be. That is, they presuppose an already articulated (or assumed) reflective structuring of all of experi-

ence, be it Platonic, Aristotelian, Newtonian, mechanistic, evolutionary–
progressive, or "process"; and then, on the basis of that "universe" as so
understood, they conclude that "God" (or whatever is here established) is
necessary or suggested to that universe. If one accepts that metaphysical
vision of things, then the proof of God probably holds; if one does not
accept that vision—or if one concludes that metaphysics is impossible—then
the proof of God as essential to the universe as so understood never gets
started. Such proofs are persuasive as well as viable when a common structuring of the world can be widely assumed; but proofs accomplish little of
what they intend (they may still instruct about what is here believed) if there
is a wide plurality of competing visions abroad in the land. The same failure
to persuade may result if—as in our case—many intellectuals suffer under
the illusion that they share in no general metaphysical vision but that through
the special sciences they can "see things as they are." If we are to develop
further an answer to what nature, as understood in modern science, might
imply about God, then we must move from the ontic (special sciences) to
the ontological. That is, we must represent the aspects of nature listed above
in more inclusive, universal form, as principles of all experience, categories
applicable to all entities, symbols that represent the "universal traits of
being"—"what it means for anything to be," as Aristotle put it, or "those
principles from which actuality never takes a holiday, that are there and
never not there."[10]

With this in mind, I here rephrase those aspects of nature as suggestions
for a possible metaphysics or ontology. Were this the beginning of an ontology rather than the end of a treatise on religion and science, I would have to
enlarge these suggested principles into a coherent and adequate articulation
of all of experience. And if I were seeking to provide a full philosophical
theology, I would have to justify such ontological principles not only in
relation to the width of experience but, even more, in relation to the
implications of relevant Christian symbols about God and God's relation to
nature, history, and human being.[11]

There are, I suggest, five fundamental ontological characteristics of all
that is in our experience—of all of finite actuality or, in theological language, all of "created reality."

1. Temporality or passage: the appearance of what is, the vanishing of
   what is, and the further appearance of what is new.
2. The definiteness and determinedness of actuality as the given: what is
   achieved in process is definite, a new unity in and for itself and so
   effective beyond itself—and (as characteristic 1 makes clear) then it
   vanishes.

3. Possibility and novelty there are genuine, relevant possibilities that have not been actual before, and then they become as actualities. One cannot understand nature as process or human existence in history as open and intentional without the category of possibility as a paradoxical aspect of "reality."[12]

4. Order as "self-maintaining": that is, order as an aspect of the nature and the behavior of actualities in passage (there are no police), spanning and so transcending the dichotomies of past and present, of achieved actuality and possibility, and of the vanishing present and the impinging future.

5. Self-determination: in actuality there is a self-constitution at each level of being, from the spontaneity evident in inorganic existence through self-direction in organic and social life to the self-choosing and autonomy of human existence. On each level given conditions (destiny) inexorably set the terms and limits for spontaneity or freedom.[13] We are never free to choose more than the possibilities inherent in the given, more than the possibilities provided by our "destinies"—we can only, as Søren Kierkegaard said, "choose ourselves."

This last ontological characteristic is known more vividly from the inside, in our experience and awareness of ourselves as subjects, of personal relations, of choices, of inquiry and reflection, and of political and historical activities. There nature—for we are nature—is known from the inside, and on that basis nature can be reinterpreted throughout its extent both in terms of self-awareness and in terms of the awareness of the other as person. The same categories of definiteness and spontaneity, of the given and open alternatives, of destiny and freedom make their appearance analogously and at different levels all around us in nature. If spirit is the result of nature and hence an illustration of nature's mystery, then these analogical signs of "spirit," in spontaneity and in self-direction, may be taken as "signs" of the ontological or metaphysical relevance of spirit as it is known in personal awareness and in personal relations.

These hints and traces of reality as a temporal becoming characterized by spirit and meaning, as well as by power and causality, are universal throughout nature. They become clearer in personal and historical experience where the dimension of moral ultimacy—as reality and as demand—is ever present.[14] The question now, however, is whether what has been said here about nature has any persuasive implications for the reality and the nature of God. Granted that this is only the dimmest of glimpses of the mystery of God, what might that mystery begin to look like?

What, then, of God in our age? Are there grounds in the preceding for speech about God or for the search for God, for confirmed commitment to God? Beyond—and through—the abstractions of the scientific understanding of nature, nature's reality has manifested itself as *power;* as spontaneity or *life;* as *order;* and also as implying a redemptive principle, a strange dialectic of sacrifice, purgation, redemption, and rebirth. In nature each of these appears to us in creaturely guise, as vulnerable and ambiguous as well as creative, as nonbeing as well as being. Each therefore represents a trace of God—a "limit question" to which, I believe, God remains the sole reasonable answer. Each leads to an ontological principle or structure, which appears to characterize all that is.

First, the power of nature is the power of existence, the power to be. Yet existence and its power are radically temporal. Existence comes, and then as quickly it goes; it is energy becoming matter, in process. It is here in the present, and then it vanishes into the past and so into nonbeing. It is, and then as quickly it is not. How, then, does the past, which immediately has vanished, at the same time so thoroughly ground the existence and shape the character of the present? How is it that the conditioning, the causing, the effecting and affecting of the present by the vanishing past happens? How is it that we can understand our common experiences of continuity and continuing presence, of causality and influence—of our being and our action from the past into the future?

Some deeper, more permanent power must exist and continue from moment to moment if this "temporal power"—this power to be over time, this power of finite existence—which is known to science, to all our common experience, and in our inner sense of ourselves, is to be possible. What is present vanishes away, and yet its effect helps to form the oncoming present; what power that does not vanish spans the gulf of past and present, given that temporality is so real and so fundamental? God is, first of all, the name for that omnipresent, ever-continuing, and so eternal power, the necessary and hence noncontingent source of contingent, temporal being. Reality as temporal and radically passing must also be reality as permanent if our experience is to be made intelligible; but the finite, vanishing realities around us have no such capacities. Therefore, as Thomas Aquinas said, some necessary being is inescapable in explaining this experienced contingency.[15]

Second, this power manifests itself originally as spontaneity and later as life. It is determined, caused, and "frozen" once it appears and becomes definite; but it is undetermined, open, as it becomes what it is to be. It exhibits jumps and unexpected turns; it faces options and alternatives that cannot be predicted. The past is fixed and set; the future is scarily but also

luringly open. This openness we experience from the inside as the inescapable pressure for decision, to choose among the options facing us in each
impinging moment coming to us from the future. In us this power, latent in
nature's spontaneity and in its capacity for the new, becomes what we term
freedom: reflection, deliberation, and decision among real alternatives. Process becomes out of the past; but in the present it constitutes itself out of
possibilities before it in its future, bringing together in present actuality
alternatives that once were only possibilities.

Events around us, when we look at them, all appear to be determined,
caused; they are, of course, in the past. Events happening inside us are open;
nature in us, facing its future, is open and not determined. Even science, as
a creative human project, requires deliberation and decision, reflection and
assent; and so, in analogous ways do all human activities and hence all of
political and historical existence. Thus for science, the future is open. Hence
it is that in both nature and history, genuine novelty is possible; the new
appears and becomes actual. Novelty and openness lie in the spontaneous
power of the present to determine itself, to be self-creative, to be a relative,
dependent, yet creative source of what is original and unique.

Neither the achieved past nor a set future can account for this spontaneous power to become, the power of each present to constitute itself—lest we
return again to determinism and lose novelty. Science is always tempted to
speak only of determinism as it looks carefully at its objects of investigation,
all of which, of course, lie as objects in the immediate past. But science as a
human project, as the creative work of human subjects, is laced with openness, with deliberation, with centered actions, with self-constituted freedom—directed at the future and its projects for the future.

God is the name for this continuing ground of freedom, of spontaneity in
nature, and of self-constitution in humans and so in history. We do not
create our freedom, our power to choose ourselves and to shape our future;
such power of self-constitution is given to us as an essential aspect of
ourselves, of being selves at all—and we cannot, try as we may, avoid it. This
human experience of *dependence* in our very freedom, a deeply religious
experience of the sacred gift of freedom, is analogously disclosed in all the
evidence of spontaneity and mutation in nature's life. This freedom or self-
constitution is, therefore, given to us from a source beyond ourselves, our
world, and our past, as is our existence itself. This source lies beyond both
the world that our choices affect and our freedom, which does not create
itself.[16] This source must include both world and freedom, both determined
past and open future, as the creative ground of each and the principle of
unity of both. This is, as Friedrich Schleiermacher argued, another sign or
pointer to God, now as the continuing ground of our freedom.

Third, this spontaneity or freedom—this openness leading to novelty—remains mysteriously within an order, an order that pervades the objective cosmos, our inner deliberating consciousness, and external history. The presence of real novelty within a dependable and calculable order and the presence of intelligible order characterizing the unexpected yet pervasive appearance of novelty are genuine "wonders," even miracles. How random spontaneity and genuine freedom can unite with continuing order is a puzzle to scientific inquiry and philosophical reflection alike, as it is to observers of history. God is, therefore, the name for that unlimited reality spanning the entire ordered past and the entire open future, uniting into an ongoing order achieved actuality, on the one hand, with the open possibilities of the novel future, on the other; uniting destiny from the past with freedom in and for the future.[17]

God is thus the unconditioned power to be[18]—yet present in each puff of existence; God is the transcendent ground of freedom[19]—yet creative in each quantum jump as in each human decision; God is the eternal source of order amid novelty, uniting the determined past with the possibilities latent in the open future.[20] Without this transcendent yet immanent principle active in all events, we face the very nest of contradictions I have outlined: a determined world outside of us, impossibly coupled with the creative mind and the shaping, self-constituting spirit of those who know and manipulate that world. Neither the determined world of material causality nor the ungrounded mind implied by science is true to our experience; this view, not reflected by experience, in which stark opposites are posed in uncoordinated juxtaposition represents on both sides the most extreme sort of abstraction and an incoherent and perilous dualism. On the grounds, then, of coherence of basic ideas and adequacy to experience, theism seems more philosophically reasonable than its far more popular alternatives.

God is only dimly known here, barely perceived and stumblingly described—as is the wonder and mystery of nature through which God is thus known. As I have demonstrated, nature is an image of God; a creaturely reality of immense creative power, order, and value; an image of the sacred and hence a finite reality or value for itself. Nature is also the instrument through which God created us and now sustains us. Nature is, for itself and for us, the medium through which God's power, life, and order are originally and universally communicated.

To the religious consciousness, however, there is more than this: more of nature, more of us, and especially more of God. God is more deeply, clearly, and truly known (as is appropriate) in our personal and communal existence; and we also are more deeply and clearly known there. There God is more vividly to be known as the creative power of our own existence in

time, the source of the freedom that makes us ourselves, the ground therefore of our responsibility that makes us persons, and so as the ordering or
moral principle of our temporal and yet free existence. And finally, central
to all we know of God, God is now known as redemptive love, bringing us
back to unity again. Here lies the center of our Christian message: in
conscience, law, promise, prophetic judgment, incarnation, teachings, atonement, and resurrection. But it is the same God who can, by eyes that search
there, be seen dimly but pervasively in the wonders of nature. To know God
truly is to know God's presence also in the power, the life, the order, and
the redemptive unity of nature. Correspondingly, to know nature truly is to
know its mystery, its depth, and its ultimate value—it is to know nature as
an image of the sacred, a visible sign of an invisible grace.

Notes

CHAPTER 1
ISSUES OF LANGUAGE AND TRUTH

1. During the 1930s and 1940s, in Japan, Germany, and the Soviet Union, an impressive scientific establishment (faculties, defense research, industrial research) supported and aided a national effort motivated and directed by the religion of Shintoism and the ideologies of Nazism and Marxism. In each case, the ideology manifested a religious character, labeled opposing views as heresy, and required assent and obedience to its own orthodoxy from all its adherents. The cooperation between advanced technology and science, on the one hand, and these quasi-religions, on the other, was not only unexpected to our post-Enlightenment culture—which held science to be like a detergent, antithetical to religious faith—but also scary. For a further discussion of these sorts of unexpected cooperation, see Langdon Gilkey, *Creationism on Trial: Evolution and God at Little Rock* (Minneapolis: Winston, 1985), chap. 6.

2. For a definition and discussion of the concept of "establishment" in relation to contemporary science, see Gilkey, *Creationism,* 162–71, 173–90.

3. For a further discussion of the "religious" as an aspect of any given culture (e.g., its political ideology, its nationalism), as opposed to a "religion," a particular tradition with beliefs, rites, ceremonies (e.g., Judaism, Christianity, Buddhism), see Gilkey, *Creationism,* 171–73, 190–208; and Langdon Gilkey, *Society and the Sacred* (New York: Crossroad, 1981), chaps. 2, 7, and 8.

4. For a more thorough account of creation science as at once a pseudo-science and a faulty theology, cf. Gilkey, *Creationism,* the account of my participation as a witness in the trial at Little Rock.

5. This remark, not at all unusual among scientists, was made to me in 1990 by Carl Sagan, a most charming as well as intelligent spokesperson of important science. This view is reminiscent of John Locke's statement concerning "lovers of truth," echoing clearly the rationalism of the Enlightenment: "How a man may know whether he be so in earnest, is worth inquiry . . . the not entertaining any proposition with greater assurance, than the proofs it is built upon will warrant. Whoever goes beyond this measure of assent, it is plain, receives not truth in the love of it; loves not truth for truth's sake, but for some other end" (*Essay Concerning Understanding*, in E. A. Burtt, *The English Philosophers from Bacon to Mill* [New York: Modern Library, 1939], p. 396). In Locke's case, this view included all sorts of "demonstrations" besides scientific ones (e.g., moral and religious propositions), as the essay makes plain; for Sagan, it has been

reduced to validated (or at least, not falsified) hypotheses of empirical "science"—a difference between rationalism and positivism.

6. "The Cosmos is all that is or ever was or ever will be" is the first sentence of Carl Sagan's *Cosmos* (New York: Ballantine, 1980), p. 1.

7. John D. Barrow and Frank J. Tipler, *The Anthropic Cosmological Principle* (Oxford: Clarendon, 1986), pp. 138–39.

8. Quoted with approval from Steven Weinberg, *The First Three Minutes*, by Heinz R. Pagels in his enthralling description of "the beginning" in *Perfect Symmetry* (New York: Bantam, 1986), p. 383.

9. The claim that the reality that the natural sciences know, as they know it, is all of reality is what most persons in the humanistic disciplines know as reductionism, that is, the reduction of reality to the conclusions of science. This is the way that this word or concept is used in this volume. It is, however, helpful to recall that for most scientists the word has another (albeit analogical) meaning, namely, the reduction of all other sciences—chemistry, biology, geology, astronomy, psychology, and so forth—to physics. This issue is frequently debated in contemporary science (as in Barrow and Tipler, *Anthropic Cosmological Principle*); the larger and far more important humanistic version of reductionism is not. Presumably, as in Sagan's case, that larger reductionism is assumed to be a legitimate, even an indisputable claim.

10. Note Imre Lakatos's insistence that an "objective" science requires the distinction (a metaphysical distinction?) between what Gottlob Frege and Karl Popper call "three worlds": the physical world, the world of consciousness, and the "Platonic" world of objective spirit, the world of ideas (*Mathematics, Science and Epistemology*, ed. J. Worral and G. Currie [Cambridge: Cambridge University Press, 1978], pp. 108, 226). The second and third worlds are denied by the positivists to be aspects of reality. If they are not part of reality, one is left with the intriguing metaphysical problem of conceiving coherently and in the light of experience the mode of the unity of the three. Perhaps René Descartes was not as far off as is modern positivistic naturalism (or as Descartes's frequent humanistic critics insist).

11. Alfred North Whitehead, *Science and the Modern World* (New York: Macmillan, 1925), p. 72.

CHAPTER 2
CHANGES IN TWO WAYS OF KNOWING

1. This is a familiar theme for students of Scripture, but no one has stated it more forcefully than G. E. Wright, who declares not only that Christian confession and theology are essentially narration but that, as opposed to ancient myth with its mythical time, Christian narration is a story of events in actual past history: "Christianity has always taught that in a real history of what once

happened in the ancient world, God came and revealed himself. Hence the Bible presents factual history in which is seen the work of the living God" (G. Ernest Wright and Reginald H. Fuller, *The Book of the Acts of God* [Garden City, N.Y.: Doubleday, 1957], p. 16). He adds: "In other words, when biblical man confessed his faith, he did so by telling the story of his past, interpreted by his faith. He learned to present his faith in the form of history" (p. 21).

Christian theologians long built most of their concepts concerning human nature and its powers, possibilities, and problems around discussions of the figure of Adam. In developing these doctrines, they merged philosophical, religious, and factual elements without question and probably without conscious awareness. Unique to this Christian theological tradition is the way that ontological structures characteristic of humanity are in many cases affirmed to be rooted in historical or "ontic" events and thus treated merely as historical fact. Irenaeus (born ca. 130 C.E.) in the following shows a sensitive but patient literalism: "And he [Adam] would no doubt have retained this clothing [scratchy fig leaves] . . . if God . . . had not clothed them with tunics of skins instead of fig-leaves. For this purpose, too, He interrogated them, that the blame might light upon the woman; and again, He interrogates her, that she might convey the blame to the serpent . . . wherefore also He drove him out of Paradise, and removed him from the tree of Life, not because He envied him the tree of life . . . but because He pitied him [and did not desire] that he should continue a sinner forever, nor that the sin which surrounded him should be immortal, and evil interminable and irremediable. But He set a bound to his [state of] sin, by interposing death, and thus causing sin to cease . . . so that man, ceasing at length to live in sin, and dying to it, might begin to live to God" (*Against Heresies* 3.23.5–6; in *The Ante-Nicene Fathers*, ed. Alexander Roberts and James Donaldson [Grand Rapids: Eerdmans, 1950], 1:457).

Augustine offered a confident statement as to how and in what numbers the human race had its origin: "Now that we have solved as well as we could, this very difficult question about the eternal God creating new things, without any novelty of will, it is easy to see how much better it is that God was pleased to produce the human race from the one individual whom He created, than if He had originated it in several men. . . . And therefore God created only one single man, not, certainly, that he might be a solitary, bereft of all society, but that by this means the unity of society and the bond of concord might be more effectually commended to him, men being bound together not only by similarity of nature, but by family affection" (*The City of God* 12.21; in *Basic Writings of St. Augustine*, ed. Whitney J. Oates [New York: Random House, 1948] 2:203–4).

Thomas Aquinas's discussion of the origin of the world and the origin of man includes symbolic, philosophical, and factual elements, the last of these in principle based on revelation (see *Summa Theologica* 1.46.2); the following quotation, dealing with the "when" of the creation of the soul of Adam, is typical: "Therefore, if we admit the opinion of Augustine about the work of the six days, we may say that the human soul preceded in the work of the six days according to a certain generic likeness, so far as it has intellectual nature in common with the angels; but it was itself created at the same time as the body. According to other saints, however, both the body and the soul of the first man were produced in the work of the six days" (*Summa Theologica* 1.90.4; cf. also 1.91–102; in *Basic Writings of St. Thomas Aquinas*, ed. Anton C. Pegis [New York: Random House, 1944], 1:869). And John Calvin assumes the same fundamental factuality to his theological account of the beginning of the human race (note his typically existential concern and his surprising—in comparison to Thomas— dualistic viewpoint): "And first let it be understood, that, by his being made of earth and clay, a restraint was laid upon pride; since nothing is more absurd than for creatures to glory in their excellence, who not only inhabit a cottage of clay, but who are themselves composed partly of dirt and dust and ashes. But as God not only deigned to animate the earthen vessel, but chose to make it the residence of an immortal spirit, Adam might justly glory in so great an instance of the liberality of his Maker.

"That man consists of soul and body, ought not to be controverted. By the 'soul' I understand an immortal, yet created essence, which is the nobler part of him" (John Calvin, *Institutes of the Christian Religion*, trans. John Allen [Philadelphia: Presbyterian Board of Christian Education, 1930], 1:203).

2. The surprising exception is Karl Rahner, who, even as late as 1961, continued to assume that certain "facts" could be communicated by revelation and were thus dogmatically certain; see his article "Theological Reflexions on Monogenism," in idem, *Theological Investigations*, trans. Cornelius Ernst (London: Darton, Longman & Todd, 1961), 1:229–96. In this article, Rahner tries to assess whether the doctrine that the human race begins with one man and one pair is (1) directly probable, certain, absolutely indispensable in tradition, in Scripture, in encyclicals, and so on and (2) indirectly implied in other directly binding doctrines (e.g., that of original sin). In the process, he enunciates the following interesting principle: "It is utterly unacceptable from the viewpoint of Catholic theology to regard some object (or the inquiry into it) as dogmatically or theologically irrelevant just because it is also to be found in the field of the profane sciences or has such a scientific aspect or consequence" (p. 274). That is, if it has on its own grounds good reasons for asserting a matter of fact, dogmatic theology must regard itself as able and bound so to do. Thus on the same ground as that propounded by Augustine (see n. 1, above), Rahner concludes that there was in fact one pair from which the human race has descended: "Scripture knows of such a common situation of salvation and ruin only in so far as men are of one stock" (p. 279). His main argument, however, is that original sin, as a necessary doctrine of Christianity, is "inconceivable" unless it concerns the act of one parental pair who are the sole progenitors for all

humans, i.e., that this doctrine no longer will rationally explain sin (as well as symbolize it) if it does not refer, first, to a historical act and, second, to an act of a particular and so single pair, and if it is not the act of the original pair (pp. 279–84). In all of this Rahner shows that on the question of whether we can assert matters of fact on dogmatic grounds he was at this stage "premodern" and thus did not yet reflect the immense pressures of modernity that are cited herein. Subsequently, however, he modified this position and has in fact been followed in it by no important "liberal" Catholic theologians.

3. An earlier presentation of this thesis appeared in Langdon Gilkey, *Religion and the Scientific Future* (New York: Harper & Row, 1969), chap. 1 (reissued in 1981 by Mercer University Press).

4. As a stunning example of the perpetuation into recent times (and in surprising places) of the identity of biblical truth with cosmological and historical facts, cf. the "world" (now "lost") of Thomas Jefferson and his circle of scientists at the end of the eighteenth century, a world ironically almost identical with that of the contemporary Creationists: that is, this world was only six thousand years or so old, it was characterized by stable and unchanging astronomical and geological structures, and it contained permanent species going right back to the beginning. Jefferson was no biblicist; but the assumption that such cosmological and historical "facts" could be provided for us authoritatively in Scripture held among most educated people well into the early part of the nineteenth century. Cf. Daniel J. Borstin, *The Lost World of Thomas Jefferson* (1948; reprint, Chicago: University of Chicago Press, 1981). Another surprising example of the authority of Scripture with regard to historical facts among leading members of the Enlightenment is this footnote from Immanuel Kant: "In any case, the sacred books of this people [the Jews] will doubtless also be preserved and will continue to possess value for scholarship if not for the benefit of religion: since the history of no other people dates back, with some color of credibility, so far as this does into epochs of antiquity (even to the beginning of the world) in which all secular history known to us can be arranged" (*Religion within the Limits of Reason Alone*, trans. T. M. Green and H. H. Hudson [New York: Harper Torchbooks, 1934], p. 154).

Concerning the happy relation of science and religion, John C. Greene quotes John Ray (1627–1705), the eminent biologist, as follows: "Science and religion were in perfect accord, 'The number of species being in nature certain and determinant, as is generally acknowledged by philosophers, and might be proved also by divine authority, God having finished His works of creation, that is, consummated the number of species in six days.'" Commenting on Carolus Linnaeus (1707–1778), another past founder of biology, Greene says, "In his *Philosophia botanica* he defined species as primordial types created by divine wisdom and perpetuated by generation from the beginning to the end of the world" (*The Death of Adam* [Ames: Iowa State University Press, 1959], pp. 131–

33). For the accord of the biblical view of time with early geology, cf. Charles Gillespie, *Genesis and Geology* (New York: Harper Torchbooks, 1959), esp. chap. 1 and pp. 41–43.

5. Gillespie, *Genesis*, pp. 46, 48. For the horror with which most early geologists regarded Hutton's abandonment of the literal text of Genesis as asserting "scientific facts," cf. Gillespie's account (chap. 3) of the "Neptunist" theories of Richard Kerwan, president of the Irish Royal Society (1799–1819), and Jean André Deluc (ca. 1740–1809).

6. Ibid., pp. 46–49 and, with regard to Charles Lyell's clarification of this, pp. 125–31. It is interesting as a note on the fallibility of even the most "infallible" science that many of the physicists in the nineteenth century refused to grant to Lyell, and later to Darwin, the sort of duration of the cosmos that developments in both geology and biology seemed to require. Cf. Loren Eiseley, *Darwin's Century* (Garden City, N.Y.: Doubleday, 1958), chap. 9; and Greene, *Death of Adam*, p. 296.

7. For a full account of these developments in paleontology, cf. Greene, *Death of Adam*, chap. 4. The different viewpoints elicited by the sight of these bones are well illustrated in the quotations that head Greene's chapter: "Such is the economy of nature that no instance can be produced of her having permitted any one race of her animals to become extinct; of her having formed any link in her great works so weak as to be broken" (Thomas Jefferson, 1785); "Therefore, we are forced to submit to the concurring facts as the voice of God—the bones exist, the animals do not!" (Rembrandt Peale, 1803).

8. Friedrich Schleiermacher, *On Religion: Speeches to Its Cultured Despisers*, trans. Richard Crouter (Cambridge: Cambridge University Press, 1988).

9. Ibid.; and idem, *The Christian Faith*, trans. H. R. MacIntosh and J. S. Stewart (1825; reprint, Edinburgh: T. & T Clark, 1948), esp. secs. 15, 30, 32.

10. Schleiermacher, *The Christian Faith*, sec. 19: "Dogmatic Theology is the science which systematizes the doctrine prevalent in the Christian Church at a given time."

11. Cf., e.g., Harry Emerson Fosdick, *Guide to the Understanding of the Bible*; and Bernard Anderson, *Understanding the Old Testament* (Englewood Cliffs, N.J.: Prentice Hall, 1975).

12. E.g., Walter Eichordt, *Theology of the Old Testament*, 2 vols. (Philadelphia: Westminster, 1961–1967). See also Gerhard von Rad, *Old Testament Theology*, 2 vols. (New York: Harper & Row, 1962–1966): "The Old Testament writings confine themselves to representing Yahveh's relation to Israel and the world in only one aspect, namely as a continuing divine activity in history" (1:106).

13. E.g., Karl Barth, *Church Dogmatics: The Doctrine of the Word of God*, trans. G. T. Thomson (Edinburgh: T. & T. Clark, 1936), vol. 1, part 1, secs. 4 and 5; part 2, sec. 19 (esp. pp. 508–12); cf. also Emil Brunner, *The Divine Human Encounter*, trans. A. W. Loos (Philadelphia: Westminster, 1943), chaps. 1 and 2.

14. Schleiermacher, *The Christian Faith*, sec. 38.

15. I refer here to my first work, *Maker of Heaven and Earth*, which presented precisely the symbolic interpretation here described but omitted—to my present surprise and chagrin—any discussion of the *process* of creation implied in that symbolic understanding, i.e., any articulation of the immanent working of God through the developing process. In fact, I have discovered in that volume only one paragraph that discusses that obvious and necessary immanence (if one holds a developmental view of cosmic process). Most of the book concerns the implications of the symbol of creation for human existence, for history, for the methods of science, and for the other symbols of Christian doctrine: incarnation, atonement, and redemption.

16. This example is in the *Bridgewater Treatises*, a series of treatises by scientists in the first half of the nineteenth century, designed to demonstrate the "power, wisdom and goodness of God" through evidence from each of the main branches of science. Cf. Gillespie, *Genesis*, pp. 208–16.

17. Henry Morris, ed., *Scientific Creationism* (San Diego: Creation-Life Publishers, 1978), pp. 218–20, 229–30; idem, *The Bible Has the Answer* (San Diego: Creation-Life Publishers, 1975), pp. 92, 95, 100; and Duane Gish, *Evolution? The Fossils Say No!* (San Diego: Creation-Life Publishers, 1977).

18. Cf., as an early example, Reinhold Niebuhr, *Beyond Tragedy* (New York: Scribner's, 1936), chaps. 1 and 2; and idem, *Nature and Destiny of Man* (New York: Scribner's, 1941), chaps. 1, 5, 6, and 7; Emil Brunner, *Man in Revolt*, trans. Olive Wyon (1937; reprint, Philadelphia: Westminster, 1947); main sec. 1; Paul Tillich, *Systematic Theology* (Chicago: University of Chicago Press, 1951, 1957), vol. 1, part 2.b 1–3, esp. p. 252; vol. 2, part 3.1.b, esp. p. 29.

19. Cf. n. 18, above; and Paul Ricoeur, *The Symbolism of Evil*, trans. E. Buchanon (New York: Harper & Row, 1967), esp. Introduction and part 2.

20. For vigorous insistence that the biological categories of *random* mutations and *natural* selection exclude in principle any "further" teleological principle working through or behind these natural factors, cf. Stephen J. Gould, *The Panda's Thumb* (New York: Norton, 1980), secs. 1 and 2; idem, *Hen's Teeth and Horse's Toes* (New York: Norton, 1983), secs. 1 and 3; Michael Ruse, *Philosophy of Biology Today* (New York: SUNY Press, 1988), chaps. 5 and 8; Richard Dawkins, *The Blind Watchmaker* (New York: Norton, 1986).

21. Cf. esp. Holmes Rolston III, *Science and Religion* (New York: Random House, 1987), chap. 3, esp. pp. 119–24.

22. Cf. the fascinating conversations (1920–1922) between Wolfgang Pauli, Niels Bohr, and Werner Heisenberg about the difficulty, not to say impossibility, of expressing conceptually (linguistically) the new physics they were developing, recorded in Werner Heisenberg, *Physics and Beyond*, trans. A. J. Pomerans (New York: Harper Torchbooks, 1971), chap. 3, esp. pp. 36–37, 40–41.

23. A colleague, Professor Wendy Doniger, and I had an interesting experi-

ence some years ago with the physics department at the University of Chicago. In possession of a grant to study the problem of the "comprehensibility of physics" by the "ordinary" layperson, the department had invited about thirty faculty colleagues—"who are obviously intelligent, but know nothing of physics," as they assured us—to listen to three introductory lectures on physics and then to tell them why the concepts in those lectures were, as reputed, "so difficult." The reason was plain enough to Wendy and to me, both students of religion and religious speech—though, to our surprise, it was not at all plain to members of other faculties. The reason was that the language of contemporary physics was wildly, even violently *analogical*: e.g., "fields," "jumps," "waves," as well as the endlessly frustrating example of the moving train in the station. This language moves from ordinary experience to express relations far beyond that experience; and not knowing the mathematics, the lay listener or reader doesn't know how to "anchor" the analogy, how to translate the "metaphors," and how thereby to give intelligible meaning "to the myth." Anyone used to these problems in religious discourse, where ordinary language also is used to express what transcends ordinary experience, recognizes these difficulties at once. I was interested that my friends in the physics department, most grateful for our comments, admitted that they had never before thought of their language as analogical.

24. Rolston, *Science and Religion*, pp. 59, 61–63.

25. Cf. the very helpful description of "classical" philosophy of science in Harold I. Brown, *Perception, Theory and Commitment* (Chicago: University of Chicago Press, 1979), part 1. For examples of such an understanding of science, cf. Rudolf Carnap, *Philosophical Foundations of Physics* (New York: Basic Books, 1966); Herbert Feigl and May Brodbeck, eds., *Readings in the Philosophy of Science* (New York: Century-Crofts, 1953); Morris Cohen and Ernst Nagel, *An Introduction to Logic and the Scientific Method* (London: Routledge & Kegan Paul, 1949); Ernst Nagel, *The Structure of Science* (New York: Harcourt, Brace & World, 1961); Karl Popper, *The Logic of Scientific Discovery* (New York: Harper & Row, 1959); Hans Reichenbach, *Experience and Prediction* (Chicago: University of Chicago Press, 1938); Israel Scheffler, *The Anatomy of Inquiry* (Indianapolis: Bobbs-Merrill, 1963); and idem, *Science and Subjectivity* (Indianapolis: Bobbs-Merrill, 1967).

26. E. A. Burtt, *The Metaphysical Foundations of Modern Science* (Garden City, N.Y.: Doubleday, 1954); R. G. Collingwood, *The Idea of Nature* (Oxford: Oxford University Press, 1945), esp. part 3; idem, *An Essay on Metaphysics* (Oxford: Oxford University Press, 1940), esp. part 3c; Herbert Butterfield, *The Origins of Modern Science*, rev. ed. (New York: Free Press, 1957); Thomas S. Kuhn, *The Structure of Scientific Revolutions* (Chicago: University of Chicago Press, 1962); cf. also A. N. Whitehead, *Science and the Modern World* (New York: Macmillan, 1925); chaps. 3–6.

27. Michael Polanyi, *Personal Knowledge* (New York: Harper & Row, 1964);

idem, *The Tacit Dimension* (Garden City, N.Y.: Doubleday, 1957); idem, *Knowing and Being*, ed. Marjorie Grene (Chicago: University of Chicago Press, 1969); N. R. Hanson, *Patterns of Discovery* (Cambridge: Cambridge University Press, 1958); idem, *Observation and Exploration* (New York: Harper & Row, 1971); Bernard Lonergan, *Insight* (London: Longmans, 1964); Paul Feyerabend, *Against Method* (London: New Left Books, 1975); idem, *Realism, Rationalism and Scientific Method: Philosophical Papers* (Cambridge: Cambridge University Press, 1985), vols. 1 and 2; Stephen Toulmin, *The Philosophy of Science* (New York: Harper & Row, 1953); idem, *Foresight and Understanding* (New York: Harper & Brothers, 1965); idem, *Human Understanding* (Princeton, N.J.: Princeton University Press, 1972); cf. also Richard J. Bernstein, *Beyond Objectivism and Relativism* (Philadelphia: University of Pennsylvania Press, 1983), esp. parts 1 and 2.

28. Cf. Imre Lakatos's interesting critique of this view, namely, that an emphasis on the subject of knowing, especially on the necessity of preunderstanding, makes science an elitist operation, dependent on the correct "conditioning" of the knower in order that the knower know. Thus the understanding of science becomes a matter of psychology, social psychology, and sociology (he could well have added history—but that, of course, is not authentic "science"), and science loses both its objectivity and its independence. Why training and expertise (preunderstanding) and not mathematics create "elitism" is not clear to me; nor is it clear why the scientific community and its conclusions, alone among intellectual and spiritual communities, should *not* be understood also in terms of psychology and sociology and history—certainly religion and theology are so understood! Cf. Imre Lakatos, *Mathematics, Science and Epistemology*, ed. John Worral and Gregory Currie (Cambridge: Cambridge University Press, 1978), 112ff.

29. Polanyi, *Personal Knowledge*, esp. chaps. 5–8, 10.

30. Ibid., pp. 204ff.

31. The humiliation of Dr. Richard Ballantine, Nobel laureate and recently resigned president of Rockefeller University, is merely the latest example of the ease with which brilliant and virtuous scientists can be "lured" into negligence, falsification, and ultimately a disingenuous cover-up by all the temptations of scientific power and wealth.

32. Although they view many important issues differently, Thomas Kuhn and Stephen Toulmin agree that each "epoch" or "stage" of scientific inquiry is dominated by a particular understanding of order and that those forms of order determine what are or are not relevant data, what sorts of explanation are possible, and what sorts of demonstration are required. Cf. Kuhn's category of "paradigm," which defines each period of science, and Toulmin's similar "forms of order." Kuhn, *Scientific Revolutions*, chaps. 3, 9, and 10; and Toulmin, *Foresight*, chaps. 3 and 4.

33. As the subsequent discussion makes clear, I am neither a Kantian nor

interested in defending Kant's particular epistemology. Insofar as Kant represented a "critical realist" position, however, this volume shares that viewpoint with him. By "critical realism" is meant the view that experience and knowing are a response to an external world but also a response in human signs, symbols, categories, i.e., in human language.

34. Rolston, *Science and Religion*, p. 66.

CHAPTER 3
THE NONSCIENTIFIC BASES OF SCIENCE

1. "Prehension" is A. N. Whitehead's word for (1) this most fundamental of relations, one of "feeling" or "experiencing," and (2) a relation that is also the basis of cognition, i.e., our awareness of the fundamental structures of actuality: "Prehension is a felt relation but one not yet, so to speak, a conscious relation" (A. N. Whitehead, *Process and Reality* [New York: Macmillan, 1929], pp. 35–37; cf. esp. chap. 6 and part 3). Gottfried Leibniz used the word *apperception* for an analogous concept. Two factors are important here: (1) an awareness that is not yet explicit is nevertheless basic to knowing (to use Michael Polanyi's word, *tacit*); and (2) to describe such an awareness we must resort to an analogical use of language. As Whitehead also remarks, our ordinary language is based on our ordinary experience of objects; hence to express more fundamental structures than ontic objects (or even atoms), we need analogies: "We habitually observe by the method of difference. Sometimes we see an elephant, sometimes we do not. . . . The metaphysical first principles never fail of exemplification. We can never catch the actual world taking a holiday from their sway" (pp. 6–7).

2. David Hume, *An Enquiry Concerning Human Understanding*, secs. 4–7, in *Enquiries Concerning Human Understanding and Concerning the Principles of Morals*, ed., L. A. Selby-Bigge, rev. P. H. Nidditch (Oxford: Clarendon Press, 1975). But see Whitehead's reply to (refutation of?) Hume in A. N. Whitehead, *Adventures of Ideas* (New York: Macmillan, 1933), pp. 232–35.

3. This is the point made clearly and forcefully by Bernard Lonergan in *Insight* (London: Longmans, 1964): "By consciousness we shall mean that there is an awareness immanent in cognitional acts . . . cognitional process is not merely a procession of contents but also a succession of acts. . . . Seeing . . . is a response that consists in becoming aware of color and shape. . . . But one cannot deny that, within the cognitional act as it occurs, there is a factor or element or component over and above its content, and that this factor is what differentiates cognitional acts from unconscious occurrences" (pp. 320–21).

4. For Paul Tillich, the self becomes a self (i.e., spirit) in the moral act, i.e., in the act where the self recognizes and assents to moral norms "over" the self. In turn, this recognition of the norm and the self's obligation to the norm itself arises in community, in the encounter of the self with the other: "Personal life

emerges in the encounter of person with person and in no other way." In this sense, human participation in community, assent to its standards and goals, and cooperation in its endeavors arise in personal interaction, a moral interaction of I and Thou in association with one another and obligation to one another. See Paul Tillich, *Systematic Theology* (Chicago: University of Chicago Press, 1963), 3:40–41. For further elaboration of this point, cf. Langdon Gilkey, *Gilkey on Tillich* (New York: Crossroad, 1989), pp. 160–64. For a quite different mode of expressing this same identification of personal relatedness, community, and morality, cf. Emanuel Levinas, *Totalité et Infinité* (The Hague: Nijhoff, 1968), sec. 1, a and b; sec. 3, b and c; cf. also Michael Polanyi, *Personal Knowledge* (New York: Harper & Row, 1964).

5. There are many stirring passages in Whitehead on this faith in order, "necessary to civilized life": e.g., "That we fail to find in experience any elements intrinsically incapable of exhibition as examples of general theory is the hope of rationalism. This hope is not a metaphysical premise. It is the faith which forms the motive for the pursuit of all sciences alike, including metaphysics" (*Process and Reality*, p. 67). Cf. also A. N. Whitehead, *Science and the Modern World* (New York: Macmillan, 1925), pp. 26–27.

6. In terms of the "three worlds" discriminated by Imre Lakatos's "demarcationism," these models of science belong not in the first "physical" world or even in the second "psychological" world but in the third "world of ideas"; see Imre Lakatos, *Mathematics, Science and Epistemology*, ed. John Worral and Gregory Currie (Cambridge: Cambridge University Press, 1978), pp. 108–226.

7. It was the conception—and the accompanying excitement—of an invariant, certain, even absolute form of knowledge, unsullied by the vagaries of sense and change, that led first to the conception of "spirit" or "soul" in Greek philosophy and of an order within "inwardness" as crucial to human fulfillment, namely, *arete*. One sees this development first in Plato's dialogues, e.g., *Gorgias*, *Theaetetus*, and *Meno*, where knowledge of virtue is modeled on medicine and mathematics and is a "spiritual" knowledge of the eternal forms of things. This development culminates in Aristotle where real knowledge—of the changeless form of any substance—is an act of the agent or active intellect that abstracts the pure form from its sensible, material embodiment. Usually, inwardness and soul are associated with religious existence, with ethics, and with the hope for immortality; and, to be sure, one root of the Platonic concept was certainly the Orphic tradition. But the other root of the concept of a separable soul was the gradual development of mathematical and medical (scientific) understanding, an understanding, it was assumed, of changeless and universal forms and thus a spiritual act and power of which only a purely immaterial principle was thought to be capable. Cf. the Platonic dialogues *Protagoras*, *Meno*, *Gorgias*, and *Theaetetus*; and Aristotle, *De Anima* 3. 3–7 (where Aristotle shows the necessity of an active intellect as part of the soul, if knowledge is to be possible). Cf. also

Werner Jaeger, *Paideia*, trans. G. Highet (New York: Oxford University Press, 1943), vol. 2, chap. 7; and idem, *Aristotle*, trans. T. R. Robinson (Oxford: Oxford University Press, 1948), esp. chap 8. For the final Hellenistic development of this tradition, cf. Plotinus, *The Enneads*.

CHAPTER 4
WHATEVER HAPPENED TO IMMANUEL KANT?

1. The cosmologies include John D. Barrow and Frank J. Tipler, *The Anthropic Cosmological Principle* (Oxford: Clarendon, 1986); Richard Dawkins, *The Blind Watchmaker* (New York: Norton, 1986); Loren Eiseley, *The Immense Journey* (New York: Vintage, 1957)—this is not an example in this discussion; Heinz Pagels, *Perfect Symmetry* (New York: Bantam, 1986); Carl Sagan, *Cosmos* (New York: Ballantine, 1980); and Steven Weinberg, *The First Three Minutes* (New York: Basic Books, 1977).

2. For examples of such critiques, cf. Langdon Gilkey, *Religion and the Scientific Future* (New York: Harper & Row, 1969), chap 3; idem, *Society and the Sacred* (New York: Crossroad, 1981), chaps. 6–8; idem, *Creationism on Trial: Evolution and God at Little Rock* (Minneapolis: Winston, 1985), esp. chap. 7.

3. Cf., for discussion of these changes, Harold I. Brown, *Perception, Theory and Commitment* (Chicago: University of Chicago Press, 1979); N. R. Hanson, *Patterns of Discovery* (Cambridge: Cambridge University Press, 1958); Thomas S. Kuhn, *The Structure of Scientific Revolutions* (Chicago: University of Chicago Press, 1962); Michael Polanyi, *Personal Knowledge* (New York: Harper & Row, 1958); Stephen Toulmin, *The Philosophy of Science* (New York: Harper & Row, 1953); and idem, *Foresight and Understanding* (New York: Harper & Brothers, 1961). For further philosophical discussion, cf. Richard Bernstein, *Beyond Objectivism and Relativism* (Philadelphia: University of Pennsylvania Press, 1983); Richard Rorty, *Philosophy and the Mirror of Nature* (Princeton, N. J.: Princeton University Press, 1980), esp. chaps. 7 and 8; Bernard Lonergan, *Insight* (London: Longmans, 1964); and Mary Gerhart and Allan Russell, *Metaphoric Process* (Fort Worth: Texas Christian University Press, 1984). For a strong defense of the objectivist position, cf. Israel Scheffler, *Science and Subjectivity* (Indianapolis: Bobbs-Merrill, 1967); and Ernst Nagel, *The Structure of Science* (New York: Harcourt, Brace & World, 1961).

4. A. N. Whitehead, *Science and the Modern World* (New York: Macmillan, 1925), pp. 72ff.; and idem, *Process and Reality* (New York: Macmillan, 1929), p. 11.

5. Pagels, *Perfect Symmetry*, pp. 10, 367–73.

6. Cf. e.g., Werner Heisenberg, *Physics and Beyond*, trans. A. J. Pomerans (New York: Harper Torchbooks, 1971), esp. chaps. 3, 10, and 11.

7. Cf. R. G. Collingwood, *The Idea of Nature* (Oxford: Oxford University Press, 1945), esp. Introduction: idem, *An Essay on Metaphysics* (Oxford: Oxford

University Press, 1940); Whitehead, *Science and the Modern World*, chaps. 1, 4, 5, 9, 12; idem, *Adventures of Ideas* (New York: Macmillan, 1933), pp. 150, 182–87; idem, *Function of Reason* (Princeton, N. J.: Princeton University Press, 1929), p. 57; idem, *Process and Reality*, pp. 500–502; idem, *Modes of Thought* (Cambridge: Cambridge University Press, 1938), pp. 145–46.

8. Barrow and Tipler, *Anthropic Cosmological Principle*, pp. 15 and 55.

9. Pagels, *Perfect Symmetry*, pp. 35ff.

10. As Brown implies, there seem to be no humans at work in this understanding of science: first, in shaping or constructing the perceptions on which scientific facts are dependent, in organizing the schemes of order within which they become facts, and in envisioning the mystery of existence in terms of the underlying assumptions about the whole that make inquiry possible; and second, in following experienced "hunches" about possible answers, in acknowledging anomalies, in recognizing events of falsification and relative verification, and in seeing through educated guesses the fruitfulness of hypotheses. Cf. Brown, *Perception*, chaps. 1, 6, 7, 9; and esp. cf. Polanyi, *Personal Knowledge*.

11. E. A. Burtt, *The Metaphysical Foundations of Modern Science* (Garden City, N.Y.: Doubleday, 1954), chap. 3.

12. Barrow and Tipler, *Anthropic Cosmological Principle*, p. 123. As an explanation of the grounds of the hostility referred to, this quotation leaves much to be desired. And if Whitehead is right in insisting that a confidence in order is requisite to science, then all scientific advances are in debt to a cosmic principle of order—and our confidence in it—if not to a more particular, "valuational" interpretation of that principle. Cf. Whitehead, *Process and Reality*, pp. 16 and 21.

13. Barrow and Tipler, *Anthropic Cosmological Principle*, p. 183. Clearly, there is lacking here any sense of the different status of arguments concerning the foundations or presuppositions (epistemological and metaphysical) of science from the status of arguments in science. There is also no consciousness of the fact that any foundation of empirical science (any relevant metaphysical principle) will be consistent with any scientific result, i.e., any proposition developed under the assumption of that principle.

14. Barrow and Tipler, *Anthropic Cosmological Principle*, pp. 138–39.

15. One of the clearest examples of this realism and of its anthropocentric implications is in current scientific speculation about other life in the universe. Whether the presence of such life is probable or not I do not know; I hope it is. Nevertheless, there are many assumptions in this area that are, surprisingly, taken for granted: e.g., that such life is probable (it having arisen in our case); that if present, it will have "advanced" from primitive and archaic levels to the scientific and technical level (as it did in our case); and hence that it will, if older, be more advanced in "scientific and technological matters." A "cosmic law of development"—of galaxies, of solar systems, of life, and then of civilization toward a technological civilization—seems to be here assumed. There is then

the even more surprising assumption that "their" science and mathematics will be the same as ours, if a little further along the same road. The reason for this astounding similarity (nothing else may be the same, as Sagan says) is that "the same laws of the universe surround them as us," and hence their understanding of these laws will be similar. Presupposed here is an amazing isomorphism between nature and all so-called laws; i.e., our scientific understanding of these patterns and that of any other "intellectual" life in the cosmos. Cf. Carl Sagan, *The Cosmic Connection* (New York: Doubleday, 1973), pp. 215–29; and Marguerite Poynter and Michael Klein, *Cosmic Quest* (New York: Atheneum, 1984), pp. 49, 65–76.

16. Sagan, *Cosmos*, p. 1.

17. Dawkins, *Blind Watchmaker*, pp. 4–5.

18. Pagels, *Perfect Symmetry*, p. 383.

19. After his retirement, distinguished astronomer Harlow Shapley lectured at many universities, including Vanderbilt, where I heard him. The purpose of his lecture, he said, was to proclaim the "truth" that he had uncovered as an astronomer, namely, that science shows us "there is no God up there." However, he continued, science can only exclaim to us (and here Shapley, wearing his white coat, raised his arms in awe): "What a universe it is!" Scientists are not dogmatic within science, and that is their glory; but many become unintentionally dogmatic about their understanding of science, about its power and its limits, and especially about their own metaphysical or ontological interpretations of its meaning. Interestingly, dogma here enters where philosophy and theology enter, that is, precisely as science leaves its own modes of certainty— where, as Toulmin puts it, science shades into "myth" (cf. Stephen Toulmin, "Contemporary Scientific Mythology," in idem, *Metaphysical Beliefs* [London: SCM, 1957]; reprinted in his excellent book *The Return to Cosmology* [Berkeley: University of California Press, 1982], part 1). This is ironic, because one major reason scientists become rightly irritated at religionists is the "dogmatic certainty" of the latter, where, say their critics, "they have no right to be so certain," their "beliefs" (i.e., metaphysical and theological propositions) not being provable as science understands proof. A goodly number of scientists fall into the same trap and become uncharacteristically dogmatic, even apodictic ("Paley is simply wrong"; "the Cosmos is all there is"), where they have no right to be. This is no longer science but precisely where the religionists, the objects of their scorn, had also been dogmatic, namely, in the area of beliefs, views of the whole based on experience but not provable by empirical testing.

20. Barrow and Tipler, *Anthropic Cosmological Principle*, pp. 138–39.

21. Whitehead, *Science and the Modern World*, pp. 71–79.

22. Cf. Pagels, *Perfect Symmetry*, pp. 24, 135, 355; also pp. 265–68, 375–76.

23. Cf. the following from Pagels's discussion: "The nothingness 'before' the creation of the universe is the most complete void that we can imagine. . . . It is

a world without place, without duration or eternity, without number. . . . Yet this unthinkable void converts itself into the plenum of existence—a necessary consequence of physical laws. Where are these laws written into that void? What 'tells' the void that it is pregnant [?]. It would seem that even the void is subject to law, a logic that exists prior to space and time. . . . Someday the physical origin and the dynamics of the entire universe will be as well understood as we now understand the stars. . . . [Steven Hawking] said that the major problems of the universe may be solved in several decades" (ibid., pp. 365–67). A little change of language could convert these initial sentences into the speculative philosophy (or myth!) of Plotinus, for whom the One is "pregnant" with Logos, the Logos with Soul, and the Soul (sadly) with matter! Cf. Plotinus, *The Enneads*, trans. Stephen Mackenna, comp. Grace Turnbull (New York: Oxford University Press, 1948), esp. Ennead 4.

24. No absolute beginning is possible for Aristotle; every "now" is preceded by a "before," so time extends endlessly backwards—as it also does forward; cf. Aristotle, *Physics* 8. 1.252–20. And because time is the "number of motion" in respect of "before" and "after," the endlessness of time means that motion or change is also endless—i.e., there was and could be no beginning (*Physics* 4. 2. 219b; and, explicitly, 8. 1.251b 10): "How can there be any before and after without the existence of time? Or how can there be any time without the existence of motion? If, then, time is the number of motion or itself a kind of motion, it follows that, if there is always time, motion must also be eternal." Cf. also *Physics* 1. 9.182a 28.

25. Interestingly, Whitehead—the great modern opponent of Aristotle—agrees on this point: for philosophical reason, "there can be no absolute beginning. . . . It is a contradiction in terms to assume that some explanatory fact can float into the actual world out of nonentity. Nonentity is nothingness. Every explanatory fact refers to the decision and to the efficacy of an actual thing" (*Process and Reality*, p. 73). Cf. also the "Category of Explanation XVIII," the so-called ontological principle: "actual entities are the only reasons" (ibid., pp. 36–37).

26. Pagels, *Perfect Symmetry*, pp. 353–59, 365–68, 375–76.

27. For Whitehead, reason requires coherence *within* the given system of things; hence a metaphysical articulation of ultimate principles (categories) is possible and rationally necessary. However, reason cannot go *beyond* the system of things, outside of it, to inquire about its origins. Hence that metaphysical rationality is, for reason itself, undetermined, "irrational"! "There is a metaphysical need for a principle of determination, but there can be no metaphysical reason for what is determined" (*Science and the Modern World*, pp. 249–50). This limitation on metaphysics to the given and already operating system of things holds a fortiori for all science.

28. The prejudice against religion in these volumes is fairly astounding. With regard to ideas held generally in Western culture in the past by scientists,

philosophers, literary persons, and clerics (e.g., that species were permanent and did not die out), it is the clerics that are blamed: "Traditional western religious opinions stoutly maintained the contrary [i.e., of the mortality of species], as for example the 1770 opinion of John Wesley" (Sagan, *Cosmos*, p. 16n). For evidence that the view that species had not changed since the beginning was widely held among the intelligentsia and not just in the ecclesia, cf. the cases of John Ray (1627–1705) and Carolus Linnaeus (1707–1778), both of whom believed in unchanging species; and also the classical statement from Thomas Jefferson when presented with bones from a prehistoric mastodon (see n. 7 in Chapter 2, above; also n. 4 in Chapter 2). Cf. John C. Greene, *The Death of Adam* (Ames: Iowa State University Press, 1959), pp. 122, 127–37. On this point also cf. Dawkins, who speaks of the "small-mindedness" and "conceit" of medieval Christians for thinking the human race was favored by God (*Blind Watchmaker*, p. 143).

29. Pagels, *Perfect Symmetry*, p. 167. Pagels describes any nonreductionist ontology, be it established on metaphysical grounds or religious grounds, as representative of a "closed mind," as opposed to the open-mindedness of the scientist. Along the same lines, Sagan gives us his explanation of the "myths" about superior beings who inhabit the skies and give directions to human beings how to order their affairs, "that among other advantages, such legends permit the priests to control the people" (Sagan, *Cosmic Connection*, p. 205). Thus rival ideologies interpret each other in exclusively negative terms, each seeing its rivals as established by "demons," external or, in this case, internal. And thus, probably with equal reasonableness, the antiscientific members of our culture interpret science and scientists.

30. When I was at Little Rock as an "expert" witness for the plaintiffs (the American Civil Liberties Union [ACLU] and the mainline churches), I spoke with a couple who were creationists. In reply to the query "Why did you become Creationists?" they said, "When our daughter came home from high school and told us that today the science teacher had said in class, 'Now we know that the book of Genesis was wrong,' *then* we joined the movement." Thus an overenthusiastic, possibly arrogant science breeds creationism! One wonders how much that science teacher, before stating authoritatively not only what *the* meaning of Genesis was but, even more, that it was false, knew about how a Jewish, Catholic, Methodist, or Presbyterian congregation might interpret that document. Most preachers have long since learned not to make such ill-informed statements about science!

31. Pagels, *Perfect Symmetry*, pp. 365–75.

32. Ibid., pp. 77, 159. I have been fascinated to learn recently that physics recognizes how essential nonorderly processes, such as chaos and quantum probabilities, are throughout the universe.

33. Whitehead argues throughout his works that the assumption of a con-

tinuing and omnipresent order throughout actuality is a necessary basis for science ("Thus yardsticks in Cambridge are good even in New Haven"), that this is the "hope of rationalism" and the "motive for the pursuit of all sciences alike," and that this hope is itself based on a "faith in reason"—a faith that establishes culture as a whole, as well as metaphysics (*Process and Reality*, p. 67). "This faith cannot be justified by any inductive generalization. It springs from direct inspection of the nature of things as disclosed in our own immediate present experience" (*Science and the Modern World*, p. 26). It is the task of the metaphysics of each age to elaborate the "world" established and upheld by this faith in reason and so to provide a rational basis for the sciences and for the culture that depends upon it.

Interestingly, philosopher of science Alexander Rosenberg, who has written what is to me a most intelligible and balanced survey of the philosophical issues in biological science, agrees that what Barrow and Tipler call "ontological reductionism" and "ontological determinism"—in fact, scientific realism—represent, unbeknownst to most biologists, an assumed metaphysics and not empirical science at all: "Provincialism [the view that biology can be reduced to physics] is a response to the epistemological embarrassment of the Positivists: It holds that where biological theory cannot be, in principle at least, connected to physical theory the biology should be negated as unscientific. But the grounds for this claim are sheer metaphysics: Nature is nothing but what physics tells us it is, so any account of nature, including animate nature, that is not reducible to physics must be wrong" (*The Structure of Biological Science* [Cambridge: Cambridge University Press, 1986], p. 23; cf. also pp. 72, 90).

34. Pagels, *Perfect Symmetry*, pp. 77, 158–59. Clearly, Whitehead's point that no observation *could* controvert the assumption of order because all "observing" that spans moments and spaces depends on assumption of "law" had not occurred to Pagels.

35. Sagan, *Cosmos*, pp. 1–2. The feeling for the predominance of knowledge (i.e., scientific knowledge, not wisdom) and so, of course, for the observer and knower in human affairs is always a breathtaking aspect of scientific literature, but Sagan is a master at it. Science and its knowledge are not only the prize issues of evolution but they represent the be-all and end-all of human worth. For example: "If we lived on a planet where nothing ever changed . . . there would be no impetus for science. And if we lived in a unpredictable world . . . again, there would be no such thing as science" (p. 32). When one considers all of the aspects of life that would never be—including life itself, probably all finite existence, and certainly all human relations—without change and without order, to place science at the top of the list is bizarre indeed! It reminds me of the priestly castes, which always gave as the reason for creation itself the establishment of valid liturgical worship.

36. Sagan, *Cosmos*, p. 32.

37. Dawkins, *Blind Watchmaker,* p. 143.

CHAPTER 5
SCIENCE, PHILOSOPHY, AND THEOLOGY

1. Cf. the excellent summary of this point in Harold Brown, *Perception, Theory and Commitment* (Chicago: University of Chicago Press, 1979), chaps. 6–8. Cf. also n. 3 in Chapter 4, above.

2. Cf. R. G. Collingwood, *The Idea of Nature* (Oxford: Oxford University Press, 1945), part 3; idem, *An Essay on Metaphysics* (Oxford: Oxford University Press, 1940), part 3c; Thomas Kuhn, *The Structure of Scientific Revolutions* (Chicago: University of Chicago Press, 1962); Stephen Toulmin, *The Philosophy of Science* (New York: Harper & Row, 1953); and idem, *Foresight and Understanding* (New York: Harper & Brothers, 1965).

3. This is the major theme in Richard Rorty, *Philosophy and the Mirror of Nature* (Princeton, N. J.: Princeton University Press, 1980), esp. chaps. 7 and 8. It is also a major theme in Richard Bernstein, *Beyond Objectivism and Relativism* (Philadelphia: University of Pennsylvania Press, 1983), parts 1 and 2.

4. E. A. Burtt, *The Metaphysical Foundations of Modern Science* (Garden City, N.Y.: Doubleday, 1954), chap. 3.

5. Immanuel Kant, *Critique of Pure Reason,* trans. Norman Kemp Smith (New York: St. Martin's Press, 1929), part 1 first division, bks. 1 and 2, esp. chap. 3; idem, *Prolegomena to Any Future Metaphysics,* trans. Paul Carus, rev. James Ellington (Indianapolis: Hackett, 1977), part 2, secs. 14–39.

6. A good number of possible answers to this question come to mind: First, science has not seen itself as in any way dependent on philosophical foundations; accordingly, its "realistic capabilities" are not challenged by philosophical criticism. Second, because neither philosophy of science nor the historical traditions of epistemology and ontology relevant to science are considered significant for science, neither philosophy of science nor history of science is taught as a required element within scientific graduate programs. Third, philosophy itself has tended to eschew epistemological and ontological matters, preferring logical and language analysis. Fourth, the reigning philosophy of science has itself been empiricist and objectivist in character. Fifth, sociologically, physical science is thoroughly established in modern technological culture; thus, intellectually, its sovereignty and independence, its theoretical "aseity," are unassailed by most voices.

7. "Nature is a dull affair, soundless, scentless, colorless; merely the hurrying of material, endlessly, meaninglessly. . . . No alternative system of organizing the pursuit of scientific truth has been suggested. It is not only reigning, but it is without a rival.

"And yet—it is quite unbelievable. This conception of the universe is surely framed in terms of high abstractions, and the paradox only arises because we have mistaken an abstraction for concrete realities" (Alfred North Whitehead,

Science and the Modern World [New York: Macmillan, 1925], pp. 77–78).

8. For A. N. Whitehead's view that the pervasive structures and order of existence are not "data" of sense or therefore of empirical inquiry, cf. his *Process and Reality* (New York: Macmillan, 1929), pp. 6–7; idem, *Adventures of Ideas* (New York: Macmillan, 1933), pp. 209 and 232; and idem, *Modes of Thought* (Cambridge: Cambridge University Press, 1938), 146–47. For derivation of the "categories" of science from unconscious perceptions (causal efficacy), cf. Whitehead, *Process and Reality*, pp. 180–81, 265–67; idem, *Adventures of Ideas*, pp. 232–37; and idem, *Symbolism: Its Meaning and Effect* (New York: Macmillan, 1927), pp. 30–49. For the dependence of the rest of experience, of civilization, and of science on recognition or "knowledge" of these pervasive structures, cf. *Adventures of Ideas*, p. 292.

9. Whitehead, *Process and Reality*, pp. 125–26, 184, 188–89, 266, 361–63; and esp. idem, *Adventures of Ideas*, pp. 232–70. As Whitehead says, this experience of the conformation of the self to its own immediate past "is the primary ground for the continuity of nature" (*Adventures of Ideas*, p. 236).

10. Whitehead, *Process and Reality*, pp. 6–7; idem, *Adventures of Ideas*, p. 209. The experience of causal efficacy is a philosophical articulation of the self-awareness that we argued in Chapter 3 is basic.

11. For discussion of ontological and technical reason, cf. Paul Tillich, *Systematic Theology* (Chicago: University of Chicago Press, 1951, 1963), 1:71ff. and 97ff., 3:55ff.; cf. also idem, *Theology of Culture*, ed. R. C. Kimball (London: Oxford University Press, 1959), pp. 127–32. For a fuller bibliography of Tillich's writings on science and technology, cf. J. Mark Thomas, *Ethics and Technoculture* (Lanham, Md.: University Press of America, 1987). For a discussion of Tillich's philosophical theology as a whole, cf. Langdon Gilkey, *Gilkey on Tillich* (New York: Crossroad, 1989).

12. Tillich's discussion of the ontological polarity of self and world and of the influence of that polarity on the possibility of cognitive knowledge of world is found in his *Systematic Theology*, vol. 1, part 1, and in 3:17–38, 57–65.

13. Tillich, *Systematic Theology*, 3:38–41.

14. Ibid., 1:168ff.

15. Whitehead, *Process and Reality*, p. 7.

16. Tillich, *Systematic Theology*, 1:189ff. On the experience of the "infinite ground of reason," see 1:79ff., 3:87ff.

17. Ibid., 3:17–28, 313ff.

18. Whitehead, *Process and Reality*, p. 28: "In the principles which actuality exemplifies all are on the same level." "The metaphysical first principles can never fail of exemplification. We can never catch the actual world taking a holiday from their sway" (pp. 7 and 168). Whitehead's defense of his method of interpreting according to the principles by which our own experience of ourselves is interpreted are here presented: "It is the accepted doctrine in physical

science that a living body is to be interpreted according to what is known of other sections of the physical universe. This is a sound axiom: but it is double-edged. For it carries with it the converse deduction that other sections of the universe are to be interpreted in accordance with what we know of the human body" (pp. 181–82). "The way in which one actual entity is qualified by other actual entities is the 'experience' of the actual world enjoyed by that actual entity, as subject. The subjectivist principle is that the whole universe consists of elements disclosed in the analysis of the experience of subjects" (p. 252).

19. Tillich, *Systematic Theology*, 1:18ff.; Whitehead, *Process and Reality*, pp. 7–8; idem, *Religion in the Making* (Cambridge: Cambridge University Press, 1927), p. 84 n.; and idem, *Adventures of Ideas*, p. 187.

20. John Barrow and Frank Tipler, *The Anthropic Cosmological Principle* (Oxford: Clarendon, 1986), pp. 1 and 13.

21. Whitehead, *Process and Reality*, pp. 125–26, 186–97, 264–79. As Whitehead puts it, contemporary [and living] occasions do not "prehend" each other (p. 95).

22. It is for this reason that the references in Pagels and in Weinberg to a "theory of everything" appear so strange and so indicative of a naive realist view of science; cf. Heinz Pagels, *Perfect Symmetry* (New York: Bantam, 1986), pp. 365–67, 373. What is pictured in such a theory is a "final" scientific understanding of nature, one isomorphic with nature and hence perfect (and incorrectable) in every detail.

23. Cf. John Dewey, *The Quest for Certainty* (New York: Minton Balch, 1929), pp. 3–20; and idem, *Experience and Nature*, pp. 161–65; and idem, *Essays in Experimental Logic*, pp. 231–41. These can be found also in *Intelligence in the Modern World: John Dewey's Philosophy*, ed. J. Ratner (New York: Modern Library, 1939).

24. "Discourse is a language, not a mirror. The images in sense are parts of discourse, not parts of nature: they are the babble of our innocent organs under the stimulus of things; but these spontaneous images, like the sounds of the voice, may acquire the function of names" (George Santayana, *Skepticism and Animal Faith* [New York: Scribner's, 1929], p. 180).

25. Ibid., pp. 180, 178.

26. Cf. Tillich, *Systematic Theology*, 1:191–92.

27. Santayana, *Skepticism*, chaps. 15–21.

28. Tillich, *Systematic Theology*, 1:168–69, 192.

29. Previous attempts to discriminate the respective tasks of philosophy and theology and to show the positive and mutual dependence of these two on each other can be found in Langdon Gilkey, *Naming the Whirlwind* (Indianapolis: Bobbs-Merrill, 1969); idem, *Religion and the Scientific Future* (New York: Harper & Row, 1969), esp. chap. 4; idem, *Catholicism Confronts Modernity* (New York: Seabury, 1975), chaps. 3 and 4; and idem, *Reaping the Whirlwind* (New York: Seabury, 1976), part 1 and Entre-Act.

CHAPTER 6
NATURE AND NATURE'S POWER

1. Cf. Stephen Toulmin, *The Return to Cosmology* (Berkeley: University of California Press, 1982), Introduction, parts 1 and 2.

2. By "naturalism" is meant the philosophical—in fact, metaphysical—view that nature represents the ultimate category of any sound reflection: nature as the *source* of all things "under the sky"; the future of nature as representing whatever *end* there may be to process. And in between, all structures, ontological and moral, are "natural." Thus naturalism disavows any relevant being transcendent to nature or any ethics that are not founded on our experienced nature. Nevertheless, a number of "naturalists," both in the past (e.g., Benedict de Spinoza, George Santayana, A. N. Whitehead, and Henry Nelson Wieman) and in the present (e.g., Charles Hardwick, William Dean, Jerome Stone), are very much concerned in different ways with the religious possibilities of naturalism. Spinoza and Whitehead could be said to represent *speculative*, "rationalistic" forms of naturalism; a more *empirical* mode could be that of Dewey and the Columbia school of "nonreductionist naturalism," which insisted on a nonreductionist view of reality but on a "continuity of analysis" (the scientific method) for all truth claims (cf. Y. Krikorian, *Naturalism and the Human Spirit* [New York: Columbia University Press, 1946], as an excellent description and analysis of this school). Finally, there are the materialistic and behavioristic naturalists, represented by Thomas Hobbes, certain French physiocrats, Ernst Haeckel, perhaps Bertrand Russell, and now Jacques Monod and B. F. Skinner. It is the materialistic or physicalist position (reductionist naturalism) that represents for me the implicit interpretation of reality of the positivist science discussed herein (reductionist and determinist), not the subtler and more inclusive forms represented by Dewey, Whitehead, Santayana, and Spinoza.

3. Recall Imre Lakatos's discrimination of "three worlds" implied in inquiring: (1) the physical world, (2) the psychological and sociological world (of the subject), and (3) the world of ideas, propositions, and formulas (*Mathematics, Science and Epistemology*, ed. John Worral and Gregory Currie [Cambridge: Cambridge University Press, 1978], pp. 108 and 226). As was argued in Part 1, many scientists have tried to do "science" with only the first world, René Descartes's "extension," and omitted the world of persons, selves, and minds (as well as the third world).

4. Ludwig Feuerbach, the most intelligent, learned, and astute of the critics of religion, argued convincingly that only when human self-consciousness had developed enough to separate humankind—at least in its obligations and destiny—from "nature" did "God" become separate from nature and so transcendent to nature. It was at this point that nature became over against the human, distinguished from the human and from what the Greeks called "art," and so another, transcendent, "all-encompassing source" was conceived and

"projected" in religion and in philosophy alike. Cf. Ludwig Feuerbach, *Lectures on the Essence of Religion*, trans. R. Manheim (New York: Harper & Row, 1967), lectures 19, 23, 26.

5. Karl Jaspers, *The Origin and Goal of History* (New Haven: Yale University Press, 1953), pp. 1–25, 55, 62, 139–40.

6. A. N. Whitehead, *Science and the Modern World* (New York: Macmillan, 1925), pp. 72ff. Ontology and metaphysics also claim universality ("being qua being," "every example of actuality"), but with a difference. They seek deliberately to include all of experienced actuality, the entire scope of experienced reality, the whole, and thus both objects and subjects, actuality and possibility, nature and history. It is just such an all-inclusive understanding, beyond the special sciences and so beyond entities merely as objects, that all of positivism (though not all of nonreductionist naturalism) denies. A reductionist naturalism is therefore left with incoherence; it is an attempt to explain the whole, including the scientist, in the positivist terms of objects alone.

7. Holmes Rolston III, *Science and Religion* (New York: Random House, 1987), pp. 52–54, 82, and chap. 4 (pp. 151–59). Cf. also Nishitani Keiji's brilliant statement of the same thesis: "Human intentions *use* determining physical laws for a higher, empowering purpose" (*Religion and Nothingness*, trans. Jan van Bragt [Berkeley: University of California Press, 1982] chap. 3, esp. pp. 77–84).

8. Two recent examples of biological–genetic efforts to "explain" (give the sufficient causes for) moral systems and religion—and thus to provide sufficient grounds for understanding them and for creatively directing and reconstructing them—are Richard D. Alexander, *The Biology of Moral Systems* (Hawthorne, N.Y.: de Gruyter, 1987); and Richard Dawkins, *The Selfish Gene* (New York: Oxford University Press, 1976).

9. This fundamental judgment—namely, that while empirical, scientific judgments come under the rubric "truth" and so "rational assessment," moral and religious judgments do not (they can be explained by their causes)—poses an interesting and fruitful question. Is this judgment itself an *empirical* judgment? Hardly—unless one pleads as evidence the plurality of morals and religion and the universality of science, a strange, unhistorical, and therefore precarious argument. Is it a judgment of reason and so an epistemological judgment or a metaphysical judgment, or both? This is probably partly the case. Or is it a judgment based on "faith," i.e., dependent on one's own (prior) worldview, a view held by conviction, by participation, and by commitment? This is even more probably the case. If this is so, then this judgment (and the efforts of Alexander and Dawkins too; see n. 8, above) represents an example of the "participation of members of the contemporary intellectual community in the 'religious substance' of modern culture"; and so, one must ask, Is *this* example of "religion" to be understood genetically?

10. Many intellectuals (even scientists), disdainful of the possibility of "truth" in religion, give biographical reasons for their disdain: e.g., "I was raised

in a conservative Presbyterian (or Jewish, Catholic, etc.) home, and I know all about religion." In partial reply to this argument, I have cited in answer to such statements the case of a young friend "whose father" I say, "was a distinguished chemistry professor and his mother a successful Freudian analyst; now the young man is a Sikh and deeply into yoga and meditation." Because this sequence is perfectly credible at the end of this century, it helps to show the irrelevance to truth claims of a biographical argument, at least of a negative argument.

11. Cf. Michael Polanyi's fascinating and original discussion of the self-set character of the norms of science, as of all fundamental communal enterprises (*Personal Knowledge* [New York: Harper & Row, 1964], pp. 183–202); such standards or norms (in this case, empirical and logical standards) determine the validity of judgment—i.e., of truth and falsehood—and are based on communal tradition, the assent of the (scientific) community, and the "passionate" adherence to the truth and to the community's agreed and common pursuit of the truth. Without these personal and communal affirmations and loyalties, there could be no relevant norms and so no science. My immediate point is that if standards are self-set, then, appropriately, each community of inquiry and so of "knowing," as of action, sets its own standards.

12. The importance of the work of Mircea Eliade, longtime colleague and friend, to the thoughts that led to this volume cannot be exaggerated; and it was in a course taught with Larry Sullivan, as in many that I taught together with David Tracy, that these views of nature first came to expression. For Eliade, cf. esp. *Patterns in Comparative Religion*, trans. R. Shed (New York: Meridian Books, 1966); *Myth and Reality*, trans. Willard R. Trask (New York: Harper & Row, 1963); *Cosmos and History* (New York: Harper Torchbooks, 1959); *The Eternal Return: Images and Symbols* (New York: Sheed & Ward, 1969); *The Quest: History and Meaning in Religion* (Chicago: University of Chicago Press, 1969); *Myths, Dreams and Mysteries* (New York: Harper & Row, 1975); and *The Sacred and the Profane* (New York: Harcourt, Brace, 1959). And cf. Lawrence E. Sullivan, *Icanchu's Drum* (New York: Macmillan, 1988); and Rolston, *Science and Religion*.

13. I am aware of the trinitarian implications of these four categories and their relation to the Augustinian triad—God as Being, as Truth, and as Love (*De Trinitate* bk. 4, Preface; *City of God* 11.24)—imaged in our own self-understanding (which is, incidentally, certain): "That I am, that I know, and that I delight in my being" (*City of God* 11.26); *Basic Writings of St. Augustine*, ed. W. J. Oates [New York: Random, 1948]. And they bear relation to Paul Tillich's symbolism of God as Being, as Living, as Logos, and as Reuniting Spirit (*Systematic Theology* [Chicago: University of Chicago Press, 1951] 1:228, 249ff.). However, I am here speaking not of God but of nature and thus at best (theologically) of the "traces" or "images" of God in nature.

14. Cf. John Herman Randall, Jr., *The Making of the Modern Mind* (Boston: Houghton Mifflin, 1940), bk. 3, chaps. 11–12; R. G. Collingwood, *The Idea of Nature* (Oxford: Oxford University Press, 1945), part 2, chap. 1; E. A. Burtt, *The*

Metaphysical Foundations of Modern Science (Garden City, N.Y.: Doubleday, 1954), esp. chaps. 3, 4, and 7; Peter Gay, *The Enlightenment* (New York: Knopf, 1967), vol. 1, esp. chaps. 6–7; vol. 2, chaps. 1–3.

15. One notes the contradiction here: it was the adage "only science knows" that effected the elimination of the divine Infinite Designer and the human self who knows—for empirical science can "know" neither one by its methods. Yet the same adage required the retention of at least the subject, what Descartes called the substance "thinking," to complement the objective substance "extension." Descartes's dualism represents a better—if ultimately incoherent—philosophical explanation of science than does the exclusively materialistic monism so fashionable among modern scientific minds.

16. The perspectival character of science in relation to the "reality" it studies is increasingly apparent here. If the goal of science, as is maintained, represents a hypothetical–deductive system, ruled by principles univocally and so "necessarily" illustrated, then that deductive and hence determined system—coherent in that sense—seems strangely at odds with the ontic character of nature, one of openness and indeterminateness, as disclosed in the actual study of nature.

17. Rolston, *Science and Religion*, pp. 46–47 and 60–61.

18. For one Christian formulation of this insight, cf. Martin Luther: "Where God works apart from the grace of His Spirit, He works all things in all men, even in the ungodly; for He alone moves, impels to act and impels by the motion of His omnipotence, all those things which He alone created" (*Bondage of the Will*, WA 753–55; trans. J. I. Packer and A. R. Johnston [Westwood, N.J.: Revel, 1957], p. 267). Cf. also the same sense of reality as animated by a divine power in descriptions of Shakti and Shiva, e.g., in Heinrich Zimmer, *Philosophies of India*, ed. Joseph Campbell (New York: Pantheon, 1961).

19. Heinz Pagels, *Perfect Symmetry* (New York: Bantam, 1986), pp. 146ff., 157ff.

20. John Barrow and Frank Tipler, *The Anthropic Cosmological Principle* (Oxford: Clarendon, 1986), pp. 173–80, 674; cf. Pagels, *Perfect Symmetry*.

21. Rolston, *Science and Religion*, pp. 67–72.

22. E. B. Tylor, *The Origins of Culture* (Gloucester, Mass.: Peter Smith, 1970), vols. 1–2; Gerardus van der Leeuw, *Religion in Essence and Manifestation*, trans. J. E. Turner (New York: Harper & Row, 1963), vols. 1–2, esp. part 1; Eliade, *Patterns*, esp. chaps. 1, 2, and 6; Tillich, *Systematic Theology*, vol. 1, part 2, II, A1 and B3; Langdon Gilkey, *Gilkey on Tillich* (New York: Crossroad, 1989), chap. 6.

23. Cf. Eliade's definition, description, and analysis of hierophanies of the sacred as manifesting or describing a different "nonprofane" level of power and so reality (*Patterns*, chap. 1). Cf. also Eliade, *Myths, Dreams and Mysteries*: "Religion begins when and where there is a total revelation of reality, a revelation which is at once that of the sacred—of that which supremely *is*, of what is neither illusory or evanescent" (p. 18).

24. Such is the extent of our understanding of and control over these powers

of nature that we are apt to forget their real and continuing presence as the absolute basis of all we can do. There is no farming without the land's fertility, despite technological agriculture; there is no medicinal science without the healing power of nature; there is no human fertility, no children, no family, no community without the power of life resident within us. Technology uses nature's powers; it cannot create them. Our dependence remains as real as it was when felt and expressed in archaic religion, except that they recognized it and we do not.

25. Cf. esp. Sullivan's extraordinary *Icanchu's Drum*, chap 2: "In myth . . . human nature in its primordial appearance makes known *that* it is, and by its very particular mode of existence, reveals itself for *what* it is" (p. 24). "Before any one of them is disclosed, the multiplicity of mythic disasters sends a message of its own: creation suffered a disaster so total, no single account can describe it adequately" (p. 57). "The rocks are memorials to the last fully manifest act, the last fleeting moment, of the primordium. For that reason, they forever evoke fear and awe; they are that ultimate experience of primordial being" (p. 82). "The whole of reality always transcends the part since the primordial wholeness, the fullness of time, was lost, maimed, stolen or destroyed" (p. 85). "Primordial reality proves inextinguishable. Its life has not ended, but rather it has changed. Symbols, the transformed presence of primordial realities, continue to reveal the meanings whose appearances once created, and now order, the universe" (p. 107).

CHAPTER 7
NATURE AS LIFE

1. Cf. the full discussion of the differentia of life according to the modern life sciences in Holmes Rolston III, *Science and Religion* (New York: Random House, 1987), pp. 82–90. For a discussion of some of the differences between physics and biology, cf. Michael Ruse, *Is Science Sexist?* (Boston and Dordrecht: Reidel, 1984), chap. 4.

2. "To use a provocative term, matter here [in life] takes on a kind of *spirit* . . . we have first located it in biochemistry, calling it *information*" (Rolston, *Science and Religion*, p. 89).

3. Cf. Richard Dawkins, *The Selfish Gene* (New York: Oxford University Press, 1976), for an especially florid use of "purposive" language in relation to the "gene": for the uses of "analogies" from human purposes, cf. pp. 40 and 67, among others; and for examples of "laundering" this teleological language back into the language of efficient causation, cf. p. 142.

4. Many biologists consider it necessary to use "functional language," understanding the part through its role in and for the whole organism, but only as a "shorthand" because the causal sequences behind this unconscious teleology are too complex to formulate. Cf., e.g., Francisco Ayala, *Studies in the Philosophy of*

Biology, ed. F. J. Ayala and T. Dobzhansky (Berkeley: University of California Press, 1974). Philosopher of science Michael Ruse agrees with this view: there are no purposes in organisms, conscious or unconscious, but we must speak as if there were because function (the purpose of organic parts) is so closely correlated with adaptation (*Is Science Sexist?* chap. 5). Alexander Rosenberg writes as if functional language were not only useful but even necessary in "explaining" biological issues, and he regards the hope of positivism exhaustively to translate all biological propositions into causal discourse as improbable and misguided; cf. his *The Structure of Biological Science* (Cambridge: Cambridge University Press, 1986), pp. 9 and 32. None of these three seems to wish to take a clear, unequivocal position in this debate. John Barrow and Frank Tipler, however, are unequivocally "causalists" in biology, as apparently is Ernst Mayr; cf. John Barrow and Frank Tipler, *The Anthropic Cosmological Principle* (Oxford: Clarendon, 1986), chap. 3, esp. pp. 132–36.

5. The geneticist in question is Lindon Eaves of the Medical College of Virginia in Richmond.

6. For this reason, it seems to me incoherent to seek to explain the origin of life, of the organic from what is inorganic, by means of the categories familiar to evolutionary explanation, especially natural selection. For examples of this use, cf. Scott, *The Origin of Life*; and Marguerite Poynter and Michael Klein, *Cosmic Quest* (New York: Atheneum, 1984), chap. 4, esp. p. 35. Cf. the same references for the appeal to an almost infinite time to explain how the improbable became probable. For Rolston's comments on these two points, cf. *Science and Religion*, pp. 93 and 111: "Longer time spans do not much help to make the improbable probable here, so long as the breakdown rate always overwhelms the constructive rate."

7. Carl Sagan writes very charmingly, as well as persuasively, about how we arise in all aspects of our being out of the cosmos and its history; cf. his *Cosmos* (New York: Ballantine, 1980), chap. 11; and idem, *The Cosmic Connection* (New York: Doubleday, 1973), p. 37. See also Poynter and Klein, *Cosmic Quest*, chap. 10.

8. Cf. the fascinating, perceptive, and (to me) very original exploration of the theme of the intertwining of energy and pain, life and suffering, life and death (and their common result: more life, new life, and new forms of life) in Rolston, *Science and Religion*, pp. 133–46.

9. Cf. John Dewey, *Intelligence in the Modern World: John Dewey's Philosophy*, ed. J. Ratner (New York: Modern Library, 1939), chap. 14; and idem, *Reconstruction in Philosophy* (New York: Henry Holt, 1920), chap. 7.

10. Cf. this surprising passage from Dewey in 1920, one almost completely out of tune with contemporary sensibilities: "The savage takes things, 'as they are,' and by using caves and roots and occasional pools leads a meager and precarious existence. The civilized man goes to distant mountains, digs channels, and conducts the water to what had been a desert. . . . He takes native

plants and by selection and cross-fertilization improves them. He introduces machinery to till the soil and care for the harvest. By such means he may succeed in making the wilderness blossom like a rose" (*Reconstruction in Philosophy*, p. 85).

11. Mircea Eliade, *Patterns in Comparative Religion*, trans. R. Shed (New York: Meridian Books, 1966), Introduction.

12. Cf. Ludwig Feuerbach's apparent agreement that in all cultural roles, acts, crafts, and arts, early men and women encountered, mimed, and so used sacred powers. Hence all of culture is originally "religious," a sequence of rituals, and the growth of civilization is accordingly the "freeing" of men and women from the illusion of divine presence and activity toward the affirmation of their own creativity in all cultural roles (*Lectures on the Essence of Religion*, trans. R. Manheim [New York: Harper & Row, 1967], lecture 23, esp. pp. 208–15). Eliade, in contrast, while agreeing that this "secular progress" has taken place, sees it as an essential and fatal loss to human existence. Cf. Mircea Eliade, *The Eternal Return: Images and Symbols* (New York: Sheed & Ward, 1969), Foreword; idem, *Myths, Dreams and Mysteries* (New York: Harper & Row, 1975), Preface and chap. 1.

13. Eliade, *Patterns*, chap. 2. Cf. also Charles Long, *Alpha: The Myth of Creation* (New York: Braziller, 1963).

14. Eliade, *Patterns*, chap. 3.

15. Ibid., chaps. 4 and 5.

16. I am fortunate to be a friend of a most original and perceptive "observer" of human existence, Thomas van Leeuwen of Amsterdam, currently professor of architectural history at Leiden. Unusually sensitive to what I could call the sacred dimension of ordinary life, Tom first wrote a widely acclaimed book on the meaning latent in the architecture of the early American skyscrapers (*The Skyward Trend of Thought* [Art, History, and Architecture Books; The Hague, 1986]), portraying the skyscraper as a Promethean burst of human energy and creativity, the attempt to scale heaven itself. Now he is immersed in the study of pools, especially the implausibly extravagant pools and grottoes characteristic of early Hollywood estates, where water (as always) communicated mystery, purification, rebirth, and ultimately the promise of eternal life.

17. Eliade, *Patterns*, chaps. 7 and 9.

18. Cf. Franz Cumont, *The Oriental Religions in Roman Paganism* (Chicago: Open Court, 1911), chaps. 2–5.

CHAPTER 8
NATURE, ORDER, AND VALUE

1. Cf. the clear ethical implications of metaphysical understanding not only in Thomas Aquinas and the subsequent Catholic tradition of natural law but also, for example, in Spinoza, Hegel, and Whitehead.

2. A lesson on the vast difference in cultural apprehension of the value of the new from that of the old or traditional was given to me on a trip in Greece. Next to me in the bus was seated an agricultural engineer from New Zealand, sent there by the United Nations to help Greek farmers and herders find the most appropriate use of their barren land. After agreeing to the beauty of these dry hills, he sighed and said they *could* be used very fruitfully if the farmers could be prevailed on to adopt new crops and new methods: "The farmers in New Zealand are eager to hear of these newer and more appropriate ways; here they merely tell me no one has ever done that before, and they turn away." The new possibility is probably forever pitted against the traditional, and it is fundamentally an implicit or unconscious view of history, either as an order held together by tradition and continuity or as one progressing by creative development, that determines the outcome. Now that we have tried the new, perhaps to excess, wiser Westerners, "burned" by their own desecration of the land, may see more value in tradition!

3. The yearning for the changeless, that which neither decays nor dies, permeated Hellenic and Hellenistic life, both pagan and Christian. One can see this beginning in Plato and Aristotle and reaching a summit in Plotinus and Augustine. It dominates most of the disputes of early Christian theology, for example, over Christology: as Athanasius (following Irenaeus) insisted, the point of the Incarnation was that the divine immortality and "incorruption" (nondecaying) made union with the human, liable to corruption (decay) and mortality, in order that we, the mortal, might become what He was—immortal.

4. This is what the sociologist Peter Berger calls the process of "legitimation," and it creates "the plausibility structure"; the world "as it is in itself"; a structure formed *historically* and important to each of us *socially*, as we have been raised in our social matrix to view the world. It is what Sigmund Freud called the "reality principle," except (it being his own) he did not view it as relative to modern culture! It is close to what Paul Tillich terms the world side of the "religious substance" of a culture. Cf. Peter Berger and Thomas Luckmann, *The Social Construction of Reality* (Garden City, N.Y.: Doubleday, 1967), pp. 61, 85, and esp. 92ff.

5. Cf. esp. Lawrence E. Sullivan, *Icanchu's Dream* (New York: Macmillan, 1988), pp. 47–101.

6. For this description of Dharma in Hindu (and later in Buddhist and Sikh) thought, cf., among others, Heinrich Zimmer, *Myths and Symbols in Indian Art and Civilization*, ed. Joseph Campbell (New York: Pantheon, 1947); and idem, *Philosophies of India*, ed. Joseph Campbell (New York: Pantheon, 1951); Kenneth Morgan, *The Religion of the Hindus* (New York: Ronald, 1953); Sarvepalli Radhakrishanan, *Indian Philosophy*, 2 vols. (London: Allen & Unwin, 1948); and, in contemporary thought, cf. Arvind Sharma, *A Hindu Perspective on the*

Philosophy of Religion (London: Macmillan, 1991), where the role of the cosmic and acosmic Dharma is (like Christian Providence) vastly reduced.

7. For this brief description of the Confucian Tao, cf. Yu-Lan Fung, *The Spirit of Chinese Philosophy*, trans. E. R. Hughes (London: Kegan Routledge & Paul, 1947); Herlee Creel, *Confucius: The Man and the Myth* (New York: Day, 1949); *The I-Ching*, trans. Richard Wilhelm and W. Baynes (New York: Pantheon, 1950); Benjamin I. Schwartz, *The World of Thought in Ancient China* (Cambridge, Mass.: Harvard University Press, 1985); Anthony Yu, "The Confucian Concept of Order," *Thought Quarterly Review* 43 (1968): 249–72; Wei-Ming Tu, *Humanity and Self-Civilization: Essays in Confucian Thought* (Berkeley: Asian Humanities Press, 1979); William Theodore de Bary, ed., *Sources of Chinese Tradition* (New York: Columbia University Press, 1960); and idem, *The Unfolding of Neo-Confucianism* (New York: Columbia University Press, 1975).

8. This account of the pre-Socratics is greatly in the debt of Werner Jaeger, *The Theology of the Early Greek Philosophers* (Oxford: Clarendon, 1947); idem, *Paideia*, trans. G. Highet, 3 vols. (New York: Oxford University Press, 1943); and idem, *Aristotle*, trans. T. R. Robinson (Oxford: Oxford University Press, 1948).

9. M. C. Nahm, *Selections from Early Greek Philosophy* (New York: Crofts, 1947), pp. 61–62; and Jaeger, *Theology*, p. 20.

10. Jaeger, *Theology*, p. 22.

11. Nahm, *Selections*, pp. 62–63; Jaeger, *Theology*, pp. 24–34.

12. Nahm, *Selections*, pp. 62–63; Jaeger, *Theology*, pp. 34–37.

13. Nahm, *Selections*, pp. 113–15; Jaeger, *Theology*, pp. 94–98.

14. Nahm, *Selections*, pp. 115–17; Jaeger, *Theology*, pp. 99–108.

15. Nahm, *Selections*, p. 89, frags. 1, 2, 4, 16–19, 91–93; Jaeger, *Theology*, chap. 7.

16. Nahm, *Selections*, p. 90, frags. 29, 60–63.

17. Ibid., p. 91, frags. 41–42, 44, 46.

18. Ibid., pp. 92–94, frags. 60–63, 66–69, 95–107.

19. For Plato, cf. esp. *Gorgias* 468–81, 503–8; *Philebus* 22–24, 63–67; *The Republic* 5–7. For Aristotle, cf. *Nicomachean Ethics* and *Metaphysics*. Cf. also Jaeger, *Paideia*, vol. 2.

20. Plato *Republic* 5. 474–75, 6. 484–87.

21. I am inescapably reminded of Reinhold Niebuhr's famous prayer: "Lord help us to accept those things we cannot change, and not to accept those things we can affect—and to be able to discern the difference."

22. Epictetus *The Manual of Epictetus*, sec. 19; in W. J. Oates, *The Stoic and Epicurean Philosophers* (New York: Random House, 1940), p. 472.

23. Ibid., pp. 273–75.

24. Ibid., sec. 34, p. 276.

25. Marcus Aurelius *Meditations*, 8.32; in Oates, *Stoic and Epicurean Philosophers*, p. 548.

26. Ibid., 5.33, 5.19 (pp. 524, 523); cf. also sec. 20 (p. 557).

27. Ibid., 8.28–29 (p. 547); cf. also 7.67–71 (pp. 542–43).

28. Ibid., 6.58 (p. 534).

29. A similar analysis could be made of the parallel transformation (while remaining elegantly "Greek") of Platonic rationality into Neoplatonic mysticism. Cf. *The Essence of Plotinus* (the six Enneads), trans. Stephen Mackenna, comp. Grace Turnbull (New York: Oxford University Press, 1948), extracts 1. 2, 4, 8; 3.7; 4.7–8; 5.8–9; 6.7, 9.

30. Cf. *1 Clement* (ca. 97 C.E.)

31. For an example of Augustine's "proof" of God through the presence of truth (at least two truths: that I am and that I live) in the soul—the *inward* soul—cf. *On Free Will* 3.7–11, 14, in *Library of Christian Classics*, ed. by C. J. Burleigh (Philadelphia: Westminster, 1953), 6.138–44; cf. also 6.149, 156–58, and esp. 159–63. For examples of the most fundamental "traces" of God in nature and the self, cf. the many references to God as Being, as Truth, and as Love and their correlates in the finite self that *exists*, that *knows* it exists, and that *loves* its existence: e.g., Augustine *On The Trinity*, bk. 4, Preface; and idem, *City of God* 11.26–28; and bk. 15, esp. chap 39.

32. For an early form of this, where Greek ethics were still united with and so defined by Christian requirements, cf. Augustine *The Morals of the Catholic Church* (380), esp. chaps. 15, 19, 21, 22, 24, 26. For a later version, where the traditional Greek virtues (courage, temperance, wisdom, and justice) have become "natural" virtues and the Christian virtues (faith, hope, and love) have become "supernatural virtues," cf. Thomas Aquinas *Summa Theologica* 1–2.58–62, 65–67. On the entire tradition of natural law in Christianity, cf. Ernst Troeltsch, *The Social Teachings of the Christian Churches*, trans. Olive Wyon (New York: Macmillan, 1949), chap. 1, sec. 3; chap. 2, secs. 1, 2, 6–8.

33. E.g., Augustine *Confessions* 1.4; 10.6–7, 17.

34. I have omitted discussion of the Reformation partly because the chapter is long but also because on the issues under discussion it continues, it seems to me, the more or less classical Christian concepts detailed here.

35. Cf. the excellent description of this "new world" in John Herman Randall, Jr., *The Making of the Modern Mind* (Boston: Houghton Mifflin, 1940), bk. 3, chaps. 11 and 12.

36. A familiar hymn, unexpectedly to many who regularly sing it, sounds this new vision of order, an order quite lacking in "secondary" qualities (note, however, the apparent absence of *sounds*, if not of *sight!*) yet illustrating a startling mathematical harmony—and not least, joy:

> The spacious firmament on high,
> With all the blue ethereal sky
> And spangled heaven, a shining frame
> Their great Original proclaim,

The unwearied sun from day to day
Does his Creator's power display,
And publishes to every land
The work of an almighty hand.

What though in solemn silence all
Move round the dark terrestrial ball?
What though no real voice nor sound
Amid their radiant orbs be found?
In reason's ear they all rejoice,
And utter forth a glorious voice:
For ever singing as they shine,
"The hand that made us is divine."

Joseph Addison (1672–1719)

37. For an excellent history of the "discovery" of the idea of Progress, exciting because written by one who believes thoroughly in that idea, cf. J. B. Bury, *The Idea of Progress* (New York: Dover, 1932), esp. chaps. 4–16.

38. Henry Drummond, *Natural Law in the Spiritual World* (New York: Pott, 1884); Lyman Abbott, *The Theology of an Evolutionist* (Boston: Houghton Mifflin, 1887); Henri-Louis Bergson, *Creative Evolution* (New York: Modern Library, 1944); Samuel Alexander, *Space, Time and Deity* (London: Macmillan, 1920); F. R. Tennant, *Philosophical Theology* (Cambridge: Cambridge University Press, 1956), vol 2; A. N. Whitehead, *Process and Reality* (New York: Macmillan, 1929); Pierre Teilhard de Chardin, *The Phenomena of Man* (New York: Harper Torchbooks, 1959).

CHAPTER 9
NATURE AS A REALM OF MEANING

1. Alfred North Whitehead, *Process and Reality* (New York: Macmillan, 1929), pp. 181–82; cf. also pp. 288, 252, and 28 for the further point that because the body is directly experienced as an intercommunion of experiences—as a "concrescence" of "prehensions"—all modes of "togetherness," in us and in nature around us, are similarly or, at least, analogously made up of "experiencing."

2. Even such a critic of a teleological view of nature (and of religion) as Richard Dawkins sees nature as saturated with needs and so "purposes," embodied in the "selfish gene" but nonetheless "meanings" that drive all organic action. If such "interests," unconscious and unfelt though they may be, are *not* there, then his rhetoric—and hence his theory—loses its substance. See Richard Dawkins, *The Selfish Gene* (Oxford and New York: Oxford University Press, 1976).

3. Holmes Rolston III, *Science and Religion* (New York: Random House,

1987), p. 118. No one has made this point more perceptively, clearly and profoundly than Rolston (pp. 115–18, and esp. pp. 133–46). This chapter is especially indebted to his thinking.

4. Cf. Franz Cumont, *The Oriental Religions in Roman Paganism* (Chicago: Open Court, 1911), chaps. 2, 6, 8.

5. Note Karl Barth's subtle discussion of the resurrection as an "event," an event not "historical" in the ordinary sense of being visible and tangible to all— as was Jesus' death—but historical as an "objective event at a particular time and in a particular space . . . [its content] cannot be grasped historically . . . but [we may] speak of a happening which is still actual and objective in space and time" (*Church Dogmatics: The Doctrine of the Word of God*, trans. G. T. Thomson [Edinburgh: T. & T. Clark, 1936], 3.1.336).

6. As one example of the obligation of self-denial and even self-sacrifice as the human response to the gift of divine grace, in effect, as the pattern of a grateful Christian example, cf. John Calvin. The Christian life, he says, is one of obedience and not of self-aggrandizement—"We are not our own but the Lord's"—and this obedience, as we are taught by Christ, is one of self-denial, of concern for and love for others and not for the self, and even of the willingness to sacrifice ourselves for God or for a righteous cause (*Institutes of the Christian Religion*, trans. John Allen [Philadelphia: Presbyterian Board of Christian Education, 1936], bk. 3, chap. 7.1; see also chaps. 6–8).

CHAPTER 10
NATURE AND THE HUMAN CARE OF NATURE

1. The author is, in the summer, a sailor on the Maine coast. There is in this activity the beginning, the merest hint, of mutuality, for one's joy in sailing is dependent on sea, wind, sun, sky, and islands; and one can quickly be at the mercy of the same wind, of waves, and of fog. Nevertheless, on a grey, stormy, southeasterly day in August, with the winds piling up rollers on the bay's rocks, candor makes one recognize the "tailored" character of that vacationer's mutuality when, peering through the cottage window, one sees the lobstermen heading out to sea—and thinks ahead five months to lobstering in that same sea in January and February!

2. Rachel Carson, *The Sea around Us* (New York: Oxford University Press, 1951); idem, *The Edge of the Sea* (Boston: Houghton Mifflin, 1955); idem, *Silent Spring* (Boston: Houghton Mifflin, 1962); Barry Commoner, *Science and Survival* (New York: Viking, 1966); idem, *The Closing Circle: Nature, Man and Technology* (New York: Knopf, 1971); idem, *Making Peace with the Planet* (New York: Pantheon, 1990); Gregory Bateson, *Angels Fear* (New York: Macmillan, 1987); idem, *Steps to an Ecology of Mind* (Northvale, N. J.: Aronson, 1987); Aldo Leopold, *Sand County Almanac* (New York: Oxford University Press, 1966); idem, *Round*

River 1953); idem, *River of the Mother of God and Other Essays*, eds. Susan L. Flacker and J. Baird Callicatt (Madison, Wis.: University of Wisconsin Press, 1991); Gary Snyder, *The Back Country* (New York: New Directions, 1968); idem, *Riprap: The Cold Mountain Poems* (San Francisco: Four Seasons Foundation, 1965); Loren Eiseley, *Another Kind of Autumn* (New York: Scribner's, 1977); Bill McKibben, *The End of Nature* (New York: Random House, 1989).

3. That the objectification of nature in science is intimately connected with nature's use (and misuse) by humans is such an important point that it is well to quote John Dewey at length: "[The modern scientific viewpoint] will regard intelligence not as the original shaper and final cause of things, but as the purposeful energetic reshaper of those phases of nature and life that obstruct social well-being. It esteems the individual . . . as the agent who is responsible through initiative, inventiveness and intelligently directed labor for re-creating the world, transforming it into an instrument and possession of intelligence" (*Reconstruction in Philosophy* [New York: Holt, 1920] p. 51). "[In modern science] it was asserted that the same laws hold everywhere, that there is homogeneity of material and process everywhere throughout nature . . . the earth is not superior in rank to the sun, moon and stars, but it is equal in dignity . . . . Being *at* hand, they are also capable of being brought *under* our hand; they can be manipulated, broken up, resolved into elements which can be managed, combined at will in old and new forms" (p. 65). "Human activity [could] conform only to ends already set by nature. It was not until ends were banished from nature that purposes became important as factors in human minds capable of reshaping existence. A natural world that does not subsist for the sake of realizing a fixed set of ends is relatively malleable and plastic; it may be used for this end *or* that. That nature can be known through the application of mechanical formulae is the prime condition of turning it to human account" (p. 70). "Only indefinite substitution and convertibility regardless of quality render nature manageable. The mechanization of nature is the condition of a practical and progressive idealism in action" (p. 72).

Two themes stand out here: first, the close dependence of the "free" or unfettered use of nature on the scientific vision of nature as mechanical and void of immanent ends or purposes, as having no ends within itself, no "for-itselfness"; and second, the intense faith of that generation in the selfless ("idealistic") intelligence with which modern technology will "manage" nature. Dewey makes proudly the same points that this book recites sorrowfully and remorsefully.

4. Herbert Marcuse, *One Dimensional Man* (London: Sphere Books, 1970), chap. 6, esp. pp. 125, 128–29, 135.

5. Lynn White, "The Historical Roots of the Ecological Crisis," *Science* 155 (March 10, 1967): 1203–7.

6. Karl Barth, *Church Dogmatics: The Doctrine of the Word of God*, trans. G. T.

Thomson (Edinburgh: T. & T. Clark, 1936), e.g., vol. 4, 1, pp. 37–38, 50–51, 126–27, 247, 466.

7. Cf. Robert Heilbroner, *An Inquiry into the Human Prospect* (New York: Norton, 1974); chap. 3, esp. pp. 93–94.

8. Keiji Nishitani, *Religion and Nothingness*, trans. Jan van Braght (Berkeley: University of California Press, 1982), chap. 3, esp. pp. 85–89.

9. Augustine *Enchiridion* 26; idem, *City of God* 14.11–18; idem, *On Original Sin* 41–42, 44–46; and cf. esp. Paul Tillich's profound reinterpretation of concupiscence away from the Augustinian emphasis on sexual lust to the broader and more destructive "lust for the whole world," "the unlimited desire to draw the whole world into one's self"; in *Systematic Theology* (Chicago: University of Chicago Press, 1957), vol. 2, chap. 2; and vol. 2, chap. 4, esp. p. 52. Cf. also Langdon Gilkey, *Gilkey on Tillich* (New York: Crossroad, 1989), pp. 128ff.

10. Rachel Carson and Carl Sagan immediately come to mind.

11. Heilbroner, *Inquiry*, pp. 132–36.

12. Martin Buber, *I and Thou*, trans. R. G. Smith (Edinburgh: T. & T. Clark, 1937).

13. Innumerable psalms make clear that all the forces of nature "praise and glorify the Lord who made them" and "declare the glory of God": e.g., Psalms 8, 19, 29, 50, 65, 77, 95–98, 103–104, 121, 136, 147–148.

14. Fyodor Dostoyevski, *The Brothers Karamazov.*

15. Keiji Nishitani, *Religion and Nothingness*, chap. 3, esp. pp. 77–95; and chap. 2.

16. Ludwig Feuerbach, *Lectures on the Essence of Religion*, trans. R. Manheim (New York: Harper & Row, 1967), lectures 19, 23, 26.

CHAPTER 11
HUMAN VIABILITY IN A NATURE THAT IS MORTAL

1. For a very illuminating discussion of the contingency of all of creation, cf. E. L. Mascall, *He Who Is* (London: Grear, 1948), chaps. 5 and 6; and idem, *Existence and Analogy* (London: Grear, 1949), chaps. 3 and 4.

2. Paul Tillich, *Systematic Theology* (Chicago: University of Chicago Press, 1951), 1:189–92.

3. For one study of the concept or symbol of *creatio ex nihilo*, cf. Langdon Gilkey, *Maker of Heaven and Earth* (Garden City, N.Y.: Doubleday, 1959).

4. A. N. Whitehead, *Process and Reality* (New York: Macmillan, 1929), p. 129; cf. also pp. 44, 304.

5. John Dewey, *The Quest for Certainty* (New York: Minton Balch, 1929), pp. 74–92, 139; and idem, *Science and the Future of Society*, in *Intelligence in the Modern World: John Dewey's Philosophy*, ed. J. Ratner (New York: Modern Library, 1939), pp. 343ff.

6. Cf. Whitehead, *Process and Reality*, pp. 28 and 116, where God is an actual entity and so in process, as are all others (p. 46), and in fact "in the grip of the metaphysical categories." Cf. also A. N. Whitehead, *Religion in the Making* (Cambridge: Cambridge University Press, 1926), p. 71.

7. Whitehead, *Process and Reality*, pp. 181–82.

8. For John Dewey, philosophy was not a "superknower," a mode of cognition "higher" or more "universal" or "timeless" than science. Philosophy's role rather was ethical and social, i.e., through intelligent reflection, first, to make the varied and momentary "wants" of life into "real values" (wants now made real by rational assessment) and, second, to secure these values by the intelligent application of scientific knowledge. On this new role for philosophy, cf. John Dewey, *Philosophy and Civilization* and idem, *Experience and Nature*, in Ratner, ed., *Intelligence*, pp. 245–74; and idem, *Reconstruction in Philosophy* (New York: Holt, 1920), chap. 1. It is interesting that for "naturalists" such as Dewey, philosophy is "not a knower"; yet it was this precise principle that later, when wielded by the logical positivists and language philosophers, unseated Deweyite naturalism in the late 1940s and 1950s. For this further step away from speculative philosophy, cf. Richard Rorty, ed., *The Linguistic Turn* (Chicago: University of Chicago Press, 1967), esp. Introduction.

9. Nils Eldridge, *The Monkey Business* (New York: Washington Square, 1982), pp. 48–50, 73–76 (an excellent book despite its title!).

10. Dewey, *Reconstruction in Philosophy*, p. 85.

11. Cf. as an example Julian H. Steward, "Cultural Evolution Today," in *Changing Man: The Threat and the Promise*, ed. Kyle Haseldon and Philip Hefner (Garden City, N. Y.: Doubleday, 1967), esp. pp. 49–62.

12. I wrote this sentence on December 27, 1991, two days after the official dissolution and burial of the Union of Soviet Socialist Republics with Mikhail Gorbachev's resignation on Christmas Day.

13. Augustine *The City of God* 14.28; 15.1–7; 19.12–17; 20.1–2.

14. Cf. Langdon Gilkey, *Shantung Compound* (New York: Harper & Row, 1966) esp. chaps. 5–8.

CHAPTER 12
NATURE AS THE IMAGE OF GOD

1. Cf. esp. Thomas Torrance, *Calvin's Doctrine of Man* (London: Lutterworth, 1952), chaps. 3–5: "There is no doubt that Calvin always thinks of the imago in terms of a *mirror*" (p. 36). Torrance goes on to say: "In what we have called the wider sense of the imago, imago dei may be used of anything in the universe created by God. Both the world as a whole and the tiniest creature are said to image the glory of God" (p. 37). He continues: "And, the only reason this imaging of God in the universe as a whole has been downplayed if not ignored

is that due to sin, man has been blind to this imaging in the nature around him and her" (pp. 39–40). For the rest, however, Torrance, like Calvin and the entire tradition, concentrates on the human as the *imago dei*.

2. Cf., e.g., Reinhold Niebuhr's important discussion of "self-transcendence" as the *imago dei* in human being in *Nature and Destiny of Man* (New York: Scribner's, 1941), chap. 6; and Emil Brunner, *Man in Revolt*, trans. Olive Wyon (1937; reprint, Philadelphia: Westminster, 1947), chap. 5, where the *imago* is defined as the "personal responsibility" (capacity and responsibility to respond) characteristic of human being as a "thou" in personal encounter with God and other humans. Cf. also Emil Brunner, *The Divine Human Encounter*, trans. A. W. Loos (Philadelphia: Westminster, 1943), chap. 2. Brunner emphasizes the theme of humanity as central, as does Karl Barth, *Church Dogmatics: The Doctrine of the Word of God*, trans. G. T. Thomson (Edinburgh: T. & T. Clark, 1936), 1:273ff. In Barth, humans lose the image in sin, for the image is "conformity to God," and it is restored in Christ. Hence, for Barth, the *imago* does not define human being qua human—"humanity," of course, is retained in sin—a rather radical departure.

3. Martin Heidegger, *Being and Time*, trans. J. Macquarrie and E. Robinson (New York: Harper & Row, 1962), 4:114–212.

4. Emmanuel Levinas, *Totalité et Infinité* (The Hague: Nijhoff, 1968), sec. 1, esp. pp. 23–54.

5. A. N. Whitehead, *Process and Reality* (New York: Macmillan, 1929), pp. 4, 25, 27, 67–68; idem, *Science and the Modern World* (New York: Macmillan, 1925), p. 26.

6. This is what Paul Tillich termed "ontological reason" (as opposed to "technical reason") and Whitehead "philosophical speculation," a wider mode of understanding reality inclusive of all the ways we know and so of all of our most fundamental assumptions. Cf. Paul Tillich, *Systematic Theology* (Chicago: University of Chicago Press, 1951), vol. 1, part 1, 1A; and cf. Langdon Gilkey, *Gilkey on Tillich* (New York: Crossroad, 1989), chaps. 2 and 3.

7. Cf., e.g., Paul Tillich, *The Protestant Era* (Chicago: University of Chicago Press, 1948) p. 57; and Langdon Gilkey, *Gilkey on Tillich*, pp. 40–47, 70–71.

8. The reason for this remark is the sharp dichotomy most twentieth-century theologies have postulated between "nature" and "spirit," i.e., between the realm of the inorganic (and the organic?), on the one hand, where "necessity" ruled and scientific knowledge apparently reigned, and the human realm, the realm of history, on the other hand, where self-awareness and decision (i.e., "freedom") were present and so where existential philosophy and biblical theology became normative. Most of these theologians recognized and assented to evolution; but they did not, as does this book, seek to apply that knowledge to their interpretation of creation and of history. As a good example of this dualism, cf. Langdon Gilkey, *Maker of Heaven and Earth* (Garden City, N.Y.: Doubleday, 1959), a volume on creation; and idem, *Reaping the Whirlwind* (New York: Seabury, 1976), a volume on providence and history. Brunner also includes

short chapters on "man and evolution" and "man in the cosmos" in his massive anthropology, *Man in Revolt* (chaps. 17 and 18), but neither subject is given any important bearing on Brunner's interpretation of the creation and fall of human being.

9. Cf. Stephen Toulmin, *The Return to Cosmology* (Berkeley: University of California Press, 1982).

10. John Calvin uses frequently the image of spectacles to show how these signs are there but not seen until faith enters and clarifies what was obscure: "For, as persons who are old, or whose eyes are by any means grown dim, if you show them the most beautiful book, though they perceive something written, but can scarcely read two words together, yet, by the assistance of spectacles, will begin to read distinctly—so the Scripture, collecting in our own mind the otherwise confused notions of Deity, dispels the darkness, and gives us a clear view of the true God" *(Institutes of the Christian Religion,* trans. John Allen [Philadelphia: Presbyterian Board of Christian Education, 1930], bk. 1, chap. 6, 1). And again: "For our eyes, either through age, or dull through any disease, see nothing distinctly without the assistance of spectacles, so, in our inquiries after God, . . . without the guidance of Scripture, we immediately lose our way" (ibid., bk. 1, chap. 14, 1).

11. Cf. also Paul Tillich's interesting equation of power in humans with vitality and of vitality with meaning or purpose ("heart")—and of both with courage—in *The Courage to Be* (New Haven: Yale University Press, 1953), pp. 78–85; and cf. the fundamental correlation of courage with self-affirmation despite finitude and of both with God as the "Power of Being" in *Systematic Theology,* 1:189–98. Cf. also *Gilkey on Tillich,* chap. 5, esp. pp. 91–97; and chapter 6, esp. pp. 102–13.

12. For an interesting and persuasive discussion of these "levels" of what he called a "stratified universe," cf. Michael Polanyi, *The Tacit Dimension* (Garden City, N.Y.: Doubleday, 1967), pp. 34–35; idem, *Knowing and Being,* ed. Marjorie Grene (Chicago: University of Chicago Press, 1969), esp. chap. 10 and chap. 14; and idem, *The Study of Man* (Chicago: University of Chicago Press, 1959), lecture 3, esp. pp. 73–93. Cf. also Donald Musser for a scholarly and enlightening thesis on Polanyi ("Theological Language and the Epistemology of Michael Polanyi" [Ph.D. diss., University of Chicago, 1981]).

13. For examples of the contradiction that all "morals" are the work of the genes that are "selfish"—a thesis presented in books extolling the two authors' quite different moral visions—cf. Richard Dawkins, *The Selfish Gene* (Oxford and New York: Oxford University Press, 1976), chaps. 4–6 and 11; and Richard Alexander, *The Biology of Moral Systems* (Hawthorne, N. Y.: de Gruyter, 1987), esp. chaps. 4 and 5.

14. *Francis Bacon, Novum Organum,* Aphorism, sec. 3:116, 124, 129, in E. A. Burtt, *The English Philosophers from Bacon to Mill* (New York: Modern Library, 1939).

15. Tillich, *Systematic Theology,* 1:208–10.

16. Cf. Michael Ruse, *Philosophy of Biology Today* (New York: SUNY Press, 1988), chap. 5.

17. For early Christian theology, God the source of all was both necessary and changeless, transcendent to all motion and temporal passage; yet God was the Creator, Ruler, and Redeemer of a changing temporal world. Hence the Logos, "Who was with God and was God" and yet "emptied Himself" and became incarnate, became the mediator between eternity and time, changelessness and change: the creative principle of God and the revealing, redemptive principle of God. In the text I am suggesting another, contemporary mediatorial role of Logos, or order, between the vast and yet coherent universe surrounding and upholding us, on the one hand, and ourselves—our minds and our wills—which also participate in this order of things, on the other hand. This meditation Tillich names Objective Logos (the order of the external universe) and Subjective Logos (the order with which our minds reflect and judge), the strange correlation that makes all cognition and science possible. Cf. *Systematic Theology,* 1:20–80.

18. "Contrast against a background of order" is the basis of beauty and so of value to A. N. Whitehead; hence novelty (as providing contrast) within a fundamental order of passage enhances value: cf. *Adventures of Ideas* (New York: Macmillan, 1933), chaps. 18 and 19. For a more technical discussion, cf. Whitehead, *Process and Reality,* pp. 424–28.

19. Steven Weinberg: "The more we [the physicists] know about the universe, the more it is evident that it is pointless and meaningless"; and Heinz Pagels adds: "This is not the conclusion of a pessimistic religion or the raving of an unhappy philosopher, but the only rational inference that emerges from our scientific view of the cosmos" (Heinz Pagels, *Perfect Symmetry* [New York: Bantam, 1986], p. 383).

20. This awareness of passing as "the ultimate evil" is beautifully expressed by Whitehead: "The ultimate evil in the temporal world is deeper than any specific evil. It lies in the fact that the past fades, that time is a 'perpetual perishing'" (*Process and Reality,* p. 517). And "according to religion, this discernment of relationship forms in itself the very substance of existence. . . . Religion insists that the world is a mutually adjusted disposition of things, issuing in value for its own sake" (A. N. Whitehead, *Religion in the Making* [Cambridge: Cambridge University Press, 1926], pp. 143–44). "Peace is then the intuition of permanence" (*Adventures of Ideas,* p. 369). Finally: "Religion is the vision of something that stands beyond, behind and within the passing flux of immediate things" (*Science and the Modern World,* p. 267).

21. This is the substance of Thomas Aquinas's two main "proofs" of God. The second proof in the *Summa Theologica* states that in no case is a thing the efficient cause of itself (i.e., it is contingent); the series of causes cannot go back to infinity; therefore it is necessary to admit a first efficient cause (*Summa*

Theologica 1.2.3). The third proof in *Summa Theologica* states that "it is impossible for these [things that may not be, "contingent" things] always to exist, for that which can not be, at some time will not be. Therefore, if everything can not be, then at one time there was nothing in existence [which is impossible] . . . therefore not all things are merely possible, but there must exist something the existence of which is necessary" (1.2.3). Cf. the brilliant analyses of these proofs in E. R. Mascall, *He Who Is* (London: Grear, 1948), chaps. 5 and 6; and idem, *Existence and Analogy* (London: Grear, 1949), chaps. 3 and 4.

22. Cf. Pagels, *Perfect Symmetry*, chap. 5, esp. pp. 359, 365–67.

23. "It is a contradiction in terms to assume that some explanatory fact can float into the actual world out of non-entity. Non-entity is nothingness. Every explanatory fact refers to the decision and to the efficacy of an actual thing" (Whitehead, *Process and Reality*, p. 73).

24. Cf. Whitehead, *Process and Reality*, part 5, esp. chap. 2, secs. 2 and 3; and H. N. Wieman, *The Source of the Human Good* (Chicago: University of Chicago Press, 1946). Implicit in this definition of God are, first, the finitude of God and, second, the near identity of God with human values.

25. For a particularly powerful statement of these questions about God and death, cf. Ernest Becker, *The Denial of Death* (New York: Free Press, 1973).

26. Cf. Becker, *Denial of Death*. Cf. also the very profound theological work of Arthur McGill.

27. This brief statement is indebted to Tillich, esp. *Systematic Theology*, 1:192–98, 206–9, 272–79. Cf. also Gilkey, *Gilkey on Tillich*, pp. 103–5.

CHAPTER 13
NATURE AND NATURE'S GOD

1. My relation to the tradition of natural theology has been a puzzle, especially to me. As an enthusiastic younger supporter of the so-called neo-orthodoxy (non-Barthian wing), I represented a strongly argued anti–natural theology position, as my books from *Maker of Heaven and Earth* to *Naming the Whirlwind* show. Then, when writing *Reaping the Whirlwind*, a volume on providence and the philosophy of history, I found it incumbent in developing that "doctrine" to think out an "ontology of historical passage." Further, it was necessary, if that ontology was to serve as the basis for conceiving an ontology of providential action (i.e., What do we *mean* by an ordinary and universal act of God?), to articulate an intelligible relation between that "empirically" derived ontology and a "biblically" derived interpretation of providence—if the former was to be "Christian" and the latter "credible." Once this relation was seen to be defensible as well as intelligible from the biblical side, it became clear that it was also defensible and intelligible from the empirical and ontological side to the biblical; that is, there appeared arguments as to why the mind was moved—even

if it did not want so to move!—from an ontology based on general experience to the reality and efficacy of God. I wrote down these three arguments late at night—at about 3:30 A.M.—confident that I would in the morning see clearly what was wrong with them. But in the morning they still appeared invulnerable—and I was stuck with them. Although the mind "freely" conceives of arguments, once they appear on the scene and appear there *as valid*, the mind can only adhere to them; thus does "freedom" breed "necessity"!

2. John Calvin, *Institutes of the Christian Religion*, trans. John Allen (Philadelphia: Presbyterian Board of Christian Education, 1930) 1.6.1.

3. Cf. Charles Hartshorne, *The Logic of Perfection* (LaSalle, Ill.: Open Court, 1962), chaps. 2, 6–9; and esp. idem, *Creative Synthesis and Philosophic Method* (LaSalle, Ill.: Open Court, 1970), pp. 29, 62ff., 1334ff.

4. A. N. Whitehead, *Process and Reality* (New York: Macmillan, 1929), esp. pp. 251–52, 340–60, 388–90; idem, *Adventures of Ideas* (New York: Macmillan, 1933), chaps. 17, 20.

5. Cf. Charles Hartshorne, *The Divine Relativity* (New Haven: Yale University Press, 1948), pp. 96–98.

6. Cf. John Dewey, *The Quest for Certainty* (New York: Minton Balch, 1929).

7. E.g., Hartshorne, *Logic of Perfection*, chap. 2; idem, *Man's Vision of God* (New York: Harper & Brothers, 1941), chap. 9; idem, *Divine Relativity*, chap. 2.

8. F. R. Tennant, *Philosophical Theology* (Cambridge: Cambridge University Press, 1956), vol. 2, chaps. 1 and 2.

9. Cf. the arguments of Augustine *Of True Religion* 52–57; Thomas Aquinas *Summa Theologica* 1.2.3; and Whitehead, *Process and Reality*, bk. 5.

10. Whitehead, *Process and Reality*, pp. 6–7.

11. For my most complete, or at least "sustained," effort to provide such a union of ontology and theology in a "doctrine" (in this case, of providence), cf. Langdon Gilkey, *Reaping the Whirlwind* (New York: Seabury, 1976), part 3.

12. Possibility, as a category separate from—even, in some measure, independent of—actuality, appears for the first time in modern philosophy, showing the coming into prominence of temporality or process and so the movement of what is real into the new. As far as I know, Gottfried Wilhelm Leibniz was the first to place possibility in a central position in ontology: the possible worlds from among which God chose our world, "the best of all possible worlds." Since then, the possible has represented a steady presence in thought, receiving its most explicit articulation in Whitehead's conception of eternal objects and in Ernst Bloch's vision of "utopia," the "not yet" that inspires, invigorates, and directs all thought, literature, and dreams. Cf. Ernst Bloch, *A Philosophy of the Future*, trans. G. J. Cumming (New York: Herder & Herder, 1970); idem, *Man on His Own*, trans. E. B. Ashton (New York: Herder & Herder, 1970); and idem, *Das Princip Hoffnung* (Frankfurt am Main: Suhrkamp, 1959).

13. For a fuller description of the polarities "freedom" and "destiny" and

their relevance to personal and historical (communal) existence, cf. Gilkey, *Reaping the Whirlwind*, pp. 43–46, 48–57, 96–98, 251–52.

14. Cf. ibid., pp. 63–69.

15. Thomas Aquinas, *Summa Theologica* 1.2.3 (second proof).

16. Cf. Friedrich Schleiermacher, *The Christian Faith*, trans. H. R. Mac-Intosh and J. S. Stewart (Edinburgh: T. & T. Clark, 1948), sec. 4.3, for a very perceptive and persuasive discussion of our experience of "freedom"—the freedom to counter the world's causality on us—as at the same time an experience of "absolute dependence," dependence on God as the ground (or cause) of our freedom, as well as the ground (or cause) of all in the world that determines us.

17. Cf. Whitehead, *Process and Reality*, pp. 514–16, 521–24; Gilkey, *Reaping the Whirlwind*, pp. 303–6.

18. Cf. Paul Tillich, *Systematic Theology* (Chicago: University of Chicago Press, 1951), 1:235–41, 246–49, 272–79.

19. Cf. Schleiermacher, *Christian Faith*; cf. also Emil Brunner, *The Divine Human Encounter*, trans. A. W. Loos (Philadelphia: Westminster, 1943), pp. 52–63; idem, *The Christian Doctrine of Creation and Redemption*, trans. Olive Wyon (London: Lutterworth, 1952), pp. 55–63 and esp. pp. 299–305.

20. Whitehead, *Process and Reality*, pp. 514–16, 521–24.

Bibliography

Works cited in this volume as well as works relevant to the volume.

1. HISTORICAL

Basalla, George, ed. *Victorian Science.* Garden City, N. Y.: Doubleday Anchor, 1970.

Borstin, Daniel J. *The Lost World of Thomas Jefferson.* 1948. Reprint. Chicago: University of Chicago Press, 1981.

Burtt, Edwin A. *The English Philosophers from Bacon to Mill.* New York: Modern Library, 1939.

———. *The Metaphysical Foundations of Modern Science.* Garden City, N. Y.: Doubleday, 1954.

Butterfield, Herbert. *The Origins of Modern Science.* New York: Free Press, 1957.

Creel, Herlee. *Confucius: The Man and the Myth.* New York: Day, 1949.

Crombie, Alistair C. *Medieval and Early Modern Science.* Cambridge: Harvard University Press, 1967.

Cumont, Franz. *The Oriental Religions in Roman Paganism.* Chicago: Open Court, 1911.

Dampier, William C. *A Shorter History of Science.* New York: Macmillan, 1944.

Dillenberger, John. *Protestant Thought and Natural Science.* Westport, Conn.: Greenwood, 1977.

Gay, Peter. *The Enlightenment,* Vols. 1, 2, 3. New York: Knopf, 1967.

Goldstein, Thomas. *The Dawn of Modern Science.* Boston: Houghton Mifflin, 1980.

Greene, John C. *The Death of Adam.* Ames: Iowa State University Press, 1959.

Gregory, Frederick. *Scientific Materialism in Nineteenth-Century Germany.* Dordrecht and Boston: Reidel, 1977.

Himmelfarb, Gertrude. *Darwin and the Darwinian Revolution.* New York: Norton, 1968.

Koyre, Alexandre. *From the Closed World to the Infinite Universe.* Baltimore: Johns Hopkins University Press, 1957.

Kuhn, Thomas S. *The Structure of Scientific Revolutions.* Chicago: University of Chicago Press, 1962.

Lindburg, David G., and Numbers, Ronald L., eds. *God and Nature.* Berkeley: University of California Press, 1986.

Moore, James R. *The Post-Darwinian Controversies.* Cambridge: Cambridge University Press, 1979.

Randall, John Herman, Jr. *The Making of the Modern Mind*. Boston: Houghton Mifflin, 1940.

2. RELIGION AND SCIENCE

Abbott, Lyman. *The Theology of an Evolutionist*. Boston: Houghton Mifflin, 1887.

Alexander, Samuel. *Space, Time and Deity*. London: Macmillan, 1920.

Ayala, Francisco. *Studies in the Philosophy of Biology*. Edited by F. J. Ayala and T. Dobzhansky. Berkeley: University of California Press, 1974.

Bachelard, Gaston. *The New Scientific Spirit*. Boston: Beacon, 1984.

Barbour, Ian. *Issues in Science and Religion*. Englewood Cliffs, N. J.: Prentice-Hall, 1966.

————. *Myths, Models and Paradigms*. New York: Harper & Row, 1974.

————. *Religion in an Age of Science*. San Francisco: Harper & Row, 1990.

Barrow, John D., and Tipler, Frank J. *The Anthropic Cosmological Principle*. Oxford: Clarendon, 1986.

Braithwaite, Richard B. *Scientific Explanation*. New York: Harper Torchbooks, 1960.

Bronowski, Jacob. *The Common Sense of Science*. Harmondsworth: Modern Library, 1960.

Brown, Harold I. *Perception, Theory and Commitment*. Chicago: University of Chicago Press, 1979.

Bury, J. B. *The Idea of Progress*. New York: Dover, 1932.

Carnap, Rudolf. *Philosophical Foundations of Physics*. New York: Basic Books, 1966.

Cohen, Morris, and Nagel, Ernst. *An Introduction to Logic and the Scientific Method*. London: Routledge & Kegan Paul, 1949.

Collingwood, R. G. *An Essay on Metaphysics*. Oxford: Oxford University Press, 1940.

————. *The Idea of Nature*. Oxford: Oxford University Press, 1945.

Davies, Paul. *God and the New Physics*. New York: Penguin, 1983.

Dawkins, Richard. *The Blind Watchmaker*. New York: Norton, 1986.

————. *The Selfish Gene*. Oxford and New York: Oxford University Press, 1976.

Denton, Michael. *Evolution in Crisis*. London: Bennett Books, 1985.

Dobzhansky, Theodosius. *The Biology of Ultimate Concern*. New York: New American Library, 1967.

————. *Evolution, Genetics and Man*. New York: Wiley, 1955.

————. *Mankind Evolving*. New Haven: Yale University Press, 1962.

Drummond, Henry. *Natural Law in the Spiritual World*. New York: Pott, 1897.

Eiseley, Loren. *Another Kind of Autumn*. New York: Scribner's, 1977.

————. *Darwin's Century*. Garden City, N.Y.: Doubleday, 1958.

———. *The Firmament of Time.* New York: Atheneum, 1960.

———. *The Immense Journey.* New York: Vintage, 1957.

Feigl, Herbert, and Brodbeck, May, eds. *Readings in the Philosophy of Science.* New York: Century-Crofts, 1953.

Feyerabend, Paul. *Against Method.* London: New Left Books, 1975.

———. *Realism, Rationalism and Scientific Method: Philosophical Papers.* Vols. 1 and 2. Cambridge: Cambridge University Press, 1985.

Gerhart, Mary, and Russell, Allan. *Metaphoric Process.* Fort Worth: Texas Christian University Press, 1984.

Gilkey, Langdon. *Religion and the Scientific Future.* New York: Harper & Row, 1969.

Gould, Stephen J. *Hen's Teeth and Horse's Toes.* New York: Norton, 1983.

———. *The Panda's Thumb.* New York: Norton, 1980.

Hanson, Norwood R. *Observation and Exploration.* New York: Harper & Row, 1971.

———. *Patterns of Discovery.* Cambridge: Cambridge University Press, 1958.

Hawking, Stephen. *A Brief History of Time.* New York: Bantam, 1988.

Heilbroner, Robert. *An Inquiry into the Human Prospect.* New York: Norton, 1974.

Heim, Karl. *Christian Faith and Natural Science.* New York: Harper Torchbooks, 1957.

Heisenberg, Werner. *Physics and Beyond.* Translated by A. J. Pomerans. New York: Harper Torchbooks, 1971.

Jastrow, Robert. *God and the Astronomers.* New York: Norton, 1978.

Krikorian, Yervant. *Naturalism and the Human Spirit.* New York: Columbia University Press, 1946.

Lakatos, Imre. *Mathematics, Science and Epistemology.* Edited by John Worral and Gregory Currie. Cambridge: Cambridge University Press, 1978.

Lester, Lane P., and Bohlin, Raymond G. *The Natural Limits to Biological Change.* Dallas: Probe, 1989.

McKibben, Bill. *The End of Nature.* New York: Random House, 1989.

Medawar, Peter B. *The Limits of Science.* New York: Harper & Row, 1984.

Musser, Donald. "Theological Language and the Epistemology of Michael Polanyi." Ph.D diss., University of Chicago, 1981.

Nagel, Ernst. *The Structure of Science.* New York: Harcourt, Brace & World, 1961.

Pagels, Heinz R. *Perfect Symmetry.* New York: Bantam, 1986.

Peacocke, Arthur. *Creation and the World of Science.* Oxford: Clarendon, 1979.

———. *Intimations of Reality.* Notre Dame, Ind.: University of Notre Dame Press, 1984.

———, ed. *The Sciences and Theology in the Twentieth Century.* Notre Dame, Ind.: University of Notre Dame Press, 1981.

Peacocke, Arthur, and Anderson, Svend, eds. *Evolution and Creation.* Aarhus, Denmark: Aarhus University Press, 1987.

Polanyi, Michael. *Knowing and Being.* Edited by Marjorie Grene. Chicago: University of Chicago Press, 1969.

————. *Personal Knowledge.* New York: Harper & Row, 1958.

————. *Science, Faith and Society.* London: Oxford University Press, 1946.

————. *The Study of Man.* Chicago: University of Chicago Press, 1959.

————. *The Tacit Dimension.* Garden City, N.Y.: Doubleday, 1957.

Popper, Karl. *The Logic of Scientific Discovery.* New York: Harper & Row, 1959.

Poynter, Marguerite, and Klein, Michael. *Cosmic Quest.* New York: Atheneum, 1984.

Rolston, Holmes, III. *Science and Religion.* New York: Random House, 1987.

Rosenberg, Alexander. *The Structure of Biological Science.* Cambridge: Cambridge University Press, 1986.

Ruse, Michael. *Is Science Sexist?* Boston and Dordrecht: Reidel, 1984.

————. *Philosophy of Biology Today.* New York: SUNY Press, 1988.

Russel, Robert J., ed. *Physics, Philosophy and Theology.* Vatican City: Vatican Observatory, 1988.

Sagan, Carl. *The Cosmic Connection.* New York: Doubleday, 1973.

————. *Cosmos.* New York: Ballantine, 1980.

Santayana, George. *Reason in Science.* New York: Scribner's, 1946.

Scheffler, Israel. *The Anatomy of Inquiry.* Indianapolis: Bobbs-Merrill, 1963.

————. *Science and Subjectivity.* Indianapolis: Bobbs-Merrill, 1967.

Schilling, Harold K. *Science and Religion: An Interpretation of Two Communities.* New York: Scribner's, 1962.

Searle, John R., *The Rediscovery of Mind.* Cambridge, Mass.: MIT Press, 1992.

Sellers, Wilfrid. *Science, Perception and Reality.* New York: Humanities Press, 1963.

Simpson, George G. *The Meaning of Evolution.* New Haven: Yale University Press, 1967.

————. *This View of Life.* New York: Harcourt, Brace & World, 1964.

Teilhard de Chardin, Pierre. *The Phenomenon of Man.* New York: Harper Torchbooks, 1959.

Theissen, Gerd. *Biblical Faith: An Evolutionary Approach.* Philadelphia: Fortress, 1985.

Tiles, Mary. *Bachelard: Science and Objectivity.* Cambridge: Cambridge University Press, 1984.

Toulmin, Stephen. *Foresight and Understanding.* New York: Harper & Brothers, 1961.

————. *Human Understanding.* Princeton, N. J.: Princeton University Press, 1972.

————. *Metaphysical Beliefs.* London: SCM, 1957.

————. *The Philosophy of Science.* New York: Harper & Row, 1953.

————. *The Return to Cosmology.* Berkeley: University of California Press, 1982.

Weinberg, Steven. *The First Three Minutes*. New York: Basic Books, 1977.

White, Lynn. "The Historical Roots of the Ecological Crisis." *Science* 155 (March 10, 1967): 1203–7.

Young, Davis A. *Christianity and the Age of the Earth*. Grand Rapids: Eerdmans, 1982.

3. THEOLOGY AND PHILOSOPHY

Anderson, Bernard. *Understanding the Old Testament*. Englewood Cliffs, N. J.: Prentice Hall, 1975.

Aquinas, Thomas. *Basic Writings of St. Thomas Aquinas*. Edited by Anton C. Pegis. New York: Random House, 1944.

Augustine. *Basic Writings of St. Augustine*. Edited by Whitney J. Oates, New York: Random House, 1948.

———. *On Free Will*. In *Library of Christian Classics*. Edited by C. J. Burleigh. Philadelphia: Westminster, 1953.

Barth, Karl. *Church Dogmatics: The Doctrine of the Word of God*. Vol. 1, 1. Translated by G. T. Thomson. Edinburgh: T. & T. Clark, 1936.

Becker, Ernest. *The Denial of Death*. New York: Free Press, 1973.

Berger, Peter, and Luckmann, Thomas. *The Social Construction of Reality*. Garden City, N.Y.: Doubleday, 1967.

Bergson, Henri-Louis. *Creative Evolution*. New York: Modern Library, 1944.

Bernstein, Richard J. *Beyond Objectivism and Relativism*. Philadelphia: University of Pennsylvania Press, 1983.

Bloch, Ernst. *Das Princip Hoffnung*. Frankfurt am Main: Suhrkamp, 1959.

———. *Man on His Own*. Translated by E. B. Ashton. New York: Herder & Herder, 1970.

———. *A Philosophy of the Future*. Translated by G. J. Cumming. New York: Herder & Herder, 1970.

Brunner, Emil. *The Christian Doctrine of Creation and Redemption*. Translated by Olive Wyon. London: Lutterworth, 1952.

———. *The Divine Human Encounter*. Translated by A. W. Loos. Philadelphia: Westminster, 1943.

———. *Man in Revolt*. Translated by Olive Wyon. 1937. Reprint. Philadelphia: Westminster, 1947.

Buber, Martin. *I and Thou*. Translated by R. G. Smith. Edinburgh: T. & T. Clark, 1937.

Calvin, John. *Institutes of the Christian Religion*. Translated by John Allen. Philadelphia: Presbyterian Board of Christian Education, 1930.

Dewey, John. *Intelligence in the Modern World: John Dewey's Philosophy*. Edited by J. Ratner. New York: Modern Library, 1939.

———. *The Quest for Certainty*. New York: Minton Balch, 1929.

———. *Reconstruction in Philosophy*. New York: Holt, 1920.

Eichrodt, Walter. *Theology of the Old Testament*. 2 vols. Philadelphia: Westminster, 1961, 1967.

Eliade, Mircea. *Cosmos and History*. New York: Harper Torchbooks, 1959.

―――. *The Eternal Return: Images and Symbols*. New York: Sheed & Ward, 1969.

―――. *Myth and Reality*. Translated by Willard R. Trask. New York: Harper & Row, 1963.

―――. *Myths, Dreams and Mysteries*. New York: Harper & Row, 1975.

―――. *Patterns in Comparative Religion*. Translated by R. Shed. New York: Meridian, 1966.

―――. *The Quest: History and Meaning in Religion*. Chicago: University of Chicago Press, 1969.

―――. *The Sacred and the Profane*. New York: Harcourt, Brace, 1959.

Feuerbach, Ludwig. *Lectures on the Essence of Religion*. Translated by R. Manheim. New York: Harper & Row, 1967.

Fung, Yu-Lan. *The Spirit of Chinese Philosophy*. Translated by E. R. Hughes. London: Routledge & Kegan Paul, 1947.

Gilkey, Langdon. *Catholicism Confronts Modernity*. New York: Seabury, 1975.

―――. *Gilkey on Tillich*. New York: Crossroad, 1989.

―――. *Maker of Heaven and Earth*. Garden City, N.Y.: Doubleday, 1959.

―――. *Naming the Whirlwind*. Indianapolis: Bobbs-Merrill, 1969.

―――. *Reaping the Whirlwind*. New York: Seabury, 1976.

―――. *Shantung Compound*. New York: Harper & Row, 1966.

―――. *Society and the Sacred*. New York: Crossroad, 1981.

Hartshorne, Charles. *Creative Synthesis and Philosophic Method*. LaSalle, Ill.: Open Court, 1970.

―――. *The Divine Relativity*. New Haven: Yale University Press, 1948.

―――. *The Logic of Perfection*. LaSalle, Ill.: Open Court, 1962.

―――. *Man's Vision of God*. New York: Harper & Brothers, 1941.

Heidegger, Martin. *Being and Time*. Translated by J. Macquarrie and E. Robinson. New York: Harper & Row, 1962.

Hume, David. *Enquiries Concerning Human Understanding and Concerning the Principles of Morals*. Edited by L. A. Selby-Bigge. Revised by P. H. Nidditch. Oxford: Clarendon Press, 1975.

The I-Ching. Translated by Richard Wilhelm and W. Baynes. New York: Pantheon, 1950.

Irenaeus. *Against Heresies*. In *The Ante-Nicene Fathers*. Vol. 1. Grand Rapids: Eerdmans, 1950.

Jaeger, Werner. *Aristotle*. Translated by T. R. Robinson. Oxford: Oxford University Press, 1948.

―――. *Paideia*. Translated by G. Highet. 3 vols. New York: Oxford University Press, 1943.

————. *The Theology of the Early Greek Philosophers*. Oxford: Clarendon, 1947.

Jaspers, Karl. *The Origin and Goal of History*. New Haven: Yale University Press, 1953.

Kant, Immanuel. *Critique of Pure Reason*. Translated by Norman Kemp Smith. New York: St. Martin's Press, 1929.

————. *Prolegomena to Any Future Metaphysics*. Translated by Paul Carus. Revised by James W. Ellington. Indianapolis: Hackett, 1977.

————. *Religion within the Limits of Reason Alone*. Translated by T. M. Green and H. H. Hudson. New York: Harper Torchbooks, 1934.

Levinas, Emmanuel. *Totalité et Infinité*. The Hague: Nijhoff, 1968.

Lonergan, Bernard. *Insight*. London: Longmans, 1964.

Long, Charles. *Alpha: The Myth of Creation*. New York: Braziller, 1963.

Mascall, Eric L. *Existence and Analogy*. London: Grear, 1949.

————. *He Who Is*. London: Grear, 1948.

Morgan, Kenneth. *The Religion of the Hindus*. New York: Ronald, 1953.

Nahm, M. C. *Selections from Early Greek Philosophy*. New York: Crofts, 1947.

Niebuhr, Reinhold. *Beyond Tragedy*. New York: Scribner's, 1936.

————. *Nature and Destiny of Man*. New York: Scribner's, 1941.

Nishitani, Keiji. *Religion and Nothingness*. Translated by Jan van Braght. Berkeley: University of California Press, 1982.

Oates, W. J. *The Stoic and Epicurian Philosophers*. New York: Random House, 1940.

Plotinus. *The Enneads*. Translated by Stephen Mackenna. *The Essence of Plotinus*. Compiled by Grace Turnbull. New York: Oxford University Press, 1948.

Radhakrishanan, Sarvepalli. *Indian Philosophy*. 2 vols. London: Allen and Unwin, 1948.

Rahner, Karl. *Theological Investigations*. Vol. 1. Translated by Cornelius Ernst. London: Darton, Longman & Todd, 1961.

Reichenbach, Hans. *Experience and Prediction*. Chicago: University of Chicago Press, 1938.

Ricoeur, Paul. *The Symbolism of Evil*. Translated by E. Buchanon. New York: Harper & Row, 1967.

Rorty, Richard. *Philosophy and the Mirror of Nature*. Princeton, N. J.: Princeton University Press, 1980.

————, ed. *The Linguistic Turn*. Chicago: University of Chicago Press, 1967.

Santayana, George. *Skepticism and Animal Faith*. New York: Scribner's, 1929.

Schleiermacher, Friedrich. *The Christian Faith*. Translated by H. R. MacIntosh and J. S. Stewart. Edinburgh: T. & T. Clark, 1948.

————. *On Religion: Speeches to Its Cultured Despisers*. Translated by Richard Crouter. Cambridge: Cambridge University Press, 1988.

Schwartz, Benjamin I. *The World of Thought in Ancient China*. Cambridge, Mass.: Harvard University Press, 1985.

Sharma, Arvind. *A Hindu Perspective on the Philosophy of Religion.* London: Macmillan, 1991.

Sullivan, Lawrence E. *Icanchu's Drum.* New York: Macmillan, 1988.

Tennant, F. R. *Philosophical Theology.* Cambridge: Cambridge University Press, 1956.

Theodore de Bary, William. *The Unfolding of Neo-Confucianism.* New York: Columbia University Press, 1975.

————, ed. *Sources of Chinese Tradition.* New York: Columbia University Press, 1960.

Tillich, Paul. *The Courage to Be.* New Haven: Yale University Press, 1953.

————. *The Protestant Era.* Chicago: University of Chicago Press, 1948.

————. *Systematic Theology.* 3 vols. Chicago: University of Chicago Press, 1951, 1957, 1963.

————. *Theology of Culture.* Edited by R. C. Kimball. London: Oxford University Press, 1959.

Torrance, Thomas. *Calvin's Doctrine of Man.* London: Lutterworth, 1952.

Troeltsch, Ernst. *The Social Teachings of the Christian Churches.* Translated by Olive Wyon. New York: Macmillan, 1949.

Tu, Wei-Ming. *Humanity and Self-Civilization: Essays in Confucian Thought.* Berkeley: Asian Humanities Press, 1979.

Tylor, Edward Burnett. *The Origins of Culture,* 2 vols. Gloucester, Mass.: Peter Smith, 1970.

Van der Leeuw, Gerardus. *Religion in Essence and Manifestation.* Translated by J. E. Turner. New York: Harper & Row, 1963.

van Leeuwen, Thomas. *The Skyward Trend of Thought.* Art, History, and Architecture Books. The Hague, The Netherlands, 1986.

von Rad, Gerhard. *Old Testament Theology.* 2 vols. New York: Harper & Row, 1962, 1966.

Wieman, Henry N. *The Source of the Human Good.* Chicago: University of Chicago Press, 1946.

Whitehead, Alfred North. *Adventures of Ideas.* New York: Macmillan, 1933.

————. *Function of Reason.* Princeton, N. J.: Princeton University Press, 1929.

————. *Modes of Thought.* Cambridge: Cambridge University Press, 1938.

————. *Process and Reality.* New York: Macmillan, 1929.

————. *Religion in the Making.* Cambridge: Cambridge University Press, 1927.

————. *Science and the Modern World.* New York: Macmillan, 1925.

————. *Symbolism: Its Meaning and Effect.* New York: Macmillan, 1927.

Winter, Gibson. *Being Free: Reflections on America's Cultural Revolution.* New York: Macmillan, 1970.

Wright, G. Ernest, and Fuller, Reginald H. *The Book of the Acts of God.* Garden City, N.Y.: Doubleday, 1957.

Yu, Anthony. "The Confucian Concept of Order." *Thought Quarterly Review* 43 (1968):249–72.

Zimmer, Heinrich. *Myths and Symbols in Indian Art and Civilization.* Edited by Joseph Campbell. New York: Pantheon, 1947.

———. *Philosophies of India.* Edited by Joseph Campbell. New York: Pantheon, 1951.

4. TECHNOLOGY, ETHICS, AND SOCIETY

Alexander, Richard D. *The Biology of Moral Systems.* Hawthorne, N.Y.: de Gruyter, 1987.

Barbour, Ian, ed. *Earth Might Be Fair: Reflections on Ethics, Religion and Ecology.* Englewood Cliffs, N. J.: Prentice-Hall, 1972.

Bateson, Gregory. *Angels Fear.* New York: Macmillan, 1987.

———. *Steps to an Ecology of Mind.* Northvale, N. J.: Avonson, 1987.

Bolding, Kenneth. *The Meaning of the Twentieth Century.* New York: Harper Collophon, 1964.

Borchert, Donald M., and Steward, David, eds. *Being Human in a Technological Age.* Athens: Ohio University Press, 1979.

Burhoe, Ralph W. *Science and Human Values in the Twenty-First Century.* Philadelphia: Westminster, 1971.

Carson, Rachel. *The Edge of the Sea.* Boston: Houghton Mifflin, 1955.

———. *The Sea around Us.* New York: Oxford University Press, 1951.

———. *Silent Spring.* Boston: Houghton Mifflin, 1962.

Cobb, John B. *Is It Too Late?* Beverly Hills, Calif.: Bruce, 1972.

Commoner, Barry. *The Closing Circle: Nature, Man and Technology.* New York: Knopf, 1971.

———. *Making Peace with the Planet.* New York: Pantheon, 1990.

———. *The Poverty of Power.* New York: Knopf, 1976.

———. *Science and Survival.* New York: Viking, 1966.

Dijksterhuis, Eduard J. *The Mechanization of the World Picture.* Oxford: Clarendon, 1961.

Ellul, Jacques. *The Meaning of the City.* Translated by Dennis Pardee. Grand Rapids: Eerdmans, 1970.

———. *The Technological Society.* Translated by John Wilkinson. New York: Knopf, 1964.

Ferkiss, Victor C. *Technological Man: The Myth and Reality.* New York: Braziller, 1969.

Ferré, Frederick. *Shaping the Future.* New York: Harper & Row, 1976.

Haseldon, Kyle, and Hefner, Philip. *Changing Man: The Threat and the Promise.* Garden City, N.Y.: Doubleday, 1967.

Huxley, Julian. *Evolutionary Ethics.* London: Oxford University Press, 1943.

————. *Religion without Revelation.* New York: Harper & Brothers, 1927.

Leopold, Aldo. *A Sand County Almanac.* Illustrated by Charles W. Schwartz. New York: Oxford University Press, 1966.

————. *The River of the Mother of God and Other Essays.* Edited by Susan L. Flader and J. Baird Callicott. Madison, Wis.: University of Wisconsin Press, 1991.

Marcuse, Herbert. *One Dimensional Man.* London: Sphere, 1970.

Meadows, Donnella. *The Limits to Growth.* New York: Universe, 1972.

Moore, Wilbert E., ed. *Technology and Social Change.* Chicago: Quadrangle, 1972.

Morgenthau, Hans. *Scientific Man vs. Power Politics.* Chicago: University of Chicago Press, 1946.

Mumford, Lewis. *Technics and Civilization.* New York: Harcourt, Brace, 1934.

Price, Don Krasher. *The Scientific Estate.* Cambridge, Mass.: Belknap Press of the Harvard University Press, 1965.

Schell, Jonathan. *The Fate of the Earth.* New York: Knopf, 1982.

Snyder, Gary. *The Back Country.* New York: New Directions, 1968.

————. *Riprap: The Cold Mountain Poems.* San Francisco: Four Seasons Foundation, 1965.

Thomas, J. Mark. *Ethics and Technoculture.* Lanham, Md.: University Press of America, 1987.

5. CREATIONISM VERSUS EVOLUTION

Bliss, Richard B. *In Search of the Origins of Life.* San Diego: Creation-Life Publishers, 1979.

Eldridge, Nils. *The Monkey Business.* New York: Washington Square, 1982.

Frye, Roland M. *Is God a Creationist?* New York: Scribner's, 1983.

Gilkey, Langdon. *Creationism on Trial: Evolution and God at Little Rock.* Minneapolis: Winston, 1985.

Gillespie, Charles. *Genesis and Geology.* New York: Harper Torchbooks, 1959.

Gish, Duane T. *Evolution? The Fossils Say No!* San Diego: Creation-Life Publishers, 1977.

Hyers, Conrad. *The Meaning of Creation.* Atlanta: John Knox, 1984.

Kofahl, Robert E., and Seagraves, Kelly L. *The Creation Explanation.* Wheaton, Ill.: Shaw, 1975.

Lammerts, Walter E. *Why Not Creation?* Nutley, N.J.: Presbyterian and Reformed Publishing, 1970.

Morris, Henry M. *The Bible Has the Answer.* San Diego: Creation-Life Publishers, 1975.

————. *The Scientific Case for Creation.* San Diego: Creation-Life Publishers, 1977.

————. *The Troubled Water of Evolution.* San Diego: Creation-Life Publishers, 1974.

————, ed. *Scientific Creationism.* San Diego: Creation-Life Publishers, 1978.

Numbers, Ronald L. *The Creationists.* New York: Knopf, 1992.

Van Till, Howard J. *The Fourth Day.* Grand Rapids: Eerdmans, 1986.

Index